Trouble at Work

Trouble at Work

Ralph Fevre, Duncan Lewis,
Amanda Robinson & Trevor Jones

B L O O M S B U R Y
LONDON · NEW DELHI · NEW YORK · SYDNEY

Bloomsbury Academic

An imprint of Bloomsbury Publishing Plc

50 Bedford Square
London
WC1B 3DP
UK

1385 Broadway
New York
NY 10018
USA

www.bloomsbury.com

Bloomsbury is a registered trade mark of Bloomsbury Publishing Plc

First published in 2012
Paperback edition first published 2013

© Ralph Fevre, Duncan Lewis, Amanda Robinson & Trevor Jones 2012

British Library Cataloguing-in-Publication Data
A catalogue record for this book is available from the British Library.

ISBN: HB: 978-1-4081-3703-1
PB: 978-1-4725-5748-3

Library of Congress Cataloging-in-Publication Data
A catalog record for this book is available from the Library of Congress.

Cover image: © Martin Novak/Shutterstock

Printed and bound by CPI Group (UK) Ltd, Croydon, CR0 4YY

Oh, how full of briers is this working-day world.
As You Like It, Act One, Scene Three

Contents

Tables and Figures

PART ONE

This book represents the most important product of the largest, specialist research programme on ill-treatment in the workplace so far undertaken. The programme dates from 2006 when the authors began work on a funding bid to the UK's Economic and Social Research Council. The project funded by this successful bid (award number RES-062-23-312) provided the bulk of the original data which are discussed in the book. Public funds also paid for the UK Government's Fair Treatment at Work Survey (FTWS) which provided valuable supporting evidence that we cite at various points. The book therefore owes its existence to public funds but its value derives from the further, unpaid contribution of thousands of British employees who spared the time to tell us about their own experiences, no matter that they sometimes found this hard, and even distressing. It is to their stories that we turn first of all.

1

A Bad Day at the Office

As part of the survey we discuss later in this book, people who told us they had been ill-treated at work were asked why they thought this had happened to them. We gave them options which included their age, gender and ethnicity, characteristics of the place they worked and about anyone whom they thought was responsible for the ill-treatment (see pp. 30–1). If none of these options fitted, they were asked to explain in their own words. A few of our respondents said it was just a 'bad day' or that someone else was 'having a bad day'. The best way to explain what this book is about is to tell the stories of a random selection of respondents who had experienced a bad day at work.[1] While the facts reported, and the feelings expressed, are given verbatim, we have made up some other details in order to preserve our respondents' anonymity; for example, all the names used here, and throughout the book, are pseudonyms. We have also imagined everything happened on the same bad day.

At 5.10 p.m., Suhuur, a 25-year-old Muslim woman of Pakistani origin, is collected by her mother outside the shop where she works. As she gets into the car, her mother can see she is upset and, as she eases into the traffic, her mum asks her what's wrong? You won't believe what happened today, says Suhuur, and then it all comes out in a rush: 'A customer asked me for something which didn't make any sense. When I went to my manager to see if she could help, the customer said a completely different thing to her than what she had said to me. We sorted out what she needed and the customer blamed me for not understanding her.' How rude, says her mother, but Suhuur says that's not the worst of it. The customer said it was my fault because of my head scarf. 'She said to me "you should unwrap that thing from around your ears so that you can hear better".'

It is now 6.30 p.m. on the same day and Tanya, a 37-year-old black Caribbean woman who has a physical disability, has just arrived home from her job as a manager in local government. As she waits in the kitchen for the kettle to boil, her eldest daughter comes in: you look tired mum, she says, bad day at work? Tanya tells her that her 'bosses harass me as a result of not meeting the unreasonable deadlines'. Her daughter is only 15 and is yet to have a job. She tells her mother it's only work and not to take it to heart, but Tanya tells her she doesn't know how bad it makes you feel when you are 'unable to meet deadlines owing to unmanageable workloads. This makes you feel incompetent'.

Half an hour after Tanya gets home, Chris rings his brother from a car rental garage in Aberdeen. Chris is white, Christian, 32 and works for an estate agent. He says, did Belinda tell you 'I flew to Scotland after work'?, and then he tells his brother that he's 'expected to drive back [the] same day – 11 hours' driving'. His brother says it's ridiculous, probably illegal, but Chris says, I know, I tried to tell them it's against health and safety but 'management took no notice, and said I could not stay at a hotel'. Well at least they've given you tomorrow off then, replies his brother. You are joking says Chris, 'when I said "could I come in late next day?" they said no; come in at your normal time'.

Terry is white, Christian, born in South Africa and 36. He is meeting his friend Wayne at the pub at 8.30 p.m. and is running late, so he rings Wayne on his mobile and tells him to get the drinks in. Wayne says, it sounds like you need one, have you had a bad day at the golf course (where Terry works)? Terry says he 'made a mistake by cutting the wrong piece of grass'. He tells Wayne his supervisor 'berated me about it, shouting at me, and he assaulted me; he struck me on the jaw with his fist'.

By 11.30 p.m. Ramsey knows he is not going to be able to sleep for an hour or two yet. He is a 43-year-old Christian of Indian origin and he has a physical disability. He checks his Blackberry and sees his brother, who is working in Korea, is already at the office, and he sends him a message to say he has had a bad day at work. His brother will not be surprised by this – he knows that Ramsey has had a long battle with his private sector employer in health and social care but has not had an update on what has happened in the past few weeks. Ramsey says, 'they said I had been sick for too much time; they then offered me a low daytime job which was not suitable for me. They then offered me redundancy.' His brother sympathises but tells him that employers do need their employees to be available for work. This is not the point, Ramsey tells him: 'Staff that came after me had more sickness but no action taken against them.'

It's 1 p.m. and Nandi is working at the hospital and things are going badly as usual. He is 28, of Indian origin, a Hindu and recently qualified as a doctor. He gets a five-minute break and uses it to go to the toilet and update his Facebook status on his i-phone. He wants it to be, 'On call – patients to be seen from A & E and then sometimes only two doctors and 20 people to be seen. Employees off, either sick or study – no proper cover'. But he hasn't time to type all this so writes 'pressure and stressed' instead.

It was C. Wright Mills (1959) who taught that it was the job of sociology to explain what bigger structural causes lay behind private troubles like those of Suhuur, Tanya, Chris and the rest, including the 1,788 survey respondents whose accounts we do not have room to discuss here. Mills explained that individuals like them could not hope to understand what was really happening in their lives from their own isolated viewpoint. The virtue of sociology was that it allowed any one of us to step outside the limitations of that individual view and find out if others shared our troubles, and what the common causes of those troubles might be. The private troubles Mills had in mind entailed an element which is common in all six examples above. In each case, a person feels their values are being threatened, and it was this threat that Mills thought could form the seed of the public issue that sociology could help people to fashion from their private troubles.

Examples of the successful translation of private troubles into public issues in the world of employment are easy enough to find. There have been public debates about unemployment, job security, working hours, health and safety, wages, income differentials and discrimination, for example. Unemployment was one of Mills's examples, but he said that it could be far from obvious how private troubles were turned into public issues, and there might be serious disagreements about the way this was done. We are now in the middle of such a period of debate and disagreement about how best to turn the troubles at work we have just described into public issues.

Mills might agree it has taken a surprisingly long time for sociologists to get involved in this process (Beale and Hoel 2011), but we must first make it clear that this late entry left the way clear for other social scientists to get to work. By far the most important contribution to this work came from psychologists and social psychologists. It is the concepts taken from these disciplines that have drawn together the private troubles of individuals into something that can be measured and investigated, and for which causes and remedies can be found. The two most influential concepts they have introduced are work-induced stress and workplace bullying.

The concept of stress conceives of workplace troubles as excessive strain on employees which impairs their ability to function normally. Ultimately, stress may harm an individual's mental and physical health. Examples of the kinds of remedies that have been proposed when the private troubles of the workplace are translated into the public issue of work-related stress are provided by the United Kingdom's Health and Safety Executive (HSE), for example, HSE (2007) which offers guidance for employers. The equivalent publications which follow from the translation of private troubles using the concept of bullying are provided by the Advisory, Conciliation and Arbitration Service (Acas). See, for example, Acas (2006).

This book is mainly concerned with showing what sociology – the latecomer to the debate – can add to the conceptualisation of workplace troubles, and there is no need to review the existing research on stress and bullying. We shall, however, use the remainder of this chapter to show how conceiving of workplace troubles by drawing parallels with the behaviour of school children[2] shapes them into a public issue. For example, we shall demonstrate that, while there is often disagreement about who and what to include, the bullying concept omits some of the examples given at the beginning of this chapter. Those troubles, and those individuals, are not to be helped by the construction of the public issue of bullying out of trouble at work. In fact, without more information (about whether the treatment of Chris was part of a long-term pattern of behaviour, for example) all six might not be regarded as bullying. This will not matter if alternative concepts are available, but we are not convinced that any of the available alternatives (including stress – see Walker and Fincham 2011) capture the essence of the private troubles that Mills drew our attention to: the threat to people's values.

In the next section, we demonstrate how thinking of troubles as bullying defines some troubles in the public issue and some out, though rarely does the debate about what is in and out seem to reach consensus. We shall demonstrate how bullying defines what troubles can be measured, and how to do it, and the available explanations and solutions for the public to pursue. We shall then show how sociologists have finally joined in the enterprise of turning private troubles into public issues. To begin with, they have done this on the ground picked by the psychologists, using the bullying concept to gather data and investigate explanations, but towards the end of the chapter we shall examine how sociologists have begun to find this concept limiting and, perhaps, in need of replacement with something more conducive to what C. Wright Mills famously called 'the sociological imagination'.

Research on workplace bullying

The field was founded on Scandinavian psychological research beginning with the works of Leymann in Sweden (1990, 1996) and Einarsen, Raknes and Matthiesen (1994), Einarsen and Skogstad (1996) and Bjorkqvist, Osterman and Hjelt-Back (1994) in Norway. Proof of the resonance achieved by bullying as a public issue (Einarsen *et al*. 2011) is easy to find and continues to grow. For example, more than a quarter of the UK newspaper references to workplace bullying in the first decade of the present century appeared in 2010 (Lexis Library). It is worth saying, however, that enthusiasm about conceptualising the issue as bullying has not been universal.

Mills would not have been surprised to learn that some people have been happier to recognise private troubles as bullying at work than others. The way in which the disagreements about the application of the label were played out was demonstrated by some, more sociological, contributions to the field. Liefooghe and Mackenzie-Davey (2001) showed how people's understandings of the bullying label were complex and derived from different experiences and perspectives, inside and outside the organisation that employed them. Lewis (2003) pointed out that bullying is a socially constructed process in which trade unionists, employees and human resource (HR) managers interpreted the causes and outcomes of bullying in remarkably different ways. Some troubles were only seen as bullying after a process of interpretation in social interaction with co-workers, family and friends. Indeed, McCarthy and Mayhew (2004) argued that some of the patchiness in the adoption of the bullying label might be due to variations in the effort put into raising awareness of it as a public issue.

The concept of bullying also had some competition within the research community, even amongst psychologists. Yet, at the time of writing in 2011, bullying had become the dominant way of conceptualising workplace troubles in many different countries (see, for example, a recent Japanese study by Tsuno *et al.* 2010). Even in North America – where concepts such incivility, abuse, mistreatment, social undermining and so on have had more support – bullying has gained ground. Sometimes this has happened in conjunction with the concept of harassment, but harassment is also used interchangeably with bullying. In French-speaking countries the same is true of '*harcèlement morale*', and in some European countries the same is true of 'mobbing' (Einarsen *et al.* 2011).

Why is it so hard to decide what counts as bullying at work? The first question to consider might be whether one can be bullied by accident. Workplace bullying researchers do not agree that there has to be a bully with intent to inflict harm for there to be bullying (Hershcovis 2010). Even if they agree, there are undoubted measurement problems because intent would seem to require verification from the alleged perpetrator (Einarsen *et al.* 2011). Ignoring the measurement problem, if there is intent, what sort of intent does it have to be? For instance, there has been a lot of debate about whether bullying necessarily implies the intention to harm (Einarsen *et al.* 2011). Establishing this might create even more challenging measurement problems (Nielsen, Notelaers and Einarsen 2011). The practical solution to these problems has been to look for circumstantial evidence of intent. Einarsen (1999), who has done more than most to define the field, argued that bullying occurs regularly and carries on for a sustained period, and attracts general agreement that it is aggressive behaviour that is intended to be hostile or could be seen as such by the person on the receiving end.

This definition of bullying could rule out one or more of the private workplace troubles described at the beginning of the chapter, even though some of the people who experienced them might consider them to be bullying. Indeed, it is possible that we would not even have gathered these data at all if we had been relying on Einarsen's definition. If researchers are not interested in irregular behaviour, or things which have happened a few times, or which are not obviously aggressive and hostile, they do not count them. Einarsen and Skogstad (1996) found the mean duration of bullying to be 18 months, while Zapf *et al.* (2011) showed a mean duration in their meta-analysis of between 12 and over 60 months. We do not know from these statistics whether shorter periods of ill-treatment – which the researchers made sure they did not count – were also experiences that people considered to be bullying.

Einarsen further refined the definition of bullying after 1999, and his refinements were widely adopted in the field. There is now widespread agreement that workplace bullying is 'harassing, offending, or socially excluding someone or negatively affecting someone's work'. Again, it has to be sustained (for six months or more) and it has to be frequent (say once a week), but the elements of aggression and hostility are de-emphasised in favour of others:

> Bullying is an escalating process in the course of which the person confronted ends up in an inferior position and becomes the target of systematic negative social acts. A conflict cannot be called bullying if the incident is an isolated event or if two parties of approximately equal strength are in conflict. (Einarsen *et al.* 2011: 22)

The notion of power disparity between perpetrator and victim was first introduced by Leymann (1996), and there seems to be agreement that it works best for the less formalised sources of power that exist simply because of personality factors which make one person more dominant than another (Einarsen 1999). Hoel and Cooper (2000) suggested that horizontally derived power from co-workers can be exploited through personal knowledge of a victim or through group behaviours that target some power deficit (Einarsen *et al.* 2011).

Applying the notion of power distance to relations between those who exercise formal authority and those who must do as they are told is, of course, more difficult. It also makes it very difficult to see how relations between employees and customers or clients could be counted as bullying. Suhuur (p. 3) had no power over her customer (but of course her troubles would have been ruled out anyway because they were not regular or sustained). But imagine a social worker who has regular and sustained contact with a client, and with every interaction the social worker remembers how unpleasant and sometimes terrifying the other person is. But when the social worker has power over the client, his or her troubles cannot count as bullying even if they have such a profound negative effect on his or her ability to do a good job (Denney 2010).

The manner in which we conceive a public issue not only rules some things in and some out, creating various measurement challenges, but the same principle applies to explanations and solutions for the public issue. One obvious place for psychologists to look for explanations for bullying is personality characteristics (Harris, Harvey and Booth 2010). For example, Baillien *et al.* (2009) identified differences in the capacities of bullies and their targets to cope with frustration. Coyne, Seigne and Randall (2000) showed how bullied victims were less extrovert, submissive, averse to conflict, quiet, reserved, less stable and more conscientious. There is no agreement, however, that personality profiles or psychological coping mechanisms are the right place to look for explanations (Milczarek 2010). Zapf (1999) and Zapf and Einarsen (2011) argued that bullying can have multiple causes and that personality is only one element. Indeed, a central strand of Leymann's original argument was that personality traits of anxiety were 'a result of and definitely not the cause of exposure to bullying' (Glasø et al. 2007: 2). In a matched sample of victims and non-victims, Glasø et al. (2007) showed how victims displayed more neurotic and less agreeable behaviours, but two-thirds of the victim sample did not differ from non-victims in their personality profiles.

In their search for explanations, psychologists have also looked beyond the characteristics of individuals to the character of their relationships. Einarsen (1999) had seen bullying as a gradually evolving process, starting with aggressive behaviour developing into bullying, stigmatisation and severe trauma. Numerous models have been produced to understand the manner in which conflict becomes bullying (Zapf and Gross 2001). The notion of bullying as a dysfunctional interpersonal dynamic has been extended beyond the dyad to include the group that is affected as the process of action and reaction continues (Tehrani 2011). Heames, Harvey and Treadway (2006) also saw dysfunctional group dynamics as present at the start of the process, for example because people do not agree on their relative status (also see Baillien et al. 2009, and see p. 10 on role conflict).

Some psychologists have extended the enquiry beyond groups of employees to consider the workplace itself as a possible explanation for bullying. Leymann (1996) had stressed the importance of the work environment as an explanation for bullying from the start. He considered it much more fruitful to investigate the ways in which work was organised, and leadership was displayed, than looking at the personality characteristics for bullies and the bullied. Especially in Scandinavia, researchers followed this lead (Einarsen et al. 1994; Hauge, Skogstad and Einarsen 2010; Vartia 1996; Zapf, Knorz and Kulla 1996). For example, in the spirit of Leymann's original thesis, poor leadership and management appeared as key elements of the explanations offered by Vartia (1996) and Einarsen, Aasland and Skogstad (2007). The destructive aspects of leadership outlined by Einarsen, Aasland and Skogstad (2007) occurred not simply because leaders were purposively destructive but often because of inaction and poor management of events on the ground, characterised as 'laissez-faire' leadership. More dictatorial forms of leadership were proposed by Ashforth (1994), who labelled this 'petty tyranny'. The autocratic leadership which was shown to be most prominent in a British study was also thought central to the explanation of bullying (Hoel et al. 2010). Salin and Hoel (2011) argued that, whereas autocratic or laissez-faire models of leadership could lead to bullying, a participative approach was much less likely to do so.

While an interest in leadership might betray the psychological bias of most research, Vartia (1996) found poor communication, and lack of participatory structures, to be important factors. Other factors that have been found to lead to bullying include high workload (e.g. Agervold and Mikkelsen 2004; Appelberg et al. 1991; Einarsen and Raknes 1997), low job control (Einarsen et al. 1994), role ambiguity (e.g. Vartia 1996) and job conflict (e.g. Einarsen *et al.* 1994; Notelaers and De Witte 2003). The last two concern whether an employee believes he or she should be working in a different way, might be doing things that are not necessary or is doing things one person thinks right and another does not (Einarsen *et al.* 1994; Hauge, Skogstad and Einarsen 2007; Vartia 1996). It is important to clarify, however, that the psychological paradigm does not suggest that these things in themselves constitute bullying. Rather, the idea is that an employee who experiences role ambiguity or job conflict will have a lower threshold for bullying (e.g. Einarsen *et al.* 1994).

From the perspective of organisational psychology, all of these factors contribute to the work environment, making bullying more likely to occur (Beale and Hoel 2011), but the existence of role ambiguity and job conflict (for example) do not necessarily imply that there is anything wrong with the way work is allocated and managed. Salin and Hoel (2011) saw things from a slightly different perspective when they suggested that work design, along with organisational culture and organisational change (see below), is closely correlated with episodes of bullying. They argued that bullying thrives where there are contradictory expectations, demands and values.

Work intensification in the form of increasing job demands and pressure of insufficient resources has been associated with bullying (Baillien *et al.* 2011). Other aspects of organisational change have also been shown to be highly correlated with bullying. More bullying is reported when there is more change taking place (Hoel and Cooper 2000; O'Connell, Calvert and Watson 2007; Skogstad, Matthiesen and Einarsen 2007). For example, a change of manager or more widespread restructuring have been shown to be associated with bullying (O'Connell *et al.* 2007; Salin and Hoel 2011). Skogstad *et al.* (2007) found an association between bullying and changes in work tasks and workplace composition. Skogstad *et al.* found that change might be associated with bullying because it caused conflicts between employees and managers, but that change also had an independent influence on bullying. Baillien and De Witte (2009) found no evidence of an independent influence and that the whole effect was mediated through role conflicts and job insecurity (note De Cuyper, Baillien and De Witte (2009) thought bullying caused insecurity rather than being caused by it). In both cases, the effect was a psychological one. When individuals found change had negative outcomes for them, this elicited victimisation.

Other researchers have been more interested in the possibility that organisational change may have a more direct relationship with bullying. Hoel, Cooper and Faragher (2001), for example, found an association with bigger, even global, shifts than those taking place in a single organisation, particularly restructuring and downsizing (Hoel *et al.* 2001). Along with others, they wanted to raise the possibility that these pressures led to work intensification and then to bullying (e.g. Harvey, Treadway and Heames 2006; Salin 2003). Salin (2003) argued that increased pressures on resources and restructuring can lead, for example, to increased competition between managers and all manner of local political struggles which make bullying more likely. In a similar vein, researchers have argued that, with or without organisational change, some workplace cultures can be particularly conducive to bullying. Thus Harvey *et al.* (2009) suggested that the reaction of others in the workplace to bullying sets the parameters for what is deemed acceptable and can encourage bullying to continue within the organisation.

In order to study the effects of workplace culture, Salin and Hoel (2011) suggested focussing on socialisation processes, communication and social climate as well as interpersonal conflicts. They cited Strandmark and Hallberg (2007) on the professional and value conflicts underpinning power struggles. Much earlier, Baron and Neuman (1996) had suggested increased workplace diversity (creating difficulties in interpersonal communication), feelings of anxiety and anger brought on by work practices such as increased computer monitoring, feelings of unjustness and unfairness related to pay cuts and unpleasant working conditions could also be conducive to bullying. A decade and a half later Einarsen *et al.* (2011) presented a theoretical model for the management and study of bullying which comprised cultural, socioeconomic, organisational and individual elements (including the characteristics of victims). The point of studies such as these was that organisational culture could not in itself encompass bullying, but that it could provide an environment in which bullying flourished (Agervold 2007).

In a review of the existing literature, Milczarek (2010: 11) concluded that 'in most of the cases of bullying, at least three or four of the following can be found: problems in work design (e.g. role conflicts); incompetent management and leadership; a socially exposed position of the target; negative or hostile social climate; and a culture that permits or rewards harassment in an organisation'. There is, in such arguments, also the potential to shift the focus away from the bullying that co-workers might subject each other to under stress. Moreover, as the knowledge base has grown, bullying has become less firmly located in a person or even a relationship. Indeed, the definition of bullying from Einarsen *et al.*, which we quoted above (p. 8), included a rider about applying the label to 'a particular activity, interaction or process' (Einarsen *et al.* 2011: 22).

Researchers such as Liefooghe and Mackenzie-Davey (2001), Hoel and Beale (2006) and D'Cruz and Noronha (2009) have argued for bullying to be seen not solely as an individualised construct but also to be recognised as an organisational one. In this regard, it is not bullies but organisational practices and processes that create the private troubles. Thus D'Cruz and Noronha concluded that it was the organisational practices of Indian call centres that demeaned and abused their employees. Lopez, Hodson and Roscigno (2009: 24) even pointed to 'routine organisational activities' as the locus of bullying. Much of the foregoing emphasis on organisational change, which we have been presenting as environmental factors causing the appearance of bullies and bullying, might actually be interpreted as processes which bully, even as evidence of bullying organisations. Here then, we have the seeds of a more sociological approach to workplace bullying. In the first instance this approach developed as a specialised application of a long-established sociological interest in industrial relations.

Enter sociology

For most of the time workplace bullying has been a public issue; it has been an article of faith that workplace bullying is not a standard industrial relations issue (Expert Advisory Group on Workplace Bullying 2005). Yet Fevre *et al.* (2009) have shown that most employees who report bullying or harassment also experience other problems with employment rights. A substantial number report unfair treatment and discrimination, including employment rights problems such as troubles with pay, health and safety grievances, hours of work, sick pay or leave, contracts and so on. Is it the job of researchers to carefully isolate bullying from these other troubles so that measurement, explanation and remedies do not become contaminated by them? Or should researchers be trying to understand if there are common causes of a wider range of workplace troubles?

Analysing a large number of ethnographic studies, mainly undertaken by sociologists, led Hodson (2001) to conclude that insufficient employee participation was a feature of many cases of ill-treatment. Mismanagement was a major cause of abuse but its effects could be tempered where managerial power was shared with workers. This would benefit organisations as a whole because managers might do anything, including ill-treating employees, in order to increase profit, whereas workers were interested in productivity and quality. In a later article, Hodson, Roscigno and Lopez (2006) argued that chaos in the workplace was a catalyst for bullying and harassment. In part, this argument recalled the environmental theories of organisational psychology since it was assumed that chaos created opportunities for bullying and harassment of those employees perceived to be weaker.

The same authors returned to the theme in Roscigno, Hodson and Lopez (2009) where they argued that organisational chaos was central to a sociology of bullying, although it did not bear the same relation to all types of 'workplace incivilities'. Moreover, these researchers argued that chaos was immanent in all workplaces because there was always the potential for tension between the goals of managers and workers. Rationalities on one side looked like irrationalities on the other:

> [I]rrationalities may easily be experienced as chaotic by those involved because the link between known causes (e.g. effort and accomplishment) and rewards

(e.g. security and advancement) are disrupted. In the resulting normative vacuum, control and co-ordination can revert to a reliance on bullying rather than use of positive inducements. (Roscigno, Hodson and Lopez 2009: 761)

Roscigno, Lopez and Hodson (2009) claimed that bullying which accompanies mismanagement and chaos can be dealt with by interventions from trades unions, for example, and by appropriate adoption of policies and practices. This conclusion might be seen as over-optimistic in Scandinavia, and the United Kingdom, where considerable evidence of bullying existed even though such policies and practices were well established (Rayner and Lewis 2011; Salin 2008), and trade unions and professional bodies, such as the Chartered Institute for Personnel Development (CIPD), and government agencies such as Acas, gave free advice and guidance to organisations and individuals to help them deal with bullying. On the other hand, Norway was one of the first nations to address bullying, and the experience there suggests that a reduction in bullying is possible through judicious use of interventions, including legislation (Nielsen *et al.* 2009). In multivariate analysis of their representative Irish sample, O'Connell *et al.* (2007) showed that there was less bullying in organisations with formal policies on bullying. However, in a similar UK study, Fevre *et al.* (2009) showed that trade union members were *more* likely to report bullying.[3]

Like Roscigno and his colleagues, Ironside and Seifert (2003) and Hoel and Beale (2006) concluded that workplace bullying should be dealt with through the industrial relations machinery. Comparing British and Swedish employers, Beale and Hoel (2010) found British managers to be more likely to intervene to prevent bullying because bullying in Sweden was most often seen as a dispute between employees, rather than between managers and employees, and because legal regulation of bullying was more explicit in Sweden. Beale and Hoel (2011) followed Ironside and Seifert's lead in focusing explicitly on the collective dimension of bullying. Bullying had a purpose – to reshape employee behaviour – and was therefore endemic to capitalist employment relations. So, despite the apparent evidence of the costs of bullying to employers, Beale and Hoel (2011: 14) proposed that employers benefited from bullying.

Rafferty went so far as to argue that bullying may be a tool chosen by employers to control their staff and that this is why it is so often associated with organisational change: 'restructuring and downsizing can magnify power imbalances and job insecurities, and encourage an atmosphere of corporate bullying. Changes of management or ownership in business can also lead to the use of bullying tactics to sweep out existing staff' (Rafferty 2001: 102). Hoel and Beale concluded from the British case, where managers were responsible for much workplace bullying, that, at the least, they would defend each other when accused of bullying, and that initial senior management sympathy towards employees who had been bullied would not lead to action when it counted.

This would make employees cynical about the fashion for high-commitment human resource management (Beale and Hoel 2011).

Sociologists are not simply interested in bullying because this seems to complement their long-standing interest in industrial relations. For example, sociologists of work and occupations might naturally be interested in any evidence that suggested bullying is more common in some jobs than others. Indeed, such occupational differences have been observed, though this observation has rarely been incorporated into a convincing theory of patterns of bullying. In the review of the literature compiled by Milczarek (2010), nurses reported a higher incidence of bullying than many other occupations. Health care workers in general, and teachers, were amongst those who might be forced out of their jobs by bullying (McCormack *et al.* 2009; Quine 1999, 2002). University employees (Bjorkqvist *et al.* 1994), civil servants or those working in public administration (Rayner 1997) have all shown relatively higher levels of bullying, while Roscigno, Lopez and Hodson (2009) showed how bullying can be the product of low occupational roles and positions. Fevre *et al.* (2009) showed that, in multivariate analysis of a representative sample of UK employees, those with more than one job were more likely to report bullying or harassment, but in their study, as in others, there was no evidence that bullying is more common in lower paid occupations. In multivariate analysis of a representative sample of the Irish workforce, however, O'Connell *et al.* (2007) showed that plant operatives and casual workers were more likely to report bullying, but this research also showed that bullying was more common amongst employees with higher levels of education.

Given the prevalence of bullying amongst nurses and teachers, it is no surprise that both education (Hubert and van Veldhoven 2001; Leymann 1996; Zapf 1999) and health and social care (Piirainen, Rasanen and Kivimaki 2003) have been shown to have higher rates of bullying in studies conducted in Sweden, Germany, the Netherlands and Finland. In their multivariate analysis, O'Connell *et al.* (2007) showed that bullying was more common in education, public administration, personal services and transport in Ireland. Citing one of their earlier works, Zapf *et al.* (2011) showed how a study of 400 German workers who reported serious bullying had a sevenfold risk of being bullied if they came from health and social services sectors, with a threefold increase for public administration workers and those employed in education. Zapf *et al.* (2011) cited some of the earliest studies of bullying in Sweden by Heinz Leymann, who reported an 'over-representation' of bullying in educational, health and administrative sectors. Leymann and Gustafsson (1996) showed in their study of post-traumatic stress disorder (PTSD) and bullying that the largest groups of patients came from health, education and social services occupations and that private sector organisations were under-represented.

Other studies found that the public sector as a whole exhibited a greater propensity towards bullying. Public sector workers were more at risk of bullying behaviours in Finland, according to studies by Vartia (1996) and Salin (2001). In the United Kingdom, Hoel and Cooper (2000) demonstrated how prison services, policing, education, health and local councils were high on the list of organisations where bullying behaviours were prevalent. Lewis and Gunn (2007) showed how UK public service workers drawn from across 13 public organisations experienced a range of negative behaviours at work, ranging from being given demeaning tasks through to humiliation and excessive criticism. In both the Lewis and Gunn (2007) study and the Hoel and Cooper (2000) research, managers were the most likely source of bullying behaviours with colleagues a distant second. In the case of the United Kingdom, for example, 'new public management' in the public sector has been associated with bullying and harassment (Burnes and Pope 2007). Other researchers have suggested that the higher rate of bullying in the public sector may be related to the extent of public sector change (Beale and Hoel 2010; Ironside and Seifert 2003; Salin 2001) and the nature of public sector employment (Zapf et al. 2003). Salin (2001) pointed out, however, that the public sector has received more attention from bullying researchers, perhaps because of the comparative ease of access to employees in that sector. McCarthy and Mayhew (2004) also suggested that the higher rate of bullying observed in the public sector may be a product of increased awareness there of bullying through policy initiatives (which also raised people's expectations of the standards they expect of behaviour in the workplace).

It is not just bullying that has been observed to vary by sector. Milczarek's review (2010) found that some of the same sectors in which bullying is believed to be more prevalent also experience more violence in the workplace from third parties such as clients. Substantially higher risks of workplace violence have been observed in health care and social work, education and public administration and defence (but also in commerce, transport, and hotels and restaurants). If there are common patterns between bullying and violence then there is no good reason, perhaps, to exclude workplace violence from the field (Einarsen and Raknes 1997).

Enter criminology

As with bullying, some studies of workplace violence have looked for explanations in the personality characteristics of perpetrators and victims (Zapf and Einarsen 2003). Other writers have emphasised factors relating to the nature of work organisation and management processes (Hodson 2001; Neuman and Baron 2003). Again in parallel to research on bullying, attention has been given to the impact of autocratic management and, of course, organisational change, including general change brought about by growing global competitive pressures, work intensification and related stresses on the social relations of work (Bowie 2010; Hoel and Salin 2003). The theories of Ironside and Seifert, and Beale and Hoel, about the predisposition of capitalist employment relations to stimulate bullying also have their counterparts in theories of violence in the workplace advanced by Bowie (2011) and others. Bowie also identified the roots of workplace violence in inconsistency in management policies, poor communication, ineffective grievance procedures, 'perceived unjust treatment of employees, lack of mutual respect among separate work teams and departments, ethnic tensions, increased workloads with diminishing resources and rewards, and poor working conditions and security' (Bowie 2010: 47).

Despite the obvious similarities between the theories advanced by writers such as Bowie and those elaborated to explain bullying, we should not assume that the violence that these writers are trying to explain always occurs between employees or even managers and employees. Critical criminologists such as Tombs (2007) have argued that harms to workers (and the general public) are much more widespread and deeper rooted than can be gauged by levels of interpersonal assault, and emerge from the structures and processes of employment relations and capitalist production. Catley and Jones (2002: 25–8) drew analytical distinctions between acts of physical interpersonal violence, violent speech acts, structural physical violence and structural 'symbolic' violence. In a similar way, Estrada *et al.* (2010) identified four separate categories of work-related violence. 'Intruder violence' includes crimes of violence against, for example, bank employees or check-out staff, and 'client-related' violence is taken to mean physical assaults by customers, patients or clients. 'Relational violence' denotes violence and harassment between workers in the same workplace, and 'structural violence' includes the broader systemic aspects of workplace harm emphasised by criminologists such as Tombs. The more specific aspects of organisational structures and cultures that expose workers to violent situations can also be seen as 'structural' forms of violence.

Bowie argued that organisations can bear responsibility for workers' exposure to client-related violence through placing employees and clients in potentially violent situations. He expressed particular concern about many workplaces which are affected by this and other aspects of structural violence:

> are part of the so called caring professions such as health, education, and social welfare. ... Often organizations where you would expect, as an employee or patient, to be treated with dignity and respect are in fact the opposite and hide an economic rationalist agenda under a veneer of service. Such abusive behavior by organizations is coming to the forefront of the current debate about healthcare provision and distribution. In such situations employers and managers might argue that they are not to blame for bad supervisors and related practices, deflecting criticism back onto supervisors and their workers. There is often no recognition or denial at the higher echelons of management regarding how the organizational climate and functioning can allow or foster a violent work environment. (Bowie 2010: 52)

There has been considerable research on client-related violence in health and social work occupations, including some recent, mixed methods research on violence against doctors, probation officers and ministers of religion. Denney and O'Beirne (2003) described the way in which managers in the probation service gave little, if any, thought to preventing violence from offenders against probation officers. Indeed, there appeared to be no acknowledgement of this violence in the training and management of probation officers except through ineffectual and piecemeal responses – for example, offering counselling – which were made when violence did occur. Elston *et al.* (2003) found that probation officers and ministers of religion who had suffered violence believed there were ways in which their jobs could be designed and resourced to make them safer. The research team found that, without such responses, the fear of violence might have many implications, including 'avoidance of mandatory work, ignoring possible risks, failing to take sufficient precautions for safety and eroding staff confidence and morale' (O'Beirne, Denney and Gabe 2004: 124).

The same research team which described the ways in which managers ignored violence also described the ways in which professionals who suffered violence often minimised it. O'Beirne *et al.* (2003) found that probation officers and ministers of religion might not disclose violence to their colleagues, still less to the police. Clergy who suffered violence did not even have a formal reporting structure available to them. Probation officers failed to report violence because they believed they would get little help from their managers, and members of both professions believed violence was something they were expected to take in their stride. As part of the same research project, Elston *et al.* (2003) reported that doctors medicalised much violence by patients, which was therefore seen as a part of their job rather than a crime. They might also be given mixed messages by other professionals; for example, a psychiatrist might encourage a doctor to report violence by a patient in order to increase the chances of that patient being treated while the police would advise the opposite.

As with bullying, variations in the conception of the public issue lead to confusion over how best to measure workplace violence. We have discussed elsewhere the contrast between levels and trends in workplace violence in crime victimisation surveys, on the one hand, and broader studies of workplace relations, on the other (Jones *et al.* 2011). For example, criminological studies based on the British Crime Survey (BCS) have suggested a low (and falling) risk of workplace assault in recent years (Budd 1999; Upson 2004). In contrast, studies from the field of management studies suggested that workplace violence has been growing in frequency and severity (Chappell and Di Martino 2006; Flannery 1996; Serantes and Suárez 2006). Crime victimisation surveys tend to focus respondents' minds onto formal legal categories of assault, and thus filter out various forms of violent behaviour – both serious and relatively minor – which for various reasons are less likely to be the subject of formal action (Jones *et al.* 2011).

It seems clear that criminological studies substantially underplay the significance of workplace violence in contemporary Britain, and as we shall see in Chapter 4, far greater numbers of workers than those suggested by the BCS are victims of violent behaviour in the workplace. That said, it may be that some estimates of spiralling workplace violence err too far in the opposite direction. Indeed, the findings of workplace surveys may reflect a lowering of the threshold of tolerance for certain forms of behaviour and a greater tendency to label problematic or otherwise harmful behaviour as 'violence'. Estrada *et al.* (2010) argued that apparent increases in workplace violence in a number of countries were related both to a greater general awareness and sensitivity to such issues, and a real increase due to changing working environments that exposed more workers to risks of violence.

Workplace bullying, violence and minorities

Research on the sociology of organisations has explored the relationship between structural power inequalities and harassment and violence in the workplace, and has often suggested that the latter bear down more heavily upon those social categories traditionally perceived as marginalised or disadvantaged (Hearn and Parkin 2001). Roscigno, Hodson and Lopez (2009: 760) found that 'both gender and minority status are significant determinants of not only sexual harassment but of managerial bullying as well'. Lopez *et al.* (2009) argued that the defence of identity and of jobs was at the core of bullying and harassment and that bullying was therefore bound up with formal and informal status hierarchies and job security. Minorities were more at risk because the biggest power differentials between employers and workers existed where the workers were drawn from minorities, and because isolation and exclusion in wider society made minorities into targets (Lopez *et al.* 2009: 20). This was, in part, a special case of powerlessness – those who suffered general social exclusion were more vulnerable in the workplace – but it also said something about the way non-minority workers reacted to sharing a workplace with minorities:

> In some kinds of situations, the association between harassment and minority workforce may be a consequence of minority workers' concentration in bad jobs, but in other settings, it is clear that harassment of minority workers serves white identity and job-protection functions in much the same way as general and sexual harassment serve male identity and job protection. (Lopez *et al.* 2009: 21–2)

Particularly conducive settings for harassment were those which involve physically demanding work. In any event,

> [bullying or harassment was part of a] larger process of social exclusion and closure. In this process of closure, mocking, barriers, and sometimes blatant

threats are used to exclude certain groups (even potentially forcing them out of the workplace) or to keep members of these groups 'in their place'. (Lopez *et al.* 2009: 23)

Hodson *et al.* (2006) suggested that it was not simply whether a respondent was a member of a minority or not, but what proportion of the workforce was made up of minorities, that affected the prevalence of bullying and harassment.

The theories elaborated by Hodson and his colleagues were founded on the assumption that bullying and harassment were more prevalent amongst minorities. They felt that what they learnt from analysis of a large number of workplace ethnographies (see p. 12) justified this assumption (Lopez *et al.* 2009: 15; also see Hodson *et al.* 2006). However, these studies were completed over a fairly long period during which patterns of overt prejudice and discrimination certainly changed, not least because of changes in legislation. Moreover, the ethnographies Hodson and his colleagues drew upon in their work were conducted in more than one society. It is possible that their method is therefore not sensitive to differences in workplace behaviour between different societies which result from variations in patterns of overt prejudice and discrimination beyond the workplace. As before, such differences may well result, for example, from differences in the anti-discrimination legislation in place in different societies.

Lopez *et al.* (2009: 24) were certainly aware of a need for additional representative studies. What other evidence do we have that employees who are members of minorities are more at risk of bullying, harassment or violence? Fox and Stallworth (2005) argued that research in this areas should be careful about distinguishing supervisor from co-worker bullying (also see Lewis and Gunn 2007), and reported their US study in which Hispanics were the only minority to report higher levels of 'general bullying' than whites, although all ethnic groups reported racial or ethnic bullying such as taunting and other forms of ill-treatment. Researchers in the United Kingdom claimed correlations between ethnicity and bullying, including racial or ethnic bullying (Hoel and Cooper 2000; Lewis and Gunn 2007). The representative study reported by Fevre *et al.* (2009) did not, however, find a correlation between bullying or harassment and ethnicity in multivariate analysis which controlled for other factors.

According to Fevre *et al.* (2009), women were 73 per cent more likely to report bullying or harassment. Other researchers have explored gender and bullying, but with mixed results dependent upon methodology and sample size, and the evidence presented in meta studies does not demonstrate such a clear gendered component. Thus research in Scandinavia and the United Kingdom showed that men and women had similar levels of exposure to bullying (Zapf *et al.* 2011). Where women are over-represented in bullying studies, this will be because occupations or sectors with a female majority have been sampled (Zapf *et al.* 2011). This could mean, however, that women are more exposed to bullying but because of the jobs they hold rather than because they are targeted for their gender (Hutchinson and Eveline 2010; Lee 2002). Hutchinson and Eveline (2010) also argued that power and hierarchy in organisations was often underpinned by a gender component. Rodríguez-Muñoz *et al.* (2010) reported just under half of 183 victims of bullying showed symptoms for the criteria for PTSD with women more likely than men to show these symptoms. Milczarek's review of research on the correlates of workplace violence suggested that men might be at higher risk of third-party violence and that men and women would usually encounter violence in different employment situations. Women were most at risk in health care, education and retail, whereas men were most at risk in police and security work, and transport (Milczarek 2010).

According to the representative study of British employees reported by Fevre *et al.* (2009), lesbian, gay and bisexual (LGB) employees were 271 per cent more likely to report bullying or harassment. This confirmed an early representative study (Grainger and Fitzner 2007) and lent credence to the suggestion from Hunt and Dick (2008) that nearly one in five lesbians and gay men experienced bullying due to their sexual orientation, with one in eight of the population reporting that they have witnessed verbal bullying of gay people in the workplace, whilst nearly one in 20 witnessed physical bullying (see also Croteau 1996). Acas (2006) suggested large minorities of LGB employees have some experience of bullying/harassment. Threats of physical abuse to LGB employees also feature in these studies (Acas 2007; Hunt and Dick 2008).

Research on the relationship between age and bullying or violence has been rather less conclusive. One early study suggested that most interpersonal conflicts were found amongst younger employees (Appelberg *et al.* 1991), and O'Connell and Williams (2001) reported that the 26- to 45-year-old age group is more likely to report bullying. In the United Kingdom, Rayner (1997) and Hoel and Cooper (2000) reported higher levels of bullying amongst younger employees, followed by those aged 35–44. Those aged 55+ are least likely to report being bullied. Age related negatively with being a target of workplace bullying in the study by Einarsen and Raknes (1997) and De Cuyper *et al.* (2009), but positively in the study by Einarsen and Skogstad (1996). Einarsen and Skogstad (1996) looked at data from 14 Norwegian surveys and found that older employees have a significantly higher risk of victimisation, than their younger counterparts, with the exception of university employees aged over 50, who were significantly less likely to report having been bullied. In the representative UK study reported by Fevre *et al.* (2009), no relationship was found between age and bullying or harassment, but those with less than a year's service in their current job were more likely to experience bullying. Milczarek's (2010) review of literature on workplace violence identified an increased risk for younger workers and those with less work experience.

Finally, we turn to research on employees with a disability or long-term health condition. Fevre *et al.* (2009) reported that those who were not disabled were less than half as likely to report bullying and harassment. Up to this point, most bullying research had conceived impairment or ill-health as the effects of bullying (Fevre *et al.* forthcoming) and not factors which might be implicated in their causes (one notable exception was Hoel, Faragher and Cooper 2004). There is certainly significant evidence for the negative consequences of exposure to bullying for mental health (Vartia and Hyyti 2002), psychosomatic illness (Zapf *et al.* 1996) and psychological well-being (Mikkelsen and Einarsen 2002). Some studies show how bullying leads to stress and as job demands rise, support and control diminish (Tuckey *et al.* 2010). This evidence strongly suggests a downward spiralling process leading to further negative psychological as well as physical ill-health. De Cuyper *et al.* (2009) argued that bullying leads to withdrawal, absence and seeking new employment as well as emotional feelings of isolation and helplessness.

On the other hand, research in Canada (Eakin 2005) and the United Kingdom (Cunningham, James and Dibben 2004; Dibben, James and Cunningham 2001; Foster 2007; James, Cunningham and Dibben 2002, 2006; Walker and Fincham 2011) also described the way in which employees with health problems and disabilities found themselves on the receiving end of ill-treatment, particularly from managers, including bullying and harassment, from which they were supposed to be protected by anti-discrimination legislation. Schur *et al.* (2009) found that employees with disabilities did not feel more marginalised or disadvantaged in companies that all employees thought were more fair and responsive. Woodhams and Corby's research showed how perceptions of disability in different workplaces were governed by the impact of an impairment or illness. Whether an impairment was disabling depended heavily on the nature of the work and workplace (Woodhams and Corby 2003). More generally, the stigmatisation of employees with disabilities may serve to reproduce the symbolic order of the workplace, reinforcing status differences and legitimating differences in power (Abberley 1987; Parker and Aggleton 2003; Walker and Fincham 2011). This, of course, recalls the theories advanced by Lopez *et al.* (2009) to explain the bullying of minorities as well as some of the earlier discussion of the causes of bullying.

Final remarks

It has been argued that the bullying concept has been widely adopted precisely because it *fails* to turn private workplace troubles into public issues in a convincing way. Thus McCarthy (2003) argued bullying in the workplace was a good fit with the *zeitgeist* of therapeutic remedies for private troubles. It was also compatible with the prevailing emphasis on codes of conduct of individuals (in this case, individual employees – see also Walker and Fincham 2011). In effect, the concept of workplace bullying did not attempt to generalise from the individual experience and, therefore, could only propose individual solutions to the issues it raised. As a result, private troubles stayed private and did not become public issues. There have been hints in the discussion that those with a more sociological interest in this field have come to a similar, pessimistic conclusion about the usefulness of the concept of workplace bullying.

We do not find modifications to the concept like 'organisational bullying' (or even 'structural violence') to be sufficient conceptual repairs and think it is more constructive to go back to the drawing board. If bullying cannot be an effective vehicle for the application of the sociological imagination, there are other contenders: counterproductive behaviour (Greenberg 1997), uncivil behaviour or incivility (Cortina and Magley 2009; Lim, Cortina and Magley 2008; Pearson, Andersson and Wegner 2001), abuse (Keashly, Hunter and Harvey 1997; Tepper 2000), negative acts (Einarsen and Raknes 1997) and mistreatment (Blase, Blase and Du 2008), for example. 'Counterproductive behaviour' seems unlikely to do the trick given what we have already discussed in relation to the benefits managers and employers may find in bullying. Perhaps people can be civil, and not abusive, but still make people's work life miserable.

Mal- or mistreatment, along with negative acts or negative behaviour (Einarsen and Raknes 1997), seems to be sufficiently inclusive for our purposes, and they usefully leave open the question of intent while indicating that people's values are under threat. In Part Two, we shall explain that we used a modified version of the negative acts questionnaire (NAQ) in our survey. The terms 'negative act' or 'negative behaviour' do, however, carry the connotation that a person is responsible. Since we do not want to rule out the possibility that practices, or even organisations, lie behind troubles at work, we prefer to standardise on an equivalent term, 'ill-treatment', where we can. This is not enough, however. More conceptual innovation is required if we are going to be able to give the sociological imagination free rein to help us turn the private troubles of Suhuur, Ramsey, Nandi and the others into a public issue which can be properly addressed.

We need a concept for what lies behind, or under, the ill-treatment that directs us to the sociological explanations we might examine. Concepts like mismanagement (Hodson 2001) are again too limited, in this case failing to encompass problems for which managers are not responsible, and also having some of the same drawbacks as the idea of counterproductive behaviour. The management that creates problems for employees may be good from the employer's point of view. The alternative we propose is to turn to the vernacular idea of trouble at work. Trouble at work is not simply an easily understood way to describe the different examples of a bad day at the office we listed at the beginning of the chapter. All the same, the fact that the term (in contrast to negative workplace behaviour) features in the vernacular tells us it has the potential to take our measurements, explanations and solutions beyond the superficial behaviours to more deep-seated, long-lasting, fundamental social patterns and relationships. Trouble at work directs us towards workplace dynamics involving managers, workers and in some cases, the clients and customers of the organisation's services that leave people feeling troubled. It also takes us to the notion of the troubled workplace in which the underlying causes of ill-treatment are built into the social relations of the workplace between employees and employees, employees and managers, managers and clients, and customers and members of the public. Best of all, both trouble at work and the troubled workplace leave us, at the onset of our research, with no need to take sides, or assign blame, in order to find evidence that shows our concepts describe real-world experiences and help us to understand and address them.

In the remainder of this book, we interrogate large data sets in order to understand how common troubles at work really are, who experiences the most troubles, why they do and what can be done about this. Although, within the troubled workplace particular kinds of workers may suffer more ill-treatment than others, the differences between troubled workplaces and other workplaces are so marked that they mask any other effects. It is, therefore, no surprise that the most effective solutions are those which address the problems of the troubled workplace.

PART TWO

In Part Two we explain the key quantitative results for different types of workplace troubles. Supporting data, for example the tables which summarise our multivariate analysis, are available at www.bloomsburyacademic.com/view/Trouble-At-Work/book-ba-9781849664677.xml. Unless we indicate otherwise, all of the data we discuss are drawn from our nationally representative survey of employees, the British Workplace Behaviour Survey (BWBS). The three chapters in Part Two are organised around themes which have been suggested by the factor analysis of our survey data which revealed three types of troubling experiences at work: unreasonable treatment (Chapter 2), incivility (or denigration) and disrespect (Chapter 3), and finally violence and injury Chapter 4). In each of the three chapters, we discuss

- how many workers were affected and how often;
- the effects of trouble at work on people in and outside work (home life, relationships, physical and mental health);
- the types of workers most likely to be affected (with special reference to the 'equality strands' which received statutory protection);
- which jobs and occupations were likely to be affected;
- which workplaces were more likely to be affected (size, sector, region, for example);
- who was responsible: subordinates, colleagues, managers or customers.

To illuminate the experiences and meanings behind the statistics, we illustrate each of the main results with interview material taken from the qualitative phase of our research (described in detail in Part Three). This introduction provides just a few important details about our survey methodology to illustrate some of the key choices we made when gathering quantitative data on trouble at work.

Conceptual challenges: when is ill-treatment the same as 'bullying'?

In Chapter 1, we explained our decision to frame our research as the study of ill-treatment, or trouble at work, rather than workplace bullying, but the question naturally arises of how much overlap exists between these concepts when they are put to work in surveys. A variety of (usually non-representative) studies have suggested that almost all behaviour that people regard as bullying can be described as ill-treatment. These studies have also suggested, however, that there is plenty of ill-treatment people would not think of as bullying. Researchers have discovered this by asking a standard battery of questions about ill-treatment such as the NAQ (Einarsen and Raknes 1997) along with a question asking respondents if they have been bullied. This technique has been used to define a threshold (particular frequency, number or seriousness of events) above which researchers can claim evidence of 'bullying', regardless of whether respondents themselves recognise they have been bullied.[1] While we were not interested in imposing a definition of bullying in this way, we used a similar methodology to explore the overlap between ill-treatment and bullying in a smaller (representative) pilot survey for our BWBS.

In the pilot survey, face-to-face interviews were conducted with 1,083 employees during the spring of 2007. They were asked the questions in the NAQ battery and whether they had been bullied at work in the past two years. Only 76 respondents answered 'yes' to the bullying question, whereas affirmative responses on the individual NAQ items ranged from 87 to 392 respondents. As Figure 1 illustrates, most people who experienced some form of ill-treatment did not label it 'bullying'.

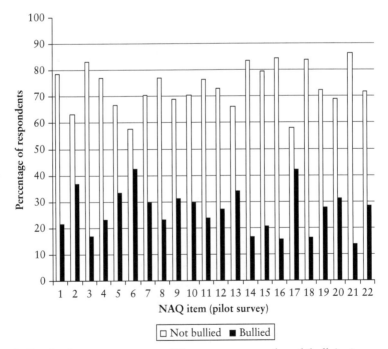

Figure 1 Overlap between measures of ill-treatment at work and 'bullying'

Figure 1 shows that there was quite considerable variation in the proportion self-identifying as bullying depending on which type of ill-treatment was reported. For example, employees were not as likely to think they had been bullied if they had experienced an unmanageable workload or impossible deadlines (Item 21) as they were when they had been ignored, excluded or sent to Coventry (Item 6) or had allegations made against them (Item 17). Do such variations indicate that the label of bullying is applied consistently and predictably?

We followed up the pilot by undertaking some 'cognitive testing' to find out more about why people answered questions about bullying and ill-treatment as they did. In particular, we wanted to know anything that might help us to understand why ill-treatment was sometimes seen as bullying and sometimes not. Cognitive testing is a form of qualitative interviewing which allows researchers to examine how far questions are understood in similar ways by respondents, whether they have sufficient information to understand and answer the questions asked, and to develop suggestions for removing ambiguity in the wording of particular questions. Sixty of these cognitive interviews were conducted in the summer of 2007 (see Fevre, Robinson, Jones and Lewis 2010 for more detail about this process). The interviews focused in particular on respondents' interpretations of different definitions of 'bullying' and the individual NAQ items. Respondents were asked about their experience of 'bullying at work', and then the interviewer initiated a discussion of what the respondent understood about the question, using probes such as 'how would you describe "bullying"?' and 'what sorts of incidents are you thinking of?'.

The cognitive interviews soon established that there were major problems with providing a comprehensive yet clear definition of 'workplace bullying' that was interpreted in similar ways by different groups of respondents. For example, some respondents reported that they viewed bullying as primarily physical abuse, whereas others saw bullying as more about verbal activities, such as teasing. One respondent argued that bullying could well be negative treatment by the organisation as a whole rather than by one or some particular individuals. When asked to define bullying, a wide variety of examples were given, including

- 'people losing their temper, violence or threats';
- 'deliberate mistreatment, or maybe not always deliberate; being treated in a way you wouldn't expect';
- 'form of abuse, abusing someone else ... a violation of someone's rights; attitude – your employer finds ways to make your life difficult at work';
- 'picking on someone for something that's not their fault';
- 'continual harassment that is personal';
- 'persistent mickey taking, always getting the worst job';

- 'making you feel frightened/embarrassed';
- 'being picked on or excluded and you can't do anything about it';
- 'made to feel inadequate'.

Many interviewees felt that all of the NAQ items might be considered 'bullying' depending on the circumstances in which they occurred. These referred to the job, the individual, how the behaviour was intended by the perpetrator and how it was received by the victim. The perception of an overlap between bullying and ill-treatment, therefore, not only varied between individuals but also changed for the same individual, depending on the circumstances.

Our pilot survey therefore suggested that there was far too much inconsistency in the application of the label of bullying for us to be able to construct a general explanation of why people regarded some, but not all, ill-treatment as bullying. Whatever limitations we, as sociologists, see in the use of the concept to further research, it seems that the bullying label is not sufficiently familiar to, and similarly understood by, British employees to allow a general explanation. One measure of this lack of familiarity and common understanding is given in Table 1, which contains three lists of typical bullying behaviours posted by organisations which consider it their

Table 1 'Official' descriptions of workplace bullying

Examples of bullying behaviour	Examples of bullying/harassing behaviour	Bullying behaviour can include the following
Constantly picked on	Spreading malicious rumours or insulting someone by word or behaviour	Persistently picking on people in front of others or in private Competent staff being constantly criticised
Humiliated in front of colleagues	Ridiculing or demeaning someone – picking on them or setting them up to fail Copying memos that are critical about someone to others who do not need to know	Regularly making the same person the butt of jokes
Regularly unfairly treated	Unfair treatment	Having responsibilities removed or being given trivial tasks to do

Examples of bullying behaviour	Examples of bullying/harassing behaviour	Bullying behaviour can include the following
Physically or verbally abused	Unwelcome sexual advances – touching, standing too close, asking for sexual favours etc.	Shouting at staff Consistently attacking a member of staff in terms of their professional or personal standing
Blamed for problems caused by others		
Always given too much to do, so that you regularly fail in your work	Deliberately undermining a competent worker by overloading and constant criticism	Setting a person up to fail by overloading them with work or setting impossible deadlines
Regularly threatened with the sack	Making threats or comments about job security without foundation	
Unfairly passed over for promotion or denied training opportunities	Preventing individuals progressing by intentionally blocking promotion or training opportunities Overbearing supervision or other misuse of power or position Exclusion or victimisation	Blocking promotion Regularly and deliberately ignoring or excluding individuals from work activities
Directgov Website	Acas Website	TUC Website

job to inform employees on whether they have been bullied or not. Not only is there some disagreement between these lists, but there is sometimes little correspondence with the patterns observed in Figure 1. Most notably, whereas only 16 per cent of employees in the pilot survey who had been given 'tasks with unreasonable or impossible targets or deadlines' considered themselves bullied, this type of ill-treatment is mentioned in all three lists of bullying behaviour.

This kind of information is, presumably, intended to help British employees reach a common understanding of what workplace bullying is, but the evidence from the lists themselves, as much as our pilot survey, suggests we are some way short of such a common understanding at present. For this reason, we are unable to say very much that can help us to understand why some forms of ill-treatment qualify as bullying in employees' minds and others do not.

Measuring trouble at work: a big survey

The BWBS is the product of the extensive piloting and refinement just described. The BWBS is a structured survey that was administered to a representative sample of UK employees (or those with experience of employment in the previous two years) during the winter months of 2007–2008.[2] The total weighted numbers responding to the BWBS were 3,979. Of these, 14.6 per cent were not employed but had experience of employment in the previous two years (the rest were currently employed to some level).

The BWBS gathered data on individual demographic factors, including age, income, ethnicity, gender and sexual orientation, along with data on job and workplace characteristics including occupation, industry, size of workplace, trade union membership, gender/ethnic/age composition of workplace and respondents' views about their levels of control over the pace and nature of their work. We also sought to ascertain workers' perceptions about those responsible for ill-treatment in the workplace and why it occurs.

The cognitive testing described above helped us to revise the NAQ for use as a battery of questions on ill-treatment (for further details on the way items were revised, see Fevre, Robinson, Jones and Lewis 2010). When they had answered all the NAQ questions, respondents were given an opportunity to confirm or deny the choices they made about which of the 21 items they had experienced; subsequently there were some small reductions to the incidence rates across the items (usually 1–2 per cent, never more than 5 per cent). Because these more conservative 'confirmed' estimates are more accurate, we use these data in all analyses presented in this book. We also asked respondents whether they had witnessed or perpetrated each of the 21 items. Finally, respondents were able to remark on any aspect of their experiences in an unrestricted way at a couple of points in the survey. So, although mostly quantitative, we do have some illuminating qualitative data.

A deeper understanding: the 'troubled minority'

A final section of the BWBS gathered information about who was responsible for perpetrating the various types of ill-treatment and why they might have done it. Details on perpetrators included their gender and ethnicity and whether they were 'internal' to the workplace (such as fellow co-workers, subordinates or employers) or 'external' (such as clients, customers or members of the public). Respondents were then able to offer their own judgement about the causes of the ill-treatment. This information was gathered by offering 20 potential reasons that respondents could select, falling into four broad categories: characteristics of the workplace (e.g. position in the organisation or feeling that 'it's just the way things are at work'), characteristics of other employees (e.g. members of a group or clique who exclude other employees from it), the respondent's demographic characteristics (e.g. race, age and disability) or other characteristics (e.g. accent and trade union membership). These categories were derived from extant research and our cognitive testing process.

Even though the funding for our project was generous, we could not gather this more detailed information from every respondent due to financial constraints. Instead, only respondents who said they had experienced three or more of the 21 types of ill-treatment were asked these follow-up questions and, no matter how many types of ill-treatment they reported, we only asked follow-up questions about three of them. A methodology was employed to select the three types that we judged to be most serious (e.g. all of those who experienced 'actual physical violence at work' as one of three or more types of ill-treatment were routed into the follow-up section of the survey). Therefore the data on perpetrators of, and explanations for, ill-treatment at work reflect (a) respondents who experienced multiple forms of ill-treatment and (b) what we considered to be the more serious types of ill-treatment. It is for this reason that we consider them to be the 'troubled minority'. Their experiences in particular enable a deeper understanding of trouble at work.

Conceptual refinement: three types of trouble at work

Having multiple measures of 'trouble at work' is a good thing. As noted in the description of cognitive testing above, getting more than one reliable measure of ill-treatment at work was no easy task. Using past research and the comments of 'people on the street' to guide our measurement of such a complex phenomenon, however, proved very useful. In Table 2 we present the final version of the 21 different items that were included in our survey. To facilitate our understanding of the items and how they potentially group together, we conducted a factor analysis which revealed three types of ill-treatment. This is a common technique in social research, including research on problems at work such as bullying. For example, using data collected in the late 1990s in the United Kingdom, Einarsen, Hoel and Notelaers (2009) found three types of bullying: personal, work related and intimidation. Researchers then use these types in order to refine their explanations of bullying (e.g. Hauge et al. 2007).

Table 2 Multiple measures of trouble at work: 21 items and three factors

Unreasonable management	Incivility and disrespect	Violence
1. Someone withholding information which affects your performance	9. Being humiliated or ridiculed in connection with your work	20. Actual physical violence at work
2. Pressure from someone else to do work below your level of competence	10. Gossip and rumours being spread about you or having allegations made against you	21. Injury in some way as a result of violence or aggression at work
3. Having your views and opinions ignored	11. Being insulted or having offensive remarks made about you	
4. Someone continually checking up on you or your work when *it is not necessary*	12. Being treated in a disrespectful or rude way	
5. Pressure from someone else *not* to claim something which by right you are entitled to	13. People excluding you from their group	
6. Being given an unmanageable workload or impossible deadlines	14. Hints or signals from others that you should quit your job	
7. Your employer not following proper procedures	15. Persistent criticism of your work or performance which is unfair	
8. Being treated unfairly compared to others in your workplace	16. Teasing, mocking, sarcasm or jokes which go too far	
	17. Being shouted at or someone losing their temper with you	
	18. Intimidating behaviour from people at work	
	19. Feeling threatened in any way while at work	
Range 0–8 Mean = 1.45 Alpha = .83	Range 0–11 Mean = 1.41 Alpha = .86	Range 0–2 Mean = 0.09 Alpha = .79

The three factors identified in our analysis are also presented in Table 2, along with some descriptive statistics indicating that they are very robust and reliable factors. In other words, we have at our disposal 21 specific items and also three broader factors with which to discuss our findings. As indicated earlier, the three factors provide the structure for the three empirical chapters that follow. It is important to note that the three factors of unreasonable treatment, incivility and disrespect, and violence and injury can be considered as distinct experiences. In other words, the data indicate that they are qualitatively different from each other and can be treated as separate entities. This is not to say, however, that some items clearly fell into only one category. Indeed, three of the items could have been placed in either the unreasonable treatment factor or the incivility and disrespect factor ('people excluding you from their group', 'hints or signals that you should quit your job' and 'persistent criticism of your work or performance which is unfair'). So, for these items, the distinction between whether they were better suited as measures of unreasonable treatment or something more akin to denigration or disrespect was a bit more blurred. It is not surprising that some items have both a social and a work-related aspect. Likewise, the item 'feeling threatened in any way while at work' could have been considered to belong to either incivility and disrespect or violence and injury. We made our choices about which items belonged to which factors based on not only an empirical but also a conceptual framework.[3] This is just worth bearing in mind, as sometimes social science cannot be as exact or tidy as we might wish.

The chapters in Part Two deal with each of these factors in substantial detail. Before considering them separately, however, it will be useful to show how they interrelate. As the Venn diagram presented in Figure 2 shows, most

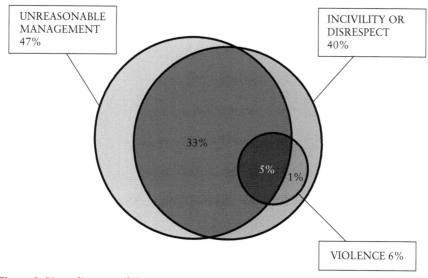

Figure 2 Venn diagram of three types of 'trouble at work'

of our respondents experienced more than one type of ill-treatment at work. For example, 33 per cent experienced both unreasonable management and incivility and disrespect. A much smaller proportion (6 per cent) experienced violence, and nearly all of them (5 per cent) experienced the other two types as well. So violence was never experienced on its own, and only when combined with some other type of ill-treatment. The diagram is useful for getting a sense of the overlapping and interlocking nature of these different aspects of trouble at work.

Before drawing this introduction to a close, it is important to note that there is also a high degree of overlap between experiencing, witnessing and perpetrating trouble at work (see Figure 3). Our analyses of the data revealed that across *all* 21 items there were significant positive correlations

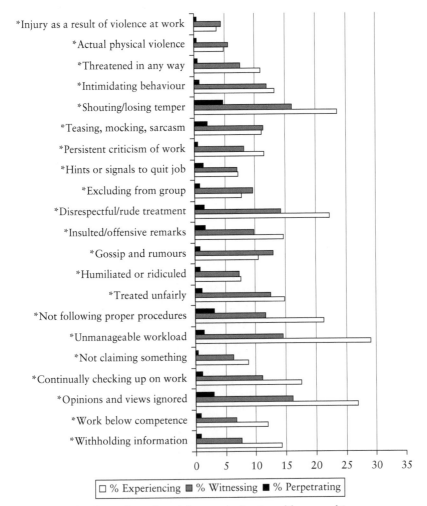

Figure 3 Experiencing, witnessing and perpetrating 'trouble at work'

(indicated by asterisks) between these three measures. In other words, people who experienced a particular type of ill-treatment were also more likely to report witnessing it and even to admit perpetrating it themselves. For example, the top three items in terms of highest incidence were very similar for experiencing, witnessing and perpetrating:

- opinions/views ignored (27 per cent experienced, 16 per cent witnessed, 3 per cent perpetrated)

- unmanageable workload (29 per cent experienced, 15 per cent witnessed, 1.5 per cent perpetrated)

- shouting/losing temper (24 per cent experienced, 16 per cent witnessed, 5 per cent perpetrated)

This is not to say that every 'victim' is also an 'offender' but rather that ill-treatment at work seems to affect people in a variety of ways – as victims, witnesses and perpetrators. This finding lends support to the main argument of our book, which is that it is the characteristics of troubled workplaces (i.e. 'hotspots') rather than of people (i.e. those especially prone to recognise, perpetrate or suffer workplace bullying) that will provide the best explanations of ill-treatment at work.

2

Fairness and Rationality at Work

Half of the British workforce experienced unreasonable treatment, the first factor identified in the introduction to Part Two, in the two years before our survey. Nearly a quarter experienced three or more different kinds of unreasonable behaviour, and one in 10 put up with five or more kinds.[1] It was unreasonable treatment, rather than disrespect or violence, which employees were more likely to say had the most effect on them. Of the six types of negative experience that they said had the most impact, four were types of unreasonable treatment. Having an unmanageable workload was said to have the most effect by more than one in five of those experiencing ill-treatment and, having their views ignored was mentioned by one in 10.

Unreasonable treatment can threaten well-being; for example, it can frustrate employees' efforts to increase earnings, achieve promotion or make their working hours a better fit with the rest of their lives. Yet unreasonable treatment did not have the worst effects on employees' health or well-being (including their finances and their relations with family and friends) in our survey. As we shall see in Chapter 3, disrespect generally had worse effects than either unreasonable treatment or violence in the workplace. We cannot therefore be certain what people meant by saying unreasonable treatment had the biggest impact – 'impact' might, for some, even be a positive thing – but we strongly suspect that many employees felt that unreasonable treatment had the biggest impact on how they spent their time and on what they learnt about themselves and their workplace. Employers measure this impact with concepts such as 'organisational commitment' and 'employee engagement' – the kind of thing they have in mind is illustrated by the views of several employees we discuss in the qualitative studies in the second half of the book. They said that, where they had once been proud to dedicate their working lives to their employer, they were now thoroughly demoralised by the unreasonable treatment they had received.

Research evidence confirms that British employees have a strong expectation that employers should behave rationally (Fevre, Grainger and Brewer 2010). They expect employers to set them goals and help them identify means to achieve them (Walker and Fincham 2011). These can be internal goals, such as the most efficient use of human or non-human resources, or external goals like the provision of a quality service or product. Both kinds of goals are frequently quoted in company websites and literature, in employee training and as part of performance management. For example, amongst its many goals, Transport for London promises to 'ensure that its staff are competent to perform their roles' but also to 'maintain robust systems for identifying and evaluating all significant risks'. British Telecom promises to 'create a diverse and inclusive work environment' and to design 'sustainable products and services that help our customers to effectively tackle social and environmental challenges'.

People do not like it when their expectations of rationality in the workplace are not met. Psychological research shows that employees have greater job satisfaction[2] when they are clear about what they are supposed to be doing – and this will involve knowing who they report to, and who reports to them, as well as what their duties are – and get recognition for doing it well (see the discussions of job/role conflicts and particularly Roscigno, Lopez and Hodson 2009 in Chapter 1). Unreasonable treatment has the potential to disrupt all of this cognitive underpinning of job satisfaction. We suspect that this is an important factor in the thinking that led employees to say unreasonable treatment had the biggest impact on them.

Our case studies illustrated some of the effects people had in mind; for example employees told us of the frustration they felt at not getting the information they needed to do their jobs properly. In this extract from one of our interview transcripts, a Banco employee, a man in his fifties, illustrated his frustration at the futility of rules regarding the use of his mobile telephone that interfered not only with his ability to do his job well but also ultimately cost the company business:

> I have to have a company mobile; I can't have my own anymore. Now I have got hundreds of clients, thousands of clients who have got my mobile number, but I can't have that because when I leave I am [allegedly] going to take all these clients with me. What a load of rubbish. So I have had rows with them, so now I have got a company mobile, a flipping great lump in my pocket. Nobody rings the company one, they ring this one [his personal mobile] because that is the number I have given them, and if I divert the calls from this one to that one it costs me money.

The irrationality of this kind of treatment was maddening, and it could be equally maddening trying to achieve the objectives set by employers if employees were given unrealistic deadlines or no clear order of priorities. A female doctor in her forties described her frustration with irrational management expectations working for Westshire NHS (National Health Service) Trust:

> And so X is overbooking clinics and keeps going on at us about doing more work, we're not hitting our targets, we've got to hit our targets, we've got to do some overtime. And waiting list initiatives are becoming, you know, what they're supposed to be, occasional extras. Yet I'm signed up to do every Saturday morning between here and the summer. I think it's unreasonable that ... And if you don't do it there's an implied management pressure. I said, 'Well you haven't tried to help us out with our waiting list targets. Why the bloody hell should I give

up my Saturday mornings?' But I have done because my patients are suffering. And my patients are suffering because Westshire won't employ enough doctors and nurses and clinics and things like that. I mean when I say doctors, they won't employ enough staff to get through the work. And that has definitely got worse over the last couple of years. But it's because the waiting times' targets have come down [i.e. government required hospitals to reduce patients' waiting times].

Sometimes employees were incensed because they believed that what had happened to them was illegal or, at the least, a flagrant breach of procedure, but more often they commented on the unfairness of what had happened to them. They knew of other employees who were not treated in this way – who were not denied recognition, who were not ignored, for example – and could not see a reason for it. At Banco, a young Asian male in his twenties outlined his frustrations at not being recognised for going the extra mile:

I mean the problem that I do have is, sometimes, I don't like the fact you don't get recognised well. It's like, I make use of my languages, when a claim comes through if the person can't speak Asian, Punjabi, Urdu, Chinese, I'll speak to them. And once I've cleared that call they are very thankful, I feel very happy but that's it. Who else is to know what I've done? What have I achieved? It's not like the company would have done it without me helping because there is another Chinese person who works here, but he can't speak Chinese so he always asks for my help. So in that sense I would like to be recognised.

For many people, the sense of unfairness and irrationality was compounded by a feeling that the organisation they worked for had no way of taking account of them as an individual. For example, they may have felt that they had been a model employee over a long career, and they needed their employer to recall their individual contribution at a difficult time in their lives or in the life of the organisation. If they were looking for 'special' treatment, it was not special in the sense of favouritism or patronage, but special in that it recognised that one employee did not have the same gifts, or values, as another. In some particularly difficult cases, individual treatment did mean that employees had different *needs*.

The existing literature on dignity at work (Bolton 2007; Hodson 2001; Hoel and Beale 2006; Peyton 2003; Rayman 2001) attempts to theorise some of the issues at stake here. In this literature, dignity is usually conceived as requiring respect (e.g. from an employer), self-respect and, sometimes, a degree of autonomy. We discuss autonomy below, but what this literature tends to leave out is the way in which employees take a great deal of persuasion to be convinced that their employer is *not* treating them reasonably. We suspect that, especially in the lower levels of organisations, employees believe that, even if they cannot discern the reason for what has happened to them, there must be a reason because the context in which their organisation operates demands it. True, this is more likely to happen in the private sector where (or so people imagine) markets will dictate rational behaviour.

The public and third sectors have to rely more on bureaucratic rules, and the judgement of professionals and managers, but there are also public, and even statutory, duties, audit and oversight, to keep such organisations rational (Fevre 2003). For these reasons, employees very often do as they are told while being determined not to reason why they should.

Of course, they do not mind covering some menial tasks because they assume that they are thereby saving on a greater cost that outweighs the temporary loss of their skills to the employer. Nor do they usually mind someone checking up on their work when it is not necessary. It would be nice if the organisation did not judge everyone by the standard of the least productive and competent, but perhaps it is better to be safe than sorry. Nor do employees mind coming in at the weekend now and then to meet an impossible deadline. As a line manager in Strand Global Systems told us, 'some of the guys in the team have been there for 40 years ... I guess their expectation is that these things are always going to be late. They're always going to be asked to do something a little bit special.' It takes a significant loss of trust for employees like these to think to question whether their employer had enough people on the payroll to meet its order book.

People higher up in their organisations may be a little more cynical about the power of markets or bureaucratic imperatives to keep their employers rational; nevertheless they expect that, if they can find it anywhere, they will find rational behaviour in the workplace. It is in this light that we should understand people's complaints of unreasonable treatment. Finding that there is no rhyme or reason to decisions, that counterproductive behaviour is rife, that money, time and effort are frittered away, is not what people are meant to find. But when people do begin to believe that they have been unreasonably treated, this is the territory they find themselves in – a strange and unsettling world in which markets and professional managers and public oversight do not apparently make organisations behave rationally – and they often find it both frustrating and upsetting. Most often, they also believe there is nothing they can do to change this. Their frustration at seeing the wrong things done or the right things omitted – service worse than necessary, equipment or talent going to waste – is made keener by their impotence. Indeed, as indicated here, it is with unreasonable treatment that we get most questioning about whether the employer is meeting the external targets set: are they selling the right financial products to people, and are they spending the taxpayers' money wisely?

Figure 4 shows how many employees experienced unreasonable treatment over a two-year period, but it does not tell us whether this was something that happened rarely: working late to maximise sales in the pre-Christmas rush, doing one's own photocopying when one's assistant was on holiday. Most employees thought that their experience of unreasonable treatment had been less frequent than once a month, but a proportion – never less than one in five, and nearly a third for unreasonable workload – of employees' experiences of

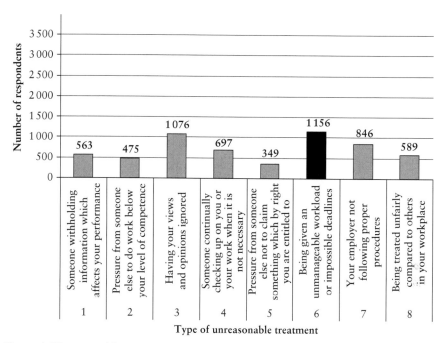

Figure 4 Unreasonable treatment

eight types of unreasonable behaviour were at least weekly, and possibly daily, occurrences.[3]

As we would expect, employers, managers and supervisors were far more likely to be responsible for unreasonable treatment than either co-workers or customers (including clients). For example, we collected data on over 1,300 incidents of unreasonable treatment from those we call the troubled minority.[4] About two-thirds of these incidents were blamed on employers, managers and supervisors (from here on we shall call this group 'managers'). The next most important group to which blame was attached for unreasonable treatment was co-workers, but these were a long way behind, accounting for about a fifth of the incidents of unreasonable treatment. Co-workers in particular were likely to be responsible for withholding information which affected performance (perhaps affecting one in 14 employees), pressure to work below one's level of competence (roughly a third of this came from co-workers), and ignoring one's opinions and views. We can surmise from the responses of the troubled minority that they thought some of the unreasonable treatment by colleagues resulted from the way the organisation was run. It would be a little misleading to call unreasonable treatment 'unreasonable management', but only a little.

Analysis of interviews with the troubled minority showed that most unreasonable treatment came from serial troublemakers, most of whom were men. Because most managers are men,[5] male troublemakers could be expected when the troublemakers were managers, and many of the issues which were the focus of ill-treatment (work allocation, communication, supervision) were recurrent. Male troublemakers were in the majority for all eight types of unreasonable treatment but were most markedly in the majority for pressure to work below one's level of competence. For all eight types of unreasonable treatment, the vast majority of troublemakers (80 per cent or higher) were white.

As we explained on p. 30, we also asked employees whether they had witnessed any unreasonable treatment of someone other than themselves on more than one occasion in the past two years. Figure 3 on p. 34 showed that more people had experienced unreasonable treatment than had witnessed it, but the witnessing rates were quite high for some types of unreasonable treatment, particularly unfair treatment and pressure not to claim something. This was not true of improper procedures and unmanageable workloads.

The proportion of the sample who said they had themselves been responsible for the unreasonable treatment of others was very low in comparison to the number who had witnessed or observed it. The only hint of a variation from this was for improper procedures and ignoring other people's opinions. Given what was said above about the expectation that people should behave rationally in the workplace, it should be no surprise that so few people admitted that they failed to live up to expectations. That people were more prepared to admit that they had failed to use proper procedures, and ignored others, may indicate where the most obvious conflicts in rational expectations were to be found. One might fail to use proper procedures if given a good reason to do so, and ignore the opinion of others if it was thought that they did not understand the objective. In any event, these low percentages remind us how foolish it would be write off the widespread nature of unreasonable treatment as in some way normal. The fact that so few people admit to having done it suggests that hardly anyone thinks of this as part of normal working life.[6]

As with all types of ill-treatment, those who experienced it were more likely both to witness it and to have done it themselves. As noted on p. 23, we think this confirms the advantages the 'troubled workplace' concept has over labels for individuals (for example as 'bullies' and 'victims' or 'targets') when we are trying to understand the causes of troubles at work. Of course, we have our own labels – the 'troubled minority' and 'troublemakers' – but these are meant to convey different experiences of a third factor, the troubled workplace, rather than setting us searching for the essential characteristics of troublemakers or troubled workers.

We discovered further evidence of troubled workplaces when we asked the troubled minority why they thought they had been subjected to unreasonable treatment. For all types of unreasonable treatment, most of the troubled minority chose one or more of these three potential explanations: 'your position in the organisation', 'it's just the way things are where you work' and 'the attitude or personality of the other person'. The only other explanations for unreasonable treatment worth mentioning were 'people's relationships at work (e.g. favouritism)' and 'your performance at work'. The former was slightly more common and particularly so where employees had experienced improper procedures and/or unfair treatment.[7]

This is an appropriate point to clarify the relationship between workplaces and the organisation which controlled them. Just over half of employees said their workplace was part of a larger organisation, and a quarter said it was not (the remainder said they did not know or refused to answer). We had anticipated that most workplaces would be controlled by larger organisations, so we knew that in some questions it would be appropriate to refer to an organisation, in others to the workplace, and in others to a vaguer formula such as 'where you work'.

Up to this point, we have been using descriptive statistics which might be encountered in marketing campaigns, and media reports of opinion polls, but we now move to multivariate analysis which allows us to control for lots of different variables at the same time. For example, if we find that unreasonable treatment is more common amongst disabled employees and public sector workers, descriptive statistics cannot tell us whether we need to look more closely at disabled workers, the public sector or both. Multivariate analysis can put everything together and tell us whether the disabled workers are only more at risk because they work in the public sector, whether the public sector is worse because it has more disabled workers, or whether it is a bit of both. Multivariate analysis can do this because it controls for every variable we put in our models.

The important lessons to learn from the multivariate analysis conducted for this chapter come in three varieties: those which refer to the individuals, jobs and workplaces associated with greater experience of unreasonable treatment. First, three characteristics of individuals were associated with greater experience of unreasonable treatment: they tended to be disabled or have a long-term illness, to be white and to be younger. Second, job characteristics associated with greater experience were earning a higher income and having managerial or supervisory responsibilities. Employees were also more likely to have experienced unreasonable treatment at work if the nature of their work had changed (or was changing), they had less control over their work, or the pace of their work had increased. Change in people's work is certainly a job characteristic but could also be a workplace characteristic. There were also employees who said that, irrespective of change, the pace of their work was too intense, which could be also be both a job and a workplace characteristic.

Third, amongst workplace characteristics associated with unreasonable treatment, employees were more likely to experience it if their workplace was outside London. There was also a strong correlation between experience of unreasonable treatment and employees telling us that their organisations always treated people as a means to an end (never an end in themselves). Another strong correlation was found between experiencing unreasonable treatment and feeling the organisation's goals were not compatible with our interviewee's moral principles. Strong as these two correlations were, perhaps the key predictor of the unreasonable treatment was that employees were not treated as individuals. As we suggested a little earlier, an employee's sense of unfairness and irrationality can be accompanied by belief that the organisation does not take account of the individual – of their talents, their values and, sometimes, their needs.

There is one thing to bear in mind before we fill in all the details of these findings. We have already explained that, although our funding was substantial, we could not afford to ask all the questions we wanted to find answers to in the whole sample. For example, the questions about who caused the trouble they reported were only asked of the troubled minority. That means that one of the things we were not able to control for in the multivariate analysis being discussed in the next section is who the troublemakers were.

What kind of employees experienced more unreasonable treatment?

One group of employees stood out as being far more likely to receive unreasonable treatment: employees who had impairments, including learning difficulties, or had a long-term serious health condition such as cancer or heart disease or, indeed, diabetes or clinical depression. We shall now describe this group as employees with disabilities. This group also stood out in the FTWS conducted on behalf of the UK government shortly after the BWBS (see Fevre *et al.* 2009), and for the same reason. In both surveys, the relationship between having disabilities and being unreasonably treated was beyond doubt, and the increased risk of being unfairly treated was substantial. At this point it may be tempting to conclude that this is a problem for a small minority. While employees with disabilities made up a minority of our sample, the proportion of the workforce with disabilities rises with age and, since we shall all, with luck, become older workers one day it may not be wise to write off the plight of employees with disabilities as someone else's problem.

When we simply compare those who had disabilities with those who did not, it becomes clear that some subgroups of workers with disabilities were more likely to suffer unreasonable treatment than others. Figure 5 shows that employees with physical and other health conditions were significantly more likely to be associated with unreasonable treatment than the non-disabled, but it was those with psychological problems and learning difficulties who had the most problems. Figure 6 shows what the relationships were when controlled for other factors. The association between having a disability and

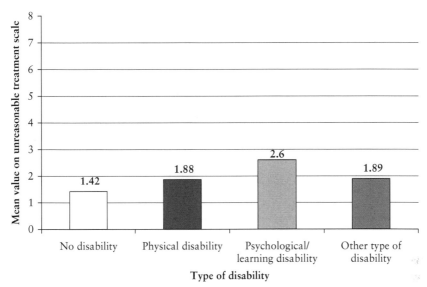

Figure 5   Unreasonable treatment of employees with disabilities

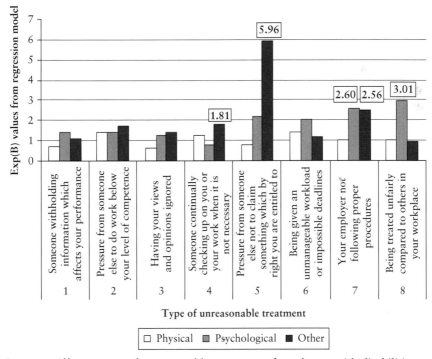

Figure 6   Different types of unreasonable treatment of employees with disabilities

being unreasonably treated does not disappear, but it does become much more specific. For example, employees with psychological problems and learning difficulties were four times as likely to be treated unfairly, and employees with other health problems (those long-term conditions including the life-threatening ones) were seven times more likely to say they have been pressured to not claim something to which they were entitled (perhaps sick leave or sick pay).

It is possible that some of these relationships may be the result of 'health effects', meaning employees acquired their impairments or health problems as an effect of the unreasonable treatment they had received. For example, the imposition of unmanageable workloads or impossible deadlines might have affected the mental health of some employees. In a paper which discusses the situation of disabled employees in detail (Fevre *et al.* forthcoming), we explain that there is often a vicious spiral of ill-treatment and health problems, and it may often be a thankless task to determine which of these originally caused the other. The situation may also be complicated in some cases by the possibility that employees with health problems may be more likely to perceive behaviour as ill-treatment because of what psychologists call 'negative affect'. Someone with clinical depression, for example, may be more likely to perceive certain treatment more unreasonable than a colleague who experiences the same treatment but does not have depression. All these finer points aside, Figures 5 and 6 suggest that some employees with disabilities were simply being treated unreasonably.

If some disabled employees were very much more likely to be unreasonably treated, should we naturally assume that this was an expression of stigma and a form of discrimination (Walker and Fincham 2011)? Only a very small number of the people with disabilities in our sample considered their impairment or ill-health was a factor causing their experiences of any kind of ill-treatment at work. This was despite the fact that they could 'tick all that apply' when citing factors they felt to be contributing towards their ill-treatment. Workers with disabilities, like the majority of other types of workers in our sample, were most likely to attribute their ill-treatment to the nature of the workplace, for example, citing, 'It's just the way things are at work.'

Like the employees in our survey, we do not think that most of the unreasonable treatment we discovered was the result of managers and employers targeting people with disabilities or chronic illness in workplace hate crimes. We agree with them that most unreasonable treatment follows from a failure to accommodate people with disabilities and chronic illness in the workplace, but we are not convinced that this has nothing to do with stigma and discrimination. Some stigmatisation certainly occurred at the point when employers failed to accommodate employees who had such conditions. This was not stigmatisation of them for their disabilities but rather for their failure to meet their employers' expectations, for example, of their work and attendance (Walker and Fincham 2011). We think this is why items like pressured not to claim due entitlements, being continually checked up on and one's employer failing to follow proper procedures loomed so large in this analysis.

We have already noted that those with 'other' disabilities or health conditions – like cancer, diabetes, hypertension, stroke, heart disease, pulmonary conditions, asthma and digestive/bowel disorders – were seven times more likely to say that they had been pressured not to claim something they were are entitled to. They were also nearly three times more likely to report someone was continually checking up on them. Both employees with 'other' disabilities or conditions, and those with psychological conditions, were three times as likely as the non-disabled to say their employer had not followed proper procedures. Earlier in this chapter, we suggested that, for some workers, the experience of unreasonable treatment might be combined with what they felt to be a denial of their qualities, values and needs. We think this is particularly likely to be the case amongst such employees. Their complaints about entitlement, about checking up, and about procedures may refer, in part, to just such issues, for example, to an employer applying the most rigid interpretation of their sickness absence policy to a long-serving employee who was, up to this point in their lives, considered invaluable.

In one example from the qualitative case studies, a Britscope worker had recovered from breast cancer but suffered a collapsed lung and pneumonia. She forced herself to go back to work before being issued an official warning. Like many employers, Britscope have a policy of dismissing when three warnings have been issued to staff about absence. This woman told us you never knew what was going to happen in the future so you did not want to incur a warning unnecessarily:

> I knew I hadn't been very well and I'd been to the doctor and they knew I had something. I didn't actually know it was that bad and … they gave me a sick note … for a week, but I went back before that … had run out because I thought I don't want to get a warning. And of course I went to work and then they realised that I've come back and said, 'well you are still supposed to get a … warning'. And I said 'well I've come back early, before my sick note ran out, hang on a minute'. The next thing I know, I'm escorted off the premises … He said, 'go back to your doctor and get a sick note to sign you back off' [and then I], sign back on so I can go back to work … On the Monday I was going back to work, I went to the doctor but I'd got really ill by then. But the funny thing was, the manager had said to me 'look I appreciate, it's off the record, I appreciate the fact that you have come back', he said … 'We'll take that into account when I come to issue a … warning and you do look alright.' Yeah, 'I look alright', I had a collapsed lung! Oh I got so ill in the few days after that. I was really ill and I'd gone back to work to try to make sure I saved my job.

In the way they deal with sick leave, employees returning to work after sickness absence, the management of ongoing conditions (e.g. providing time off to attend hospital or other sources of therapy), and the 'reasonable adjustments' to work and the workplace required by UK legislation, organisations were seen to be behaving far from rationally. Confirmation of this finding was given by the Fair Treatment Survey, which showed a correlation between bullying and/or harassment and disability and that employees with disabilities were nearly twice as likely to say they had a range of problems with employment rights. Simple bivariate analysis showed that disabled employees were particularly likely to say they had experienced problems with sick leave or pay but also with holidays, rest breaks, number of hours or days they worked, pay, contracts, complaints procedures, grievance procedures, health and safety, and retirement (Fevre *et al.* 2009). While problems with employment rights do not necessarily entail unreasonable treatment, we strongly suspect that it was issues like these that much of the unreasonable treatment disabled employees experienced in our survey referred to. In such cases, we would argue, the stimulus to unreasonable treatment was the disappointment of employers' expectations which their employees believed were unreasonable given their disability or health condition.

We do not think it an oversimplification to suggest that most unreasonable treatment that employees with disabilities experienced occurred when they tried to make their work a better fit with their disability or condition. For example, they encountered it when they took sick leave or when they wanted to negotiate changes in their work to accommodate their disability or condition. It is, however, possible that subsequent changes to British legislation improved the situation documented in our survey and the FTWS. The Equality Act 2010 attempted to clear up some of the confusion surrounding 'reasonable adjustments', but it also made it possible for disabled employees to argue that an employer's unreasonable expectations amount to illegal, indirect discrimination (Part 2, Chapter 2, Paragraph 19 of the Act). If disabled employees have particular problems in respect of complaints or grievance procedures, the 2010 Act opened up the possibility that such problems may amount to victimisation (Part 2, Chapter 2, Paragraph 27).

The other characteristics that made employees more likely to experience unreasonable treatment in our survey – age and ethnicity – had nowhere near as strong a relationship as having a disability or long-term health condition, but the ethnicity effect was the stronger of the two and its direction was surprising. In multivariate analysis, non-white employees were less likely to experience unreasonable treatment. Most of this was the result of employees with Asian backgrounds being much less likely to experience unreasonable treatment than anyone else. Indeed, Asians were significantly less likely to experience half of the various types of unreasonable treatment. It is as well, at this point, to remember that most unreasonable treatment originated with managers and co-workers.

It might be ventured that, in a 'politically correct' society, people will manage their public behaviour in such way that they rule out any possible accusation of racism. In this case, it could be imagined ethnic minority employees as a whole would be better treated, but this does not really help us to explain why the effect should only be visible for employees of Asian origin. Is it the case, perhaps, that it was less likely for Asians to be unreasonably treated wherever they happened to work, or was it because they were less likely to work in troubled workplaces? Non-white employees, and particularly Asians, were significantly less likely, compared to white workers, to witness the unreasonable treatment of others in the workplaces. This might suggest that they did indeed work in less troubled workplace and that this was why they did not experience as much unreasonable treatment. It might even suggest that Asian employees take steps to avoid taking jobs in troubled workplaces. We return to these possibilities later in the book (p. 217).

We suggested (p. 44) that getting old might be associated with an increased risk of experiencing unreasonable treatment because older people are more likely to suffer impairments and illness. In fact, once we control for disabilities and long-term conditions, increased age slightly reduced experience of unreasonable treatment amongst our sample. Increased age reduced (though not by much) the experience of six out of eight types of unreasonable treatment across the board. This was not a question of getting used to how things were in a particular job because the reduction in unreasonable treatment was not related to length of job tenure. Nor was it to do with getting better treatment with more seniority, or inducting successive generations into the culture of the workplace, because the (albeit small) reduction in unreasonable treatment continued beyond the years in which people joined the labour force for the first time.

Perceptions of treatment as reasonable or not might change with age. Older workers might know from their experiences in other jobs that the treatment they received in their current job could hardly be described as unreasonable. The age factor might also be a 'cohort effect', meaning that successive generations have been more likely to perceive their treatment as unreasonable throughout their careers. That is, people born in the 1970s will always perceive more unreasonable treatment than people born in the 1950s, no matter how old they are when you ask them. These are theoretical possibilities but throughout our analysis of the survey we have found that we have eventually tended to discard explanations of our data couched in terms of different perceptions because they do not fit other survey data or the findings of our qualitative research. We see no reason why this case should be any different, and therefore we think the simple explanation of the age effect is probably the most likely: workers are more reasonably treated as they got older, perhaps because they demand this.

One of the fitters we interviewed at Strand Global Systems was a woman in her early twenties who thought her manager was 'very ageist'. She found it 'really irritating' that he talked 'completely differently' to younger people and treated them differently because he expected them 'to act like young people'. She felt he was also holding her back, not letting her learn and progress at her own pace and not listening to her opinions. She could not object because her career depended on his decisions. She could not be 'mouthy' because she would not get on – indeed she wanted to be a manager herself. The older employees could be mouthy because they were stuck and would never be promoted. The young woman said, 'they just baby you', and she did not like having her abilities underestimated and would have liked the chance to prove that she had learnt a lot from studying ahead on her own, but her boss was 'always spying on you from afar, he's never there knowing that you've gained this knowledge. So he's always assuming that you're still just a rooky when you're not'.

By accident, we happened to interview the assistant to this young woman's manager, so we heard his slant on what she told us about being given a menial job because she was young: 'They wouldn't have asked any of the older ones to do it because they know they would have told them to go away.' Why was she given what she called 'just child's work ... just silly'? He said it wasn't silly at all – it was all about encouraging customers 'by having a world-class workplace'. So why did the older fitters not have to do it? 'Some were quite happy to get involved; in fact a majority were quite happy to get involved, but when it comes to actually getting on your hands and knees and scraping up a bit of old tape that was on the floor, then a few people did draw the line at that. But we just honoured that.'

Being younger, disabled and white put employees in our sample at greater risk of unreasonable treatment. The survey is better able to tell us why the employees with disabilities were at risk than white workers and younger workers, but these are not the only puzzles the survey data threw up. For example, it might have been easy to assume at the outset that the members of other 'equality strands' would be more likely experience unreasonable treatment. The results for Asian employees may go a long way to explaining why non-Christians and those born outside the United Kingdom were no more likely to experience unreasonable treatment, but the fact that women were no more likely to experience unreasonable treatment could be just as much a conundrum as the surprising finding.

Which jobs were more prone to unreasonable treatment?

Like age, the level of income an employee earned in his or her job was a low-level effect but with significance across several different types of unreasonable treatment. Yet, where getting older reduced the experience of unreasonable treatment, higher income made it more likely. Multivariate analysis showed that, irrespective of age, job tenure and so on, a slightly better paying job meant putting up with a bit more unreasonable treatment. In fact it is not so hard to imagine why earning a little more might increase exposure to someone withholding information which affects one's performance, pressure from someone else to do work below one's level of competence, pressure not to claim an entitlement or being given an unmanageable workload. The same is true of the next occupational characteristic that put employees at greater risk of unreasonable treatment.

While not being as big a risk factor as having a disability, having managerial or supervisory responsibilities clearly increased the likelihood of unreasonable treatment, particularly having one's views and opinions ignored, bearing an unmanageable workload and finding one's employer failing to follow proper procedures. Clearly, employees who did not have managerial duties might well be less likely to expect their opinions to be taken into account and less likely to know what procedures were used and what proper ones would look like. This was, after all, implied earlier in the chapter when we suggested that higher level employees might have lower expectations of rational behaviour. Similarly, it might not be hard to see why employees with managerial responsibilities, like employees with greater incomes, might be at greater risk of unmanageable workloads or impossible deadlines. As one of the senior managers from Strand said, these were a normal part of 'the management challenge'.

Now, as in the previous section, we think it is worth pointing out which findings our data did not produce. In this case we did not find that those who were in the worst jobs received the most unreasonable treatment. Once income and managerial duties were taken into account, the type of occupation they were in did not matter at all. There is nothing here to suggest worse treatment of the vulnerable, the marginalised or those who have few options in the labour market.

Which workplace and organisations were more prone to unreasonable treatment?

We have already noted on p. 45 that measures of organisational change can be considered a workplace characteristic as well as an occupational one. Change in the workplace creates plenty of opportunities for unreasonable treatment; indeed, organisational change may itself be unreasonable for some employees. It is therefore not a surprise that all three of the measures of change in our survey were predictors of unreasonable treatment. The strongest effect overall was where employees said they now had less control at work. This was also a very general effect, significant across seven of the eight types of unreasonable treatment. It is perhaps not surprising that losing control over what one does at work should be correlated with someone continually checking up on one or one's work when it is not necessary. On the other hand, having less control was just as strongly correlated with being treated unfairly. We need to remember that this finding is very definitely about employees having *less* control than they used to have, because whether an employee had a lot of, or very little, autonomy in deciding the amount, pace and choice of work, or the quality of what they did, made no difference to his or her chances of suffering unreasonable treatment.

Employees who said that the nature of their work had changed, and/or the pace of their work had increased, were also more likely to say they had been unreasonably treated, but the correlation was not as strong and covered fewer (three) of the eight types of unreasonable treatment. One other question provided further evidence that change was a less important factor in unreasonable treatment than the feeling that work was out of control. Those employees who thought the pace of their work was too intense were a lot more likely to say they had been unfairly treated than those who reported that the pace of work had increased or the nature of their work had changed. Again it is no surprise that saying the pace of your work is too much for you is correlated with an unmanageable workload but, once more, the correlation with unfair treatment was also strong.

It is also worth pointing out that these correlations held irrespective of whether people felt they had less control over the pace of their work, whether they or their manager decided how much work they did or how fast they did it, and whether or not they had control over quality. This raises the interesting question of how much of the connection between high-intensity work and unreasonable treatment involves employees who are driving themselves to work harder, perhaps because they are complying with normal expectations of their jobs. We have already heard of the shop-floor workers at Strand who were expected to do 'something a bit special' for their employer every so often. It is worth adding that some of these workers did not bother to claim back the time in lieu earned in the process. The trade union convenor for shop-floor workers told us that '[s]ome people do not want to take holidays even. We have to force them to take holidays'. In fact the company had once used this fact, before the law changed, to argue against the union in a negotiation over holiday entitlement, and 'when we used to get paid up front, there were people who booked their holidays and then come into work, have the money and then work the week as well. Oh aye. You wouldn't believe it'.

In the introduction to this chapter, we suggested that the key predictor of the troubled workplace seemed to be that individuals did not matter there. In the survey, we measured with the following three questions the degree to which this applied to the places our interviewees worked:

- Where I work, the needs of the organisation always come before the needs of people.
- Where I work, you have to compromise your principles.
- Where I work, people are treated as individuals.

Large minorities of the British workforce agreed with one or more of these statements: 39 per cent said the needs of the organisation always came first, 30 per cent maintained they had to compromise their principles and one in five stated that people were not treated as individuals where they worked. Even though so many people agreed with them, we have found these three questions to be most important to the diagnosis of workplace problems that we have given them the collective acronym of FARE questions, standing for FAirness and REspect (also see Walker and Fincham 2011: 61–2).

Figure 7 shows that there was some variation in these results between industries, with employees in utilities and public administration and defence tending to be more critical across the board. We had initially imagined that the more critical responses would be in the private sector, so the results for public administration were surprising. Overall, the private sector did come out worst in the FARE questions but, while people were less likely to say the needs of the organisation came first if they worked in health and social work or (especially) education, employees in health and social work were more likely than those in most other industries to feel they had to compromise their principles. Health and social work employees were the only ones who were more likely to say they compromised their principles than they were to say the needs of the organisation always came first (something worth bearing in mind in Chapter 7). Employees in education were, however, amongst the least likely to think they had to compromise their principles or were not treated as individuals.

We would argue that the FARE questions may be a better guide to the existence of troubled workplaces than conventional questions about job

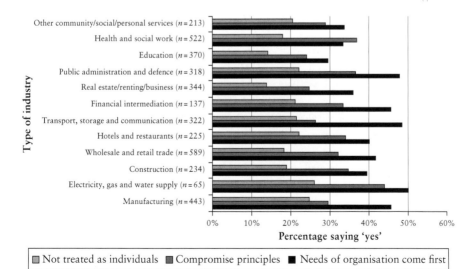

Figure 7 Fairness and respect (the FARE questions) in different industries

satisfaction, bullying or stress. For example, once we controlled for things like the difference in FARE scores between industries, all three questions were significant for all eight types of unreasonable treatment, and employees who thought people were not treated as individuals were twice as likely to report one or more types. This was the strongest predictor of unreasonable treatment across the board in our model, stronger even than having less control over one's work or having a disability. The second FARE question about compromising one's principles was just as strong as having less control and stronger than having a disability.

Of course, there will be some unreasonable treatment where the FARE questions do not indicate whether an interviewee works in a troubled workplace. We would argue that it is these, rather less frequent, situations in which the more individual, psychological or clinical models of bullying and/or stress might apply (Walker and Fincham 2011). More sociological researchers should be trying to understand the characteristics and underlying causes of troubled workplaces. This is not to say, however, that they should neglect those factors such as disability, managerial duties and reduced control over work, which were correlated with unreasonable treatment even when we controlled – as we did in all our multivariate analyses – for the answers to the FARE questions.

As we shall see in Chapter 3, the FARE questions were strongly correlated with measures of incivility and disrespect. We also suspect the FARE questions predict when employees are dissatisfied with the service their employer gives to clients and customers, or feel the organisation they work for does not contribute to the public good (perhaps they feel it is involved in corruption or environmental degradation). These are all potential indicators of the troubled workplace, just as unreasonable treatment is, but none of them explain what the source of trouble is. The case studies discussed in Part Two are designed to help us with this, however.

The other workplace characteristic which predicted unreasonable treatment in our multivariate analysis was the region in which the employee lived. Those who were resident in any region except London, but particularly Yorkshire and Humberside, and Wales, were more likely to report unreasonable treatment. The differences between regions were startling and quite unexpected. Employees in every other region than London were more likely to say their opinions and views were ignored, and they were subjected to unnecessary checking, denied entitlements, given unmanageable workloads and their employers did not follow proper procedures. Employees in Yorkshire were five times as likely as those in London to say they had an unmanageable workload and four times as likely to say their opinions were ignored.

As with the results for ethnicity, it is possible to come up with some suggestions as to why the results for region might have something to do with troubled workplaces. We know that very little unreasonable treatment originated with clients and customers. We might guess, therefore, that someone who was in a job where the behaviour of clients of customers was a major factor in determining the quality of their working lives would be less likely to report unreasonable treatment. It might matter more to them than what their managers did. Indeed, their managers might also be focused on customers and clients and used to judging whether organisational goals had been met through monitoring customer feedback. This is not always the case, even in a 'customer-facing' role in an organisation like Banco which prided itself on the standards of service it achieved. Here, a male employee who worked in one of their customer service centres a long way away from London explained how taking too long over the delivery of a service to customers caused him difficulties in meeting managers' expectations:

> So once you have taken a call this clock appears on your screen, starts ticking. As soon as you are three or four minutes in [to the call], you are not available to take another call, [the clock] alerts and then it goes red. The manager's screen will be able to see that, and then you are challenged why you are not taking a call. If that is a certain percentage that is enough to ruin your performance, and it will be looked at. So you would fall down the ladder and after three periods of not achieving those targets you would be then taken into some disciplinary action, whether it be informal or a formal decision to potentially relieve you of your duties.
>
> So what we need to do or what our role is, putting the customer first, making sure the customer experience is fantastic, we are putting them at the heart of our business decisions, we are showing empathy, you know that type of thing. How to fit that into our everyday role when we have our targets to meet, and we can't be not taking a call for a certain percentage of our day without it being detrimental to our overall performance. The two things don't meet and that is what seems to be the general sort of feel amongst all employees.

If we assume that people who worked in London were more likely to work in jobs where clients and customers were a more important factor in the quality of their working lives, the fact that Londoners were less likely to report unreasonable treatment might well have nothing to do with managers in London being more reasonable. It could simply reflect the fact that clients and customers were more important factors in the kinds of jobs done by Londoners.

The troubled minority

It is a good bet that unreasonable treatment of the troubled minority will not have the same correlates as unreasonable treatment within the wider sample. People who have experienced three or more types of unreasonable treatment are more likely to be in a troubled workplace to begin with, so the factors that distinguish troubled workplaces from untroubled ones will not show up strongly, or at all, in an analysis of the ill-treatment received. In the multivariate analysis of the troubled minority, we are not looking at the things that distinguished a troubled from an untroubled workplace – we have already distinguished them – but are looking at the things that explain who had the worst experience inside troubled workplaces. An example may make this clearer. If we imagine that Welsh people, or people with degrees, avoid working in troubled workplaces, and quit if they find themselves in one, these people will show up as less likely to be ill-treated in a national survey like ours. This does not mean, however, that Welsh people, or people with degrees, have an easier time when they do find themselves in a troubled workplace. They may actually suffer more ill-treatment – indeed, this may be why they avoid and leave such workplaces – but this difference would not show up until we looked at the troubled minority on its own.

First, what kind of employees experienced the most unreasonable treatment within the troubled minority? We know that the unreasonable treatment of employees with disabilities was far more marked within three particular types of unreasonable treatment. Even if an employee with disabilities had experienced all three, they would be no worse off than any other member of the troubled minority because experiencing three forms of ill-treatment was the qualification for entry to the minority. In short, it is not so surprising that employees with disabilities were no more likely to be unreasonably treated than other members of the troubled minority. Women, however, *were* more likely to be but only in respect of unfair treatment. This looks fairly straightforward: women were no more likely to work in troubled workplaces, but once this is out of the way, they were more likely to be unreasonably treated in this one respect. We do not know, however, whether women employees were complaining of unfairness in comparison with men, or to other employees in general. We can come back to this question in the second half of the book, however. What we cannot even attempt to explain (beyond saying their numbers in the sample were very small) was why LGB employees were more likely to experience unreasonable workloads than the rest of the troubled minority. Similarly, white employees were more likely than non-whites in the troubled minority to experience improper procedures, but we have no idea why. This does, of course, shed a little doubt on the earlier suggestion that Asians experienced less unreasonable treatment because they were less likely to work in troubled workplaces.

In what kinds of jobs did members of the troubled minority experience the most unreasonable treatment? Managerial responsibilities no longer mattered here but income did (although only for workload – which seems fairly straightforward). And there were two new significant factors: having a university degree went with pressure not to claim something; being a trade union member went with being checked upon unnecessarily. In which type of workplace could members of the troubled minority expect to experience the most unreasonable treatment? Since most, or perhaps all, of them were already in a troubled workplace, we would not expect the factors that separate out troubled workplaces from the rest to matter, and, for the most part, they did not. There were, however, a few surprises in store. Most of our measures of organisational change were irrelevant. Employees who reported an increased pace of work were more likely than other members of the troubled minority to experience an unmanageable workload, or someone checking up on them, but we would expect these responses to overlap anyway. This was certainly the case for super-intense work, which retained the correlation with an unmanageable workload, but here we had our first surprise.

Amongst the troubled minority, employees who reported super-intense work were *less* likely to say their views were ignored or that someone was continually checking on their work. Perhaps this is not that hard to explain because the troubled minority who reported super-intense work were also more likely to say they were not asked to do work below their level of competence and more likely not to be subject to pressure not to claim entitlements. This suggests to us that these workers were managing their own workloads with a considerable degree of autonomy. It might be too much to say they were choosing to work too hard, but the white-collar works convenor from Strand gives a better indication of what we meant when he explained why his members voluntarily worked longer hours for no extra pay: there is 'a bit of self-pressure as well, because you just can't walk off and leave all your jobs that are waiting'.

As expected, the region where the workplace was sited was not relevant to predicting the worst experiences of unreasonable treatment amongst the troubled minority, and this supports our suggestion that region was significant for the sample as a whole because troubled workplaces are more common in particular regions, perhaps for the reasons of work design discussed earlier. Nor, for the most part, were the FARE questions relevant to predicting variations within the troubled minority. We were again surprised, however, because some of the correlations for the feeling that people were treated as individuals appeared to stand on their heads once more. Inside a troubled workplace, thinking that individuals mattered made employees *more* likely to experience being ignored, someone checking up on them, unmanageable workload and improper procedures. It is hardly likely that this has anything to do with 'self-pressure', especially when pressure not to claim retained the same relationships as in the sample as a whole (employees were more likely to experience this if they felt people were *not* treated as individuals). We can rule out the possibility that a minority were interpreting the question about individuals to refer to favouritism because there was no suggestion of a positive correlation with unfair treatment here. It is possible, however, that they had in mind clients or customers being treated as individuals rather than employees. We shall return to this possibility much later in the book.

Conclusions

Multivariate analyses tell us which employee, job and workplace characteristics are 'really' associated with unreasonable treatment but, for many purposes, we simply need to know where the most troubled workers can be found. Where would a trade union look for unreasonable treatment amongst large concentrations of its members? In which employment sectors should a government agency, or a professional body like the CIPD, concentrate its efforts to try to reduce ill-treatment in order to get value for money? Such interventions do not have to rely on sophisticated, multivariate analyses to know where to start. Bivariate analyses, which tell us who is more likely to experience unreasonable treatment for one variable at a time, can help with this.

For example, bivariate analysis shows that the non-UK born and non-Christians were less likely to experience unreasonable treatment. This is only what we would expect – when we know how much more likely it is that white employees will experience unreasonable treatment than Asian employees – but it does allow us to conclude that we shall be less likely to find troubled employees amongst those who we might have imagined would be vulnerable because they are migrants from outside United Kingdom. Bivariate analysis also suggested that, contrary to some of the things said in Chapter 1, if we want to find workers who have been unreasonably treated we had better ask men rather than women. While this may 'really' be because women earn less than men and are less likely to have managerial responsibilities, the fact remains that women are less likely to experience unreasonable treatment than men. In addition, bivariate analysis showed unreasonable treatment was more likely in workplaces with lower proportions of women. While this was not a very strong relationship, these may, once more, be the workplaces where we would expect to find more people with managerial responsibilities and/or higher incomes.

The conclusion that unreasonable treatment was more likely amongst male employees adds to the emerging picture of unreasonable treatment as an affliction of the comparatively privileged rather than the most vulnerable sections of the workforce. As a mild corrective to this, bivariate analysis also showed unreasonable treatment to be higher amongst recent employees, and this was probably because younger workers were a little more likely to experience it. Recent employees may be new entrants to the labour market – and are therefore more likely to be younger – and younger people change jobs more often anyway. Employers may well find this useful knowledge to consider when managing new recruits.

Bivariate analysis of job characteristics revealed that unreasonable treatment was more likely amongst full-time workers and those in associate professional, professional and technical jobs. This perhaps reflects the multivariate results for age, income and managerial duties. Similar factors may also explain why bivariate analysis showed that union members were more likely to report unreasonable treatment. As we have implied before, trade unions and others who want to target large numbers who experience unreasonable treatment should concentrate on core rather than peripheral workers: full-timers in fairly good jobs who are more likely to be union members already.

If the section of the population most affected by unreasonable treatment is the aspirant middle class, it is highly unlikely that the typical workplace where unreasonable treatment goes on will be a private sector sweatshop with no human resource function and no union representation, and a low-paid and low-skilled workforce. It is therefore no surprise that bivariate analyses suggested that, if we want to find troubled workers, we ought to go to small-to-medium (50–249) workplaces rather than to workplaces which are any bigger or smaller. We also ought to bear in mind that at least 50 per cent of these workplaces were themselves part of larger organisations. Unfair treatment actually became more common as size of the organisation increased. Nevertheless, it remained the case that unreasonable treatment was more likely in highly visible organisations with human resource functions, union recognition and highly skilled and well-paid workforces.

There is no odour of the backstreet about unfair treatment. We find it, in fact, in modernity's shop window. Bivariate analyses showed that industries that have the largest proportions of workers experiencing unreasonable treatment were health and social work, public administration and defence, the utilities and financial intermediation. While this may really be because these sectors had more troubled workplaces, as indicated by higher responses to the FARE questions, there could be other factors at play.[8] Some of these industries may have been more likely to employ disabled people, for example. Others may have been more likely to employ young people, or white people, or to pay higher wages.

Bivariate analyses showed that unfair treatment was more likely to be found where employees said they did not decide how much work they did. It seems likely this was because deciding how much work one did was very closely allied to one or more of the 'real' factors at play like organisational change, the intensity of work or the FARE questions. It is still the case, however, that finding employees with little autonomy will be a practical short cut to finding trouble at work.

Finally, it is worth saying a little about our bivariate analyses of troublemakers. We would expect them to have some of the same characteristics as troubled workers, not least because we would expect them to work in the same places. By and large, this is what we found: troublemakers were more likely to have managerial duties, be full-timers, work in associate professional and technical jobs, have super-intense work, experience organisational change and did not think their organisation cared for individuals or their principles.

We also found, however, that a detailed industry breakdown showed troublemakers were spread across several industries.

The utilities and public administration were both more likely to have troublemakers, but the big concentrations were in construction and financial intermediation. These analyses used small numbers but the result for construction is intriguing. It might suggest, for example, that the managerial structure of some organisations is such that the task of re-creating a troubled workplace is quite a specialised one. In other words, that structure might only require that a senior manager, perhaps even an executive, should make a decision which results in unreasonable treatment meted out for many people. Thus one senior NHS manager can make sure dozens of people think they have an unreasonable workload, whereas, however much they want to, or have to, do it, the foreman on the building site can only make sure the workload of a small team is so affected.

This last point illustrates once more the key point we are trying to make in this chapter and, indeed, in this part of the book. For many people, and for a great deal of the time, trouble at work is not about bullies and victims or the stress endured by individual employees (Walker and Fincham 2011). It is about troubled workplaces and the sociological factors which contribute to them. So far we have isolated quite a few of these factors – age, disability, ethnicity, income, intense work, managerial responsibilities, organisational change, region and fairness and respect. It is now time to move on to incivility and disrespect, to see if the same factors carry over to a different kind of ill-treatment in the workplace.

3

Civility and Respect at Work

In Chapter 2 we noted that, as part of their expectations of reasonable behaviour in the workplace, people wanted recognition for their work. We now widen the focus to include not just recognition but also civility and respect. Whereas, outside the workplace, antisocial behaviour may go unchecked and incivility passes without comment, there is an expectation that the workplace should be different. Here, at least, it could be thought that there should be higher standards for the way people treat each other, standards which employers can enforce with sanctions and rewards. Much of this chapter will be concerned with these expectations being routinely unfulfilled but, as before, we are particularly interested in pinpointing the characteristics of the workplaces which have the most problems.

As with unreasonable treatment, the key predictor of the troubled workplace is that individuals feel they do not matter. In Chapter 2 we mentioned the literature on dignity at work, which suggested that dignity requires respect, self-respect and autonomy. While respect might more frequently be understood in terms of recognition than civility, this literature clearly spans the subjects of both the chapters. Other sociological work, which draws inspiration from the work of Durkheim, and particularly Goffman's interpretation (1956, 1968, 1972), has more relevance to this one. Thus Pearson *et al.* (2001) argue that norms of respect between workers underpin their cooperation and that workplaces are communities with shared sentiments and moral understandings. Incivilities flout those norms of respect and undermine the elements of community in the workplace.

In total 40 per cent of the British workforce experienced incivility or disrespect in the two years leading up to the survey, and nearly a quarter experienced three or more types of this behaviour. A little over 10 per cent endured five or more varieties of incivility or disrespect. It might be widespread but, as with unreasonable treatment, incivility and disrespect was not a very frequent experience for most people who experienced it, though a minority experienced it very frequently. Most people who told us they had experienced each type of incivility and disrespect said it had been less frequent than once a month, but, for all but two types, the proportion who experienced it once a week, or even daily, was at least 20 per cent.

We already know that it was not incivility and disrespect that people said had the biggest impact on them. In Chapter 2, we suggested that, when they answered the question about impact, people were thinking about the impact of ill-treatment on how they spent their time and on what they learnt about themselves and their workplace. It may be that incivility and disrespect is simply less of a surprise than unreasonable treatment. This certainly does not mean that employees were able to shrug it off. Of the various kinds of incivility and disrespect, people were more likely to admit that being shouted at or someone losing their temper had upset them most. This was not one of the three kinds of incivility or disrespect that were covered in the FTWS, but the three that were asked about certainly had worse effects on people's health and well-being than other kinds of ill-treatment. Being humiliated or ridiculed in connection with one's work had drastic consequences with 30 per cent experiencing moderate or severe effects on their finances, 40 per cent suffering moderate or severe deterioration of their physical health, 46 per cent seeing moderate or severe changes to their psychological health and the relationships of 30 per cent undergoing moderate or severe changes. The proportions for being insulted or having offensive remarks made were almost as large, and it is worth repeating that all of these effects (and those for being treated in a disrespectful or rude way) were more extreme than for actual physical violence.

As with unreasonable treatment, the type and severity of the effects of ill-treatment varied between different types of employee. Three of the categories of employees protected by equalities legislation suffered the more extreme effects of incivility and disrespect. Of particular interest were those who were significantly more likely to report effects on physical health (women, university-educated employees, permanent workers, union members, older workers) and effects on psychological health and well-being (lesbian, gay or bisexual (LGB), black and minority ethnic (BME), and university-educated employees, permanent workers, union members, and older workers). This is only bivariate analysis, of course, but it is still interesting that the people who were less likely to shrug off incivility and disrespect seemed to be older and better educated and those with little prospect of escaping the situation that was upsetting them anytime soon because they were permanent workers. Becoming a union member may be a response to ill-treatment.

Researchers rarely, if ever, have similar data to go on, but there is much scholarly literature that owes its existence to the debate over the alleged decline of civility and respect in the United Kingdom and, particularly, the United States. Most media outlets have made this the focus of their news and comment output at one time or another. Politicians of all hues have latched onto the idea that public concern about these issues is something they cannot afford to ignore. From antisocial behaviour and the 'respect agenda' to 'the broken society', politicians in the United Kingdom have experimented with the idea that promising to do something about the perceived decline in civility and respect may be a vote-winner. We do not want to intervene in this debate by saying whether we think there is more incivility and disrespect than there used to be.

For one thing, we do not have the resources to address this question as the data we draw on are cross-sectional. But we can say something about the state of common incivility and respect in the workplace, and how real the effects are on employees' health and well-being, and this has to be helpful because there is so little reliable information around.

As we have seen in Chapter 1, there is in fact very little sociological literature on incivility and disrespect between managers and employees or between co-workers in the workplace. There is, however, a large sociological literature which assumes that incivility and disrespect is an external intrusion into the workplace – probably brought in by clients and customers – but inside civility is in charge. When the outside intrudes in this way, employees will, as their employers demand, actually intensify the civility of their behaviour to compensate. This is what some of the studies in the literature on 'emotional labour' literature claim, for example, that workers who provide services in person are subject to varieties of abuse but are expected to endure it all with a smile (Hochschild 1983).

We need to know whether civility and respect in the workplace are always undermined from outside, by the actions of clients and customers, or whether some problems arise between employees or between employees and managers. As we would expect, the share of incivility and disrespect for which managers were responsible was far lower than the share of unreasonable treatment that originated with them. They remained, however, the single most important group of troublemakers. This is important and perhaps surprising. We might have imagined from the discussion at the start of this chapter that co-workers and customers (or clients) would be the main source of incivility and disrespect, but our survey suggests that this is not true at all. We reach this conclusion, once again, from analysis of over 2,600 incidents of incivility and disrespect from those we call the troubled minority who blamed 40 per cent of them on managers. Co-workers and customers/clients were each responsible for roughly a quarter of the incidents. It was only hints to quit one's job (and, perhaps, intimidating behaviour) that managers were more likely to be responsible for than co-workers or clients. Co-workers were more likely to be responsible for gossiping, excluding people, teasing and ridicule (as we might expect). Moreover, it is perhaps not surprising that customers or clients were more likely to be responsible for insults, rudeness, shouting and threatening behaviour.

Most of this analysis from the troubled minority was confirmed by the analysis of the characteristics of the self-reported troublemakers in the sample. Customers or clients were *much* more likely to go in for incivility and disrespect than unreasonable treatment. A troublemaker who was a manager was a bit more likely to adopt unreasonable treatment, but co-workers/colleagues who were responsible for ill-treatment were fairly evenly distributed between unreasonable treatment and incivility and disrespect.

Subordinates turned out to be fairly small players for any of the factors but were more likely to display incivility and disrespect than unreasonable treatment. We did, however, find incidents of ill-treatment by mixed groups – including managers, co-workers and subordinates – in our case studies. For example, a Strand project officer told us she had suffered long-term bullying from her manager when we interviewed her. This was a classic case: the manager may have seen her as a threat so brought her down a peg by promoting two people, who had reported to her, to a job she expected to get. He then gave our interviewee the poisoned chalice of a role in the teams identifying areas, and people, for redundancy and then encouraged her colleagues to ostracise her because of her new role. He was 'drip feeding them bits of information, enough for them to go off and gossip about ... and people just used to revel in it, and a couple of people would just purposely say things out loud knowing that I was within the vicinity'. Her performance deteriorated and

> I began to shut down so I just became like in a bubble, that's how I felt. And it was terrible because it really affected my home life as well because I would take it home and, although you would try not to take it home with you, it happened and I did. And it affected my marriage, because I'd go home and I'd cry and get angry and take it out on my husband, and it was all because of what was happening here.

We asked if she considered taking sick leave and she admitted ironically, 'No, because, again, with the current redundancy programme they look at sickness.'

Although this was not true of this woman's experience at Strand, more survey results from the troubled minority showed that incidents of incivility and disrespect were not dominated by repeat troublemakers in the same way that we found for unreasonable treatment. It was equally likely to be the same perpetrator or a different one across the three incidents we asked about. This makes sense because customers and clients were more important in this part of the story and were obviously a little less likely to come in contact with the employee on regular basis. We need to bear in mind that we are not talking about bullying here but trouble at work. A lot of the bullying literature concentrates on repeated ill-treatment, but one does not need to be abused by the same person over and over again to think one is ill-treated. Being treated without civility or respect by a variety of customers and/or several different co-workers is no less worthy of social-scientific attention.

Most of the people responsible for unreasonable treatment turned out to be men and, because this was partly a result of the prevalence of male managers, it might be thought that there would be more female perpetrators of incivility and disrespect because clients and co-workers had more of a presence in this type of ill-treatment. All the same, female troublemakers were never in the majority and only got close to being responsible for half of the ill-treatment for a couple of types of behaviour, in particular unfair criticism.

If we use the replies of self-identified troublemakers to examine gender, we find women troublemakers were sometimes in the majority but, in fact, only for gossip, excluding and intimidation. As in Chapter 2, the vast majority of troublemakers were white.

Witnessing incivility and disrespect in the workplace was almost as common an experience as suffering it. This kind of ill-treatment is therefore much more visible than unreasonable treatment. Indeed, the proportions witnessing someone spreading gossip or rumours, and excluding others from a social group, were higher than the proportions saying they had experienced this kind of thing. As we might reasonably expect, then, some employees who were the focus of gossip or exclusion were not aware of their ill-treatment. There was little evidence, except perhaps for shouting and losing one's temper, that people were any more likely to own up to causing this kind of trouble than they were to being responsible for unfair treatment. As in Chapter 2, this reluctance to identify oneself as a troublemaker underlines the inference we make that the vast majority of employees do not find any of this behaviour accceptable and, when they encounter it, they certainly consider it to be trouble. Given what we have already learnt about the effects of incivility and disrespect at the start of the chapter, we think it would be foolish to disagree with them.

For example, this technician who had long service at Strand after coming into the company as an apprentice told us how he had made a point of telling his colleagues that they had crossed a line when they carried on teasing him about his moral convictions. He told us in very clear terms the amount of trouble disrespect between co-workers could cause for people.

> And sometimes, although there's nothing like the bullying and all the so-called things you used to hear happening on the shop floor, like people getting dragged to the toilets and hung up [with] forklifts and things, right ... [Interviewer: This is what used to happen here or ...?] Apparently, yeah. Right, but a long time ago, and the place was apparently full of bullies on the shop floor and all that, but no different to school, it's just an extension of school. But even though none of those things happen any more, they're still ... that still happens maybe in just a verbal sense. There's still people that do it. My point is that many people think it's funny, but they don't know where to draw the line. And somebody like me, that could say look that hurts, they hear it, they might ignore it, but some people will bottle that up. And because they will say nothing, that will eat away at them. And the consequences are a lot greater than me just walking off for two weeks and not speaking to them.

We already know that, no matter what type of ill-treatment we asked about, people who told us they had experienced it were also more likely to say they had seen it happen to other people and, indeed, had done it themselves. This was a key piece of evidence in the picture we are compiling of the troubled workplace in which all sorts of ill-treatment are more likely. The importance of this concept to our analysis was confirmed by the reasons the troubled minority offered for the incivility and disrespect they experienced. The position the respondent held in the organisation registered for all of types of incivility and disrespect, confirming the importance of the workplace in any sociological explanation of this type of ill-treatment. As before, the two outstanding reasons were that it was just the way things are and the attitudes or personality of the other person. The attitudes of the other person were probably less important than just the way things are for most types of incivility and disrespect (but particularly exclusion) with the exception of shouting, rudeness (about the same) and intimidation and threats (where attitudes got a bit more of the blame). Choosing just the way things are as the reason for incivility and disrespect was probably most important for humiliation, gossip and teasing. Clearly the troubled workplace is not all about unreasonable treatment by managers.

Having made this point, position in the organisation was more marginal for a few types of incivility and disrespect, for example, teasing and unfair criticism. Performance at work appeared to be less relevant to this kind of ill-treatment than it had been suggested in Chapter 2. The only place it made a substantial appearance was where we might expect it to: unfair criticism. Nor was it much of a surprise that relationships at work were cited more often as a reason than they had been mentioned for unreasonable treatment. Relationships hardly figured as reasons for insults and rudeness but were really quite important, unsurprisingly, for gossip and excluding people.

We hope to persuade many people in this book that quite a lot of trouble at work is not connected with bullies and their victims or the stress endured by individual employees (Walker and Fincham 2011). The book deals with troubled workplaces and the sociological factors which contribute to them. In Chapter 2 we isolated quite a few of these factors – age, disability, ethnicity, income, intense work, managerial responsibilities, organisational change, region, fairness and respect. Did some or all of these same factors carry over to our analysis of the correlates of incivility and disrespect?

Perhaps it is no surprise that we lose those job characteristics (income, managerial responsibilities) that were significant for unreasonable treatment. This might be what would be expected if incivility and disrespect are, unlike unreasonable treatment, not a measure of the troubled workplace at all but all about the attitudes and personalities of individuals. However, our multivariate analysis suggests that less control over work and super-intense work were just as important here as they were for unreasonable treatment. Moreover, employee characteristics associated with incivility and disrespect were not very different from those we found for unreasonable treatment. Employees in our survey were more likely to suffer incivility and disrespect if they were younger. They were more likely to suffer incivility and disrespect if they did not have an Asian background and much more likely to suffer denigration or disrespect if they had disabilities (particularly psychological problems and learning disabilities). The difference this time is that they were also more likely to suffer incivility and disrespect if they were gay or lesbian employees. As ever, we have to bear in mind that the numbers of such employees who appeared in our sample were small.

Nevertheless, the important correlates of this kind of ill-treatment were much more obviously to do with the type of work people were employed to do. They were particularly likely to work in the public sector – where they were exposed to the antisocial clients and customers, where they had less control over their work and where the pace of their work was too intense. Once more, the FARE questions proved to be important predictors of trouble at work. There were, however, two workplace measures which had been significant in the multivariate analysis of unreasonable treatment but which were not significant for incivility and disrespect: change in the nature of work and region. In fact, the correlation for region is quite close to significance, and this makes us pause for a moment to remember the possible explanation of the significance of region in terms of whether work was customer-focused. We have already seen that, though they only made up a quarter of troublemakers, customers were much more important sources of incivility and disrespect than unreasonable treatment. This may help to explain why region slipped below significant levels in multivariate analysis of incivility and disrespect.

While the importance of less control was perhaps not quite as marked as it was in the analysis of unreasonable treatment, the importance of super-intense work was probably even greater in the analysis of incivility and disrespect. The importance of the FARE questions in our analysis differed very little between unreasonable treatment and incivility and disrespect. What is the consequence for theory that these two apparently different aspects of trouble at work should both be determined by the nature of the workplace? This certainly underlines what we have been saying about the importance of the sociological, less individualistic or clinical, contribution.

What kind of employees experienced more incivility and disrespect?

Once again we begin with a discussion of workers with disabilities and long-term health conditions which describes the findings for the sub-categories of this group and makes reference to the FTWS. Figure 8 shows, once more, that it was the psychological/learning disabilities subgroup who were most at risk – not just of unreasonable treatment but also of incivility and disrespect. Indeed, the degree of exposure of this group to incivility and disrespect was substantially greater.

As before, we need multivariate analysis to be sure of what is really going on, and Figure 9 summarises the results of this analysis. It shows that, when

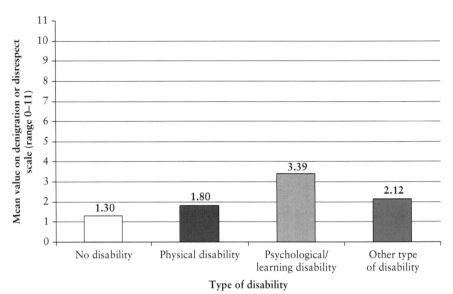

Figure 8 Incivility and disrespect suffered by employees with disabilities

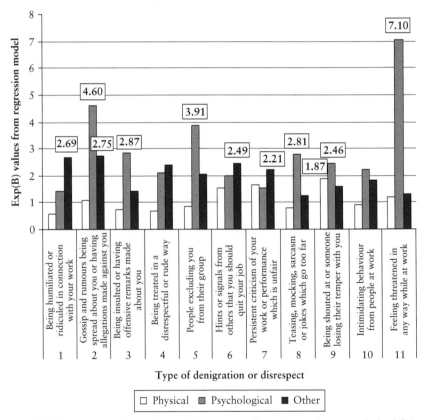

Figure 9 Different types of incivility and disrespect suffered by employees with disabilities

we controlled for all the other likely variables, people with a psychological/learning disability were significantly more likely to experience most forms of incivility and disrespect. Only three questions about incivility and disrespect were asked in the FTWS. Of these, only one type, rudeness, was seen to be correlated with psychological/learning disabilities in multivariate analysis. The correlations revealed in our survey are both wider and more substantial than this.

The increased exposure to incivility and disrespect experienced by employees with psychological/learning disabilities was extreme; for example, they were more than five times more likely to experience gossip, rumours and allegations, nearly five times more likely to experience being excluded from groups and cliques, and eight times more likely to feel threatened. However, it is possible that managers were responsible for comparatively little of this behaviour. Roughly half of the types of incivility and disrespect experienced by people with psychological problems or learning disabilities were those which customers were more likely to be responsible for. The other half were more likely to originate with co-workers. That means that people with psychological/learning disabilities were no more likely than anyone else to experience the kind of incivility and disrespect where managers were the chief troublemakers.

We shall return to what Figure 9 tells us about the other subgroups – physical disability, other disability – shortly, but we first need to consider what might lie behind the patterns we have just described. For example, was there evidence here of health effects? Is a major reason why people with psychological problems were more likely than anyone else to experience incivility and disrespect that the ill-treatment caused their mental illness? To take the most extreme example, feeling threatened might sometimes even be considered tantamount to having emotional/psychological problems.

Certainly, the high correlations we found for some types of incivility and disrespect could indicate the circular process we mentioned in Chapter 2. Ill-treatment might lead to psychological effects, and these might then be exacerbated by further ill-treatment associated with the disability. This was what one Strand engineer described to us: for years he had suffered racial harassment inside and outside the workplace which had led to mental illness and then further stigmatisation and incivility and disrespect from co-workers (Walker and Fincham 2011). However, it is unlikely that health effects played much of a part in the greater exposure of employees with learning disabilities to incivility and disrespect. Moreover, there was no evidence of health effects for the types of incivility and disrespect which managers were especially likely to be responsible for. If health effects were a major part of the explanation of why people with these disabilities reported more incivility and disrespect, we would expect them to be more likely to report the types that were more likely to originate from managers as well as customers and co-workers.

This could well suggest that their disabilities were a part of the cause rather than the effect: the high rates of incivility and disrespect resulted from co-workers and customers behaving in this way (gossiping, insulting, excluding, teasing, shouting and threatening) because someone had psychological problems or learning disabilities.

It is no more plausible that employees with learning disabilities would be more likely to perceive the behaviour of others as ill-treatment because of their condition, than that their ill-treatment was evidence of health effects. It is, however, more plausible that psychological disabilities like depression could lead to a more negative perception of behaviour that other employees might not think of as denigration or disrespect at all.

What about the other types of impairments and health conditions? People with physical impairments – the paradigm of the popular idea of stigmatisation – barely experienced more denigration or disrespect than employees without disabilities. They did not experience more insults, ridicule, humiliation or teasing, only more shouting. This clearly did not suggest the stigmatisation of people with obvious impairments, but nor did it suggest a politically correct society when such people were more likely than those without impairments to experience customers (probably) shouting at them or losing their temper. Again, rather unfortunately, we did not ask about shouting in the FTWS, but the different composition of the disability subgroups in the FTWS allowed us a second bite of the cherry, and the results are interesting. Deafness (but none of the other physical impairments) was significantly correlated with humiliation and rudeness. Physical impairment was significant for rudeness only.

In Chapter 2, we said a considerable amount about people with other health conditions in relation to ill-treatment from managers and supervisors. As Figure 9 shows, within the broad range of incivility and disrespect associated with other health conditions, we find all of those which were specially associated with managers (hints about quitting one's job and intimidation – and also persistent criticism). In addition, those with other disabilities or conditions were more likely to report humiliation, gossip and exclusion – all particularly associated with co-workers (and only rudeness was associated with clients). It seems, then, that those with other disabilities added ill-treatment by co-workers to ill-treatment by managers, which we saw in the analysis of unreasonable treatment in Chapter 2.

We can explore this further in the case study chapters, but suspect that much of this incivility and disrespect is related to managers and co-workers impressing on workers with other disabilities that, if they had different needs from other workers, they did not deserve the same rewards or, perhaps, to hold onto their jobs. We suggest that this is why they were more than three times as likely to be ridiculed in connection with their work, persistently or unfairly criticised, or be in receipt of hints that they should leave. Of course, all of this ill-treatment could be part of a package of 360° abuse which also included pressure not to claim entitlements, and not following proper procedures, as indicated in Chapter 2.

To conclude the discussion of employees with disabilities and denigration or disrespect, we shall look once more at the FTWS. Multivariate analysis revealed that other disabilities were significant for humiliation and rudeness (but not for insults, so conforming to the results for our survey). These were the only questions about incivility and disrespect which were asked in the FTWS.

The other significant individual characteristics for incivility and disrespect in the BWBS were the same ones as we observed in the multivariate analysis for unreasonable treatment: age and ethnicity – plus a new one, sexual orientation. Younger workers were a little bit more likely to experience gossip, rudeness, hints to quit, persistent criticism, teasing and being shouted at. Analysis of the FTWS confirmed this (though one type of ill-treatment actually failed to reach significance by a hair's breadth). Although, as indicated in Chapter 2, we tend towards concluding that young workers were treated differently because of their age; we should bear in mind that these were small effects which have only become visible because we had such large numbers in our sample (since almost everyone told us their age).

As before, the results for ethnicity were not what we had imagined when we first designed our research project. Employees with Asian backgrounds were much, much *less* likely to report insults, rudeness, persistent criticism, shouting, intimidation and feeling threatened. In line with our previous practice, we note that none of these were particularly associated with co-workers. The kinds of incivility and disrespect which Asian employees were less likely to experience were those particularly associated with managers and, even more obviously, with customers and clients. Might a part of this pattern reflect an anxiety on behalf of customers to avoid appearing prejudiced: if not indiscriminately racist, perhaps Islamophobic? Might they have been more cautious about appearing to disrespect Muslims as a result of post-9/11 and 7/7 political correctness? The results of multivariate analysis did not suggest that any type of religion, or none, was correlated in any way with any of the three types of ill-treatment. However, how many customers would be sure of the religion of an Asian employee?

Data from recent British Social Attitudes Surveys would not lead us to expect people to bend over backwards to avoid appearing racist. These surveys suggest that people's self-reported prejudice fell in the 1990s but rose slightly in the following decade, perhaps because of reactions to 9/11 and 7/7. When asked about perceived level of prejudice in their workplace, people were likely to say it was, if anything, higher against people of Asian origin rather than black people (Creegan and Robinson 2008). However, Ford (2008) finds little difference between prejudice against Asians and black people using the same data. Given the lack of support for the idea that differences in measures of civility and respect reflect more political correctness, we are left with the suggestion made in Chapter 2 that Asians were less likely to work in troubled workplaces – in this case, workplaces in which they would be subject to incivility and disrespect, particularly from clients or customers. As in Chapter 2, we look to the discussion of the troubled minority (p. 76 below) to shed further light on this.

The risk of incivility and disrespect for GLB employees was almost as great as it was for employees with disabilities. Figure 10 shows the bivariate results for different types of incivility and disrespect. In multivariate analysis, gay and lesbian employees were significantly more likely to experience feeling threatened and, bearing in mind the way in which significant results are hard to achieve with such small numbers, it is well worth pointing out that the results for gay and lesbian respondents were close to significance for humiliation, hints to quit, and shouting. In multivariate analysis of the FTWS, the LGB group as a whole was substantially more likely to report humiliation. In our survey, bisexuals were significantly more likely to experience hints they should quit, and intimidation, and in both cases the effects are massive. We should

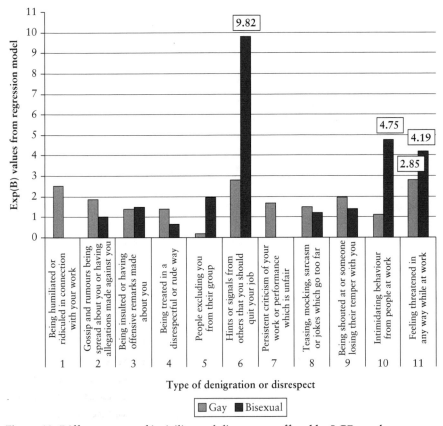

Figure 10 Different types of incivility and disrespect suffered by LGB employees

not make too much of this, but it would seem there are grounds for at least investigating whether bisexuals are particularly targeted by managers. Gay and lesbian workers may also suffer from incivility and disrespect from managers and, in addition, from customers or clients.

As in Chapter 2, we are learning that, when it comes to ill-treatment in the workplace, we should be very wary of assuming that members of the various minorities were all in the same boat. Having disabilities persistently landed one in trouble throughout but, even then, the kind of trouble one found oneself in depended on one's disability. We have just seen that the workplace could be threatening for LGB, but neither religion, place of birth nor, most surprisingly, gender provoked incivility and disrespect in the workplace. There will be many people who will have expected that the continuum of sexual harassment would extend into many of the varieties of incivility and disrespect discussed here. Yet we obtained absolutely no significant results for gender, indeed nothing even came close to significance, and this is quite remarkable when analysis of gender, like age, can draw on really big numbers to find out if even comparatively small effects are significant. The one type of incivility and disrespect that was closest to significance, at 0.09 per cent, suggested that women were *less* likely to feel threatened in the workplace. This is, however, not the last word we have to say on his topic in this chapter. We shall return to it on p. 77.

Which jobs were more prone to incivility and disrespect?

If we choose, as before, to treat organisational changes and super-intense work as the characteristics of workplaces rather than jobs, the short answer is that all jobs were equally exposed. Once again, we were struck by the lack of a result of any kind to indicate that ill-treatment was more common amongst vulnerable, or marginalised, workers.

Which workplaces and organisations were more prone to incivility and disrespect?

We saw in Chapter 2 that, when employees told us the nature of their work had changed, or the pace of work had increased, employees were significantly more likely to experience unreasonable treatment. This was not true for incivility and disrespect and this, we believe, rather knocks on the head the simple association between organisational chaos and ill-treatment, in the form of bullying, which Hodson *et al.* propose. Instead, we think this confirms what we said in Chapter 2 about the association between organisational change and unreasonable treatment being almost a semantic one – change itself can be seen as unreasonable by the people who are affected by it. There is no obvious semantic association between organisational change and any of the questions about incivility and disrespect. This is why we did not find the same association between the two that we did for unreasonable treatment.

While there is no overall association for incivility and disrespect, the individual models produced fairly weak associations for increased pace of work and insults, rudeness and shouting. All of these, as can be recalled, were particularly associated with customers or clients. This is hardly what would be predicted in the Hodson *et al.* model of organisational chaos and bullying in the workplace. Moreover, none of the individual models for the various types of incivility and disrespect produced a significant result for change in the nature of work.

Having less control over work and finding the pace of work too intense were, together, about as strongly associated with incivility and disrespect as they were for unreasonable treatment, as described in Chapter 2. It seemed obvious how these factors might be connected with unreasonable management, but what about incivility and disrespect? Less control was significant for humiliation, disrespect, exclusion, hints to quit, persistent criticism and feeling threatened. Super-intense work was correlated with humiliation, gossip, disrespect, exclusion, persistent criticism, teasing, being shouted at, intimidation and feeling threatened. Although ill-treatment by employers must have been represented in both sets of results, they were also strongly suggestive of ill-treatment by co-workers and customers. While Hodson *et al.* predicted ill-treatment by co-workers when control was lost and speed-up occurred, they (understandably) did not predict ill-treatment by customers.

But perhaps the most remarkable finding of this chapter is that the FARE questions turned out to be as, if not more, important for predicting incivility and disrespect as they were for unreasonable treatment. At least two of the FARE questions proved significant for every type of incivility and disrespect in our individual models. Indeed, so important were they across the board that it is pointless trying to discern particular patterns which might be associated with denigration or disrespect from managers, co-workers or customers. We can simply consider the headline figures: 40 per cent of incivility and disrespect was down to managers and about a quarter each to co-workers and customers. It seems that the FARE questions were equally useful for predicting incivility and disrespect from all of them.

We might pause for a moment to think about the implications of this finding for the discussion of incivility earlier in the chapter. First, respect and civility, like reason and fairness, are tied up in people's minds with recognising individuality, including variations in moral principles between individuals, and having human ends as ends in themselves. Now this might be thought to make the most radical demands of people in respect of unreasonable treatment (particularly unreasonable management – indeed, it could be argued that people who want individuality recognised in an organisational context are being unreasonable themselves!), but it is hardly straightforward in relation to respect either. If respect was considered to be due to all and sundry, it would be easy to see why people might associate lack of respect with unfairness, and people being a means to an end (and their principles not mattering), but why would they associate it with people not being treated as individuals? However, the public debate about incivility, which was alluded to at the start of this chapter, also has a companion discourse of rights and responsibilities, of *earning* and *deserving* respect. This discourse is also relevant here, and perhaps it is not so far from the fairness and justice, and moral, elements of Chapter 2, as implicit as they were.

We argue that the FARE questions are the best predictors of troubled workplaces. So far, we have argued this in respect of the type of trouble we called unreasonable treatment, but now we are arguing that troubled workplaces had a problem of denigration and respect too. We should not miss the obvious implication of this: troubled workplaces might well have (a) been less able to protect employees from incivility and disrespect and (b) actually generated incivility and disrespect from clients, employees and managers. It is as well to bear in mind, moreover, that we are suggesting that both things would be truly independent of other risk factors. In other words, a troubled workplace puts all of its employees (with or without disabilities, old or young, straight or LGB, Asian or not) at greater risk of incivility and disrespect.

In the troubled workplace people do not know that it is wrong to humiliate or ridicule people in connection with their work, treat them in a disrespectful way, shout at them and intimidate them. They do not get sanctioned for it, and they may even be actually encouraged to behave like this. For example, in many of our case study interviews, we were repeatedly told that no action was taken after ill-treatment was reported and/or that ill-treatment was a part of workplace culture. Obviously, this may not be the same as employers relying on managers and supervisors behaving unreasonably to carry out the management function (e.g. performance management or the management of sick pay). Nevertheless, although there may not be a direct line from the boardroom to disrespect on the shop floor, there can be no doubt that the troubled workplace is the employer's responsibility. HR managers and organisations like the CIPD would do well to take note that treating people as individuals, recognising their principles and their needs, is the key to not putting organisations at risk of becoming troubled.

Troubled workplaces may make all types of ill-treatment discussed thus far more likely, but the multivariate analysis of incivility and disrespect showed that, for this kind of ill-treatment, things were also made far worse when the workplace was located in the public sector. Why should this association appear here and not for unreasonable treatment? Working in the public sector puts employees at significantly greater risk of humiliation, insults, rudeness, teasing, shouting, intimidation and threats, and the bulk of this ill-treatment was strongly associated with customer or client behaviour. Clients were responsible for very little of the ill-treatment discussed in Chapter 2, and it seems that public sector workers owe their greater exposure to trouble at work to the great British public.

Finally, workplaces outside London were not significant for incivility and disrespect, whereas they were for unreasonable treatment. We speculated in Chapter 2 that it was the relative unimportance of customers and clients to the type of work found outside London that meant unreasonable management appeared to be less common there. When we moved on to incivility and disrespect, customers and clients became much more important, and the association between ill-treatment and region was no longer present in our multivariate analysis. We now have better grounds to claim that any relationship between region and ill-treatment in the workplace was probably a function of variations in the types of workplaces between the regions. These different types were associated with variations in opportunities for direct managerial control and control which was mediated by contact with customers and clients. In this case, any higher risk factor for the non-London-based workplaces is simply a result of the type of workplaces they were.

The troubled minority

From the discussion of this point in Chapter 2 we knew that, once we were dealing with the troubled minority, we were much more likely to be working with data taken from employees who had the misfortune to work in troubled workplaces. There was no point, therefore, in expecting to see the same clear patterns emerging in the analysis done when finding out which variables predicted which employees were in troubled workplaces and which were not. If we had expected to see such patterns in this chapter, we would have been disappointed. There was nothing to suggest that incivility and disrespect within the troubled workplace was related to the sector of the workplace (public or otherwise), organisational change, intense work or the FARE questions.

The most startling feature, and, indeed, the only really remarkable feature, of the analysis of incivility and disrespect in the troubled minority is the very strong, and very substantial, relationships for some equality strands. First, and for once the least remarkable, was the fact that workers with disabilities were four times more likely to receive hints to quit their jobs. Second, LGB employees were 12 times more likely than straight employees to be given hints to quit and four times more likely to be threatened. Given that we knew that there were some significant results for sexual orientation, this is not a complete surprise, but the degree of difference in the risk of these particular behaviours was breathtaking. It is hard to escape the conclusion that very many of these LGB employees were being eased out of their jobs because of their sexual orientation. This was also true of employees with disabilities of course, but, though we do not know how many LGB employees were open about their sexual orientation at work, it looks as if coming out could be an even surer route to being shown the door than acquiring a disability. But these were not the most surprising findings.

Women were four times as likely as men in the troubled minority to be insulted, and BME employees were four times as likely as non-BME employees in the troubled minority to receive hints to quit their jobs. Now, these are just the kind of results we might have expected when we designed our study. The result for BME employees lends some support to the idea that differences in Asian employees which stand out in analysis of the national sample are, in large part, a result of Asians being less likely to work in troubled workplaces. This may, in turn, be a consequence of Asian employees avoiding workplaces where they think they may be ill-treated, for example, by co-workers or the public. The results for BME employees and women amongst the troubled minority also suggest why our initial expectations turned out to be so far off the mark. That the greater risk of these types of incivility and disrespect should only be observable now shows, first of all, how overwhelming the troubled workplace factor is in all of our analysis. When we are dealing with the whole sample, that factor is given free rein and it obliterates even the slightest hint of these quite substantial relationships.

Second, it is now clear that studies which are limited to one workplace, or a few, are very unlikely to find systematic evidence of the troubled workplace factor simply because of the way they were designed. They just do not have enough cases of employees working in both kinds of workplaces for subsequent analysis to reveal the relationship between workplaces and ill-treatment. If workers in a handful of public sector workplaces in a particular locality are selected for interview, for example, researchers may have inadvertently selected only troubled workplaces, though of course they will not be aware of this. When they find that the important factors in their study are ethnicity or gender, they will understandably, but unfortunately, conclude that these results will be replicable in a nationally representative study. Not only did we read such studies before conducting our own, one of us was responsible for several such studies (Lewis and Gunn 2007, for example). This is, of course, why our initial expectations were so different from the findings which eventually emerged when we were able to conduct our own study with a nationally representative sample rather than a sample drawn from a handful of workplaces.

Conclusions

As in Chapter 2, we conclude with some bivariate analysis which shows where we might expect to find large numbers of troubled workers and, particularly, troubled workplaces. This information is useful for policy-makers and those, like trade unions and interested professional bodies, who are concerned to do something about ill-treatment in the workplace.

Was incivility and disrespect something that went on in modernity's shop window or was it something that happened in the backstreets, or the low-rent corners of unfashionable industrial estates, to vulnerable workers who were intimidated and frightened half to death by bullying managers? Or was it what the emotional labour literature would have us believe, the fate of employees, particularly young women, in customer-facing jobs? Or was it the iceberg underneath the stories of the bullying of minorities, and particularly women, in the allegedly racist and misogynist trading floors of the financial institutions? As before, the answers to these questions show us how the factors we have already discovered through our multivariate analysis played out, for example, how they created a pattern of troubled workplaces and troubled workers in the British employment landscape.

In a couple of respects, the typical denigrated worker was rather like the typical unreasonably treated one: more likely to be a man, less likely to be BME (and particularly Asian), more likely to be Christian and more likely to be born in the United Kingdom. Denigrated workers were also likely to be those in the middle of their careers. Does this mean they were definitely not vulnerable workers hidden away in a sweatshop by some ruthless employer? As before, there is the caveat about more recent employees, and of course we have to bear in mind the incivility and disrespect meted out to workers with disabilities, and particularly learning/psychological disabilities. We also have to bear in mind the results for sexual orientation. Yet, with the possible exception of employees with learning disabilities, these were not the kind of employees policy-makers and researchers usually have in mind when they describe vulnerable workers.

Bivariate analysis of job characteristics revealed exactly the same types of workers being ill-treated as for unreasonable treatment: higher than average income, managers, full-time workers, union members, three to four years in post, associate professional and technical occupations. Again, the typical workplace was in the 50–249 bracket, and incivility and disrespect went up as size increased. It is not a disease of the low-rent unit off the motorway spur but a malaise of highly visible organisations with HR functions, union recognition and highly skilled, well-paid workforces. What is more, incivility and disrespect are particularly virulent in the public sector (and next the third sector, with the private sector, sweatshops and all, the least infected). The particular hotspots of incivility and disrespect were public administration and defence, followed by health and social work. Here, in contrast to Chapter 2 on unreasonable treatment, ill-treatment by the clients of public services is a more important factor.

We shall now look at industry in more detail. What happened to the city traders and the emotional labourers? When we conducted bivariate analysis for industries where we had more than 10 respondents in each, some of this kind of thing did emerge. Hotels and catering were added to public administration and defence, health and social work (but so were mining and quarrying). When we repeated this analysis for individual items of incivility and disrespect, financial intermediation also made an appearance for humiliation, exclusion, hints to quit and intimidation. There is, therefore, some limited evidence that it is worth looking at finance as well as hotels and catering to target an ill-treatment initiative (or find people who can be helped to take their cases to an employment tribunal). All the same, it might be just as productive to visit the local hospital.

As in Chapter 2, we conclude with the limited information we have on the troublemakers. According to members of the troubled minority, a higher percentage of female than male troublemakers went in for gossip, exclusion, persistent criticism and intimidation, but the male troublemakers outnumbered female troublemakers for all types of incivility and disrespect, including these. These results were, in large part, confirmed by the information given to us by the self-identified perpetrators of incivility and disrespect. Men were significantly more likely for some but not all types (the exceptions were rudeness and intimidation); BME employees were less likely for only two (teasing and shouting). In many ways the troublemakers looked like the victims: they were more likely to be Christian, born in the United Kingdom, aged 16–35, and a couple of items suggested they were more likely to have a degree. Interestingly, most items showed high earners (£50–80K annual income) were more likely to be troublemakers, as were those with managerial duties, permanent jobs and at least 3–4 years' service. Lastly, bivariate analysis of self-identified troublemakers confirmed the importance of hotels and restaurants, a bit of financial intermediation and public administration and defence. There was one more point. As mentioned in Chapter 2, the construction industry makes an appearance at the close of our analysis. Once more, we have to wonder about the spread of control enjoyed by troublemakers in various industries and also about what a brutal, or honest, breed construction workers might be.

4

Violence and Injury at Work

In Chapter 3 we referred to the popular perception of a decline in civility and respect and the idea that, perhaps because it was a haven for rational behaviour, the workplace provided some protection against the worst effects of this decline. Despite the fact that, after peaking in the mid-1990s, violent crime in the United Kingdom has fallen back to the levels it was 30 years ago, incivility is often linked in people's minds with threatening behaviour which may spill over into casual and random violence of the type that is sometimes seen in city centres on Saturday nights. It is commonly understood that those working in the blue light services charged with keeping order in the streets, or dealing with the consequences of disorder, and others such as bus and taxi drivers, run the risk of becoming targets of this violence. There is, however, little concern about the extent of violence in other occupations. As before, expectations of rational behaviour in the workplace are assumed to provide some protection against a wider social problem.

The incidence of violence and injury in the workplace recorded in our survey certainly shows that violence was much less common than the other kinds of ill-treatment discussed in Chapters 2 and 3. We found that about 5 per cent of British employees experienced physical violence at work during the previous two years. Figure 2 on p. 33 shows the relative incidence of the three types of ill-treatment, and violence is represented as a much smaller circle in the Venn diagram than the circles for unreasonable treatment and incivility and disrespect. Nevertheless, our survey found that the overall level is considerably higher (about five times the rate) than that found in crime victimisation surveys such as the BCS.[1] The figure of 5 per cent is very similar to other large-scale studies of employees which produce estimates of 4–7 per cent.[2] Nevertheless, whilst these other studies of workplace behaviour, such as the FTWS, support the estimates of our study, it is the BCS that has been the main source of information utilised by official bodies such as the HSE when formulating policy responses to workplace violence. It is an important finding that the overall incidence of workplace violence is not as low as these policy responses assume, and significantly greater numbers of workers are affected by violence at work than has been previously recognised by the official agencies concerned with the issue.

We have discussed elsewhere the reasons why we believe that major differences have emerged between estimates of violence by studies of broader workplace behaviours and those of crime victimisation surveys (Jones *et al.* 2011). We argued that respondents to the workplace surveys may feel less tied to formal legal categories when discussing violent behaviours. Consider, for example, the descriptions given by three of the 194 respondents to the survey who told us they had experienced violence in the workplace:

- I've had fingernails dug into my skin by patients who are probably infected. You do get grabbed and punched ... you get sworn at ... I've been bitten (a white female, aged over 50, working in health/social work).

- It was a teenager looking for trouble. She abused me verbally and physically ... I was unable to fight back as she was a woman. She caused damage to the fire alarm. It took four policemen to get her arrested (white female, aged 53, working in Other Community and Personal Services).

- Disagreement about a meeting and she hit me with a file (white female, aged 35–44, working in Education).

In only one of these cases is it clear that the respondent regarded the violence as a crime. As we discuss later in the chapter, it is quite possible that those who experience relatively serious physical assaults at work, for example, from patients or distressed relatives in social care settings, may be reluctant to label these as criminal (see Estrada *et al.* 2010). This is not to say, however, that the higher levels of violence reported in employee surveys are simply inflated by the inclusion of 'minor' types of violence, such as pushing and shoving. In fact, the rates of reported *injury* in our study – presumably reflecting something more serious than pushing and shoving – were higher than those reported in crime victimisation studies.

We found that 59 per cent of those reporting violence stated that they received 'injury in some way as a result of violence or aggression at work' (compared to 42 per cent in the most recent BCS). We did not specify, as we did for the experience of violence, that the violence concerned was 'physical violence'.[3] What respondents considered an injury might range from minor to severe physical injuries, or they may have considered psychological harm or trauma as an injury and stated it as such. Thus 26 per cent of the respondents who reported sustaining injuries did *not* mention experiencing physical violence. In other words, some respondents took a broad interpretation of injury and felt they had been injured from some encounters which were aggressive but not necessarily violent. This group was largely accounted for by people who had experienced the more serious forms of incivility and disrespect, such as being shouted at, intimidating behaviour and feeling threatened.

Our data also suggests that the frequency with which physical violence is experienced at work is much higher than that suggested by crime victimisation

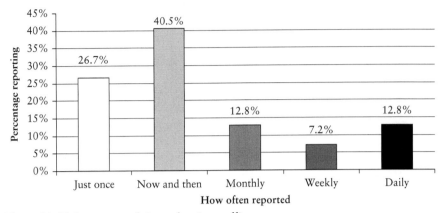

Figure 11 Violence at work is rarely a 'one-off'

studies (see Figure 11). Just 27 per cent of those reporting violence stated that this was a 'one-off' (compared to 58 per cent in the most recent BCS). A substantial proportion of respondents (41 per cent) stated that it happened 'now and then', 13 per cent that it occurred monthly, and 7 per cent that it happened weekly. Perhaps most startling was the finding that 13 per cent of respondents reported that they experienced physical violence on a *daily* basis.

In the survey, the small group of respondents who reported 'daily' experience of workplace violence was a surprising finding, and so we considered a number of possible explanations for it. For example, we explored the possibility that some respondents – including these 25 (out of the total of 194 who confirmed that they had experienced some type of physical violence at work) – might have felt so disenchanted about their work that they responded 'daily' for all the negative acts presented to them without considering them individually. Further examination revealed that these respondents had not simply answered 'daily' to every question about ill-treatment, and as a group, they shared similar characteristics overall to the others who experienced violence. It is also worth noting that out of the 25 respondents reporting daily experience of physical violence, all but one reported that they had suffered injuries as a result, and 17 of the 25 said they were injured on a daily basis.

As indicated earlier, our survey did not capture the nature of the injury (psychological or physical, for example), nor its severity. Nevertheless, it is hard to see how people confronted with violence and aggression on a daily basis would not also be injured fairly regularly as well. The qualitative accounts from particular types of workers lend further credence to this finding. For example, we have already referred to the white woman (aged over 50) who experienced violence while working in health/social work. She was injured on a daily basis, resulting from 'clients in a nursing home and hitting and punching us'.

Her work situation seemed particularly bad, given that she stated she also experienced being shouted at, being treated in a disrespectful or rude way, feeling threatened, and having insulting or offensive remarks made about her (all of these were also experienced on a daily basis!). However, she reported 'never' experiencing many of the other types of ill-treatment asked about on the survey, such as being continually checked upon or given an unmanageable workload. This lends credence to her answers and sheds some light on how particular workplaces can be especially toxic and problematic in certain ways.

At the outset of our research, we expected that many people would regard actual physical violence as the most serious end of the spectrum of harmful workplace behaviour. Yet we know from previous chapters that violence was not included in the top three types of ill-treatment in terms of producing the most negative impact on the victim, which were being given unmanageable deadlines, having opinions ignored and being shouted at. Only just over 1 per cent of our respondents reported experiencing actual physical violence at work as having the most impact (compared to the other forms of ill-treatment included in the survey). It is therefore obvious that the majority of those who experienced violence did not think it was the type of ill-treatment that had the greatest impact on them.

We noted in earlier chapters that respondents may have interpreted our very general question about impact in terms of the consequences of ill-treatment for people's feelings about their relationship with their employer and co-workers, and their feelings of self-respect. Ill-treatment which had less impact in this sense might have substantial effects of other kinds, but this does not seem to be the case in respect of workplace violence. In the FTWS, relatively low proportions of respondents reporting actual physical violence at work said that the impact was 'serious' across all of these dimensions. For example, only 11 and 15 per cent, respectively, reported 'serious' physical and psychological impact, and well over half those experiencing violence reported no physical or psychological impact at all. Perhaps surprisingly, other forms of ill-treatment were rated as having greater specific impacts on those who experienced them. For example, whilst the differences were not huge, higher proportions of those who had been humiliated or ridiculed in connection with their work reported that this caused 'serious' physical and psychological impact for them (14 and 19 per cent, respectively).

This highlights the importance of social context and the 'lived reality' of harmful behaviours in the workplace. As Waddington et al.'s (2005) study of workplace violence in a number of professions found, in some contexts verbal threats or harassment were regarded as far more upsetting and harmful than incidents of actual physical mistreatment. We also found some evidence for this in both our survey and in our case studies. For example, a white female (aged 25–34) who worked in education chose to recall 'being called a fat cow by a child' when we asked her to tell us about the most upsetting of her experiences, even though she reported experiencing violence and injuries on a daily basis at work. In similar fashion, a Westshire employee said,

> At least with physical you get a slap and it's gone. This needling, pick, pick, pick, pick, picking goes on and on and on. And if they're allowed to get away with it, like a child stealing sweets, they continue and then they steal a few more sweets. And then they steal a few more until they're stealing a box full of sweets, you know?

Of course, violence may have consequences for the organisations involved as well as the individuals. Whilst our case studies provided a small number of examples of workplace violence, those that did arise suggested that the organisational consequences could be serious although, just as with the impact on individuals, these consequences were probably no greater than the impact of the wider range of ill-treatments on the organisation concerned.

It was certainly the case that workers in 'flashpoint' areas in Westshire, and their managers, demonstrated that workplace violence had financial and managerial consequences in terms of days lost through sickness/injury (at the time of the research, two of the small security team were currently off sick with injuries received during the course of their duties). This clearly had immediate resource implications for the organisation, even before we consider the wider impact on attitudes to work and general well-being of the staff. However, as Chapter 7 (on Westshire) shows, it seems reasonable to argue that, worrying though reports of violence are, the most serious organisational consequences arise from the numerically greater incidences of non-physical bad behaviour in the workplace. The same argument could apply to Britscope, the other of our organisational case studies that gave rise to reports of physical violence. With regard to the other two organisations, Strand and Banco, reports of actual physical violence and injury were so rare that negative organisational consequences relating to bad behaviour at work were almost entirely to do with unreasonable treatment and denigration or disrespect (as discussed in previous chapters). It is worth bearing in mind, then, that most of the ill-treatment was perpetrated by managers, and comparatively little of it originated with clients or customers. It was therefore managers who were largely responsible for the organisational consequences of ill-treatment in the workplace.

The Venn diagram in Figure 2 on p. 33 depicting the interrelationship between the three types of ill-treatment shows the circle for violence firmly embedded in the other two circles, indicating that it is a significant, if less widespread, part of the more general story of ill-treatment. Our survey showed that it is rare indeed that violence happens in the absence of any other type of workplace problems (otherwise, in the Venn diagram, the violence circle would be orbiting the other two circles rather than firmly ensconced within them). In fact, we found that violence increased the likelihood of other ill-treatment items occurring to a statistically significant extent. Those reporting violence

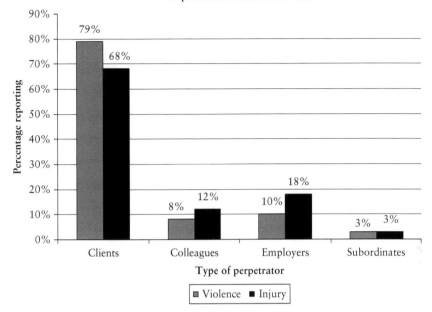

Figure 12 Violence at work is usually perpetrated by non-employees

also reported rates of the other types of ill-treatment that were at least two, and often three or four, times as high (compared to those who had no experience of violence). The most striking differences were for these types of incivility and disrespect: 'being insulted or having offensive remarks made about you', 'intimidating behaviour from people at work' and 'feeling threatened in any way while at work'.

Racial attacks and domestic violence often appear to be part of a broader pattern of harmful interactions that can include anything from relatively minor incivilities to harassment and threatening behaviour. Harm often stems from experiencing physical abuse alongside other types of encounters that are inherently emotionally damaging (Hanmer and Itzin 2000; Robinson 2010; Walby 2005). Similarly, research on racist victimisation has shown that it is better understood as a process rather than a series of discrete events, 'with both "minor" abuse and incidents of physical violence interwoven in a pattern of harassment and intimidation' (Bowling 1999; Phillips and Bowling 2007: 425). Thus, although physical 'violence' often seems the most significant of all encounters, we must not discount the pernicious effects of the combination of violence and other forms of abuse and ill-treatment.

Violence occurs along with unreasonable treatment as well as incivility and disrespect. This much is clear from Figure 2 but it also emerged in the bivariate comparison of violence with other types of ill-treatment. It was not just in relation to incivility and disrespect that violence increased the likelihood of other forms of ill-treatment. Significant differences were observed for *every one* of the 20 comparisons, including all types of unreasonable treatment. Whatever continuities we can find between incivility and disrespect and violence and injury, continuities with unreasonable treatment suggest common *organisational* causes of both violence and ill-treatment (as suggested by Bowie; discussed in Chapter 1).

The overlap between employees' experience of violence and other types of ill-treatment had an unintended methodological benefit for our study. Because respondents who reported violence and/or injury at work *always* reported further ill-treatment, they *all* fell into the group we have been referring to as the troubled minority. Some of them reported injury through violence at work but every single one of those who reported violence or injury also reported one or more additional items from the list of ill-treatment. So, although they are fewer in number, we have more comprehensive information about the experiences of everyone who reported workplace violence or injury, and this includes information about the perpetrators of incidences of violence in the workplace.

Whereas, in Chapter 3, we were surprised that customers (or clients) were not a more important source of incivility and disrespect, our expectations were less wide of the mark in respect of violence. The perpetrators of violence were rarely fellow *employees* but instead *non-employees* such as clients, customers or members of the general public.[4] More than three-quarters (79 per cent) of the violent incidents were perpetrated by these non-employees, with far fewer victims identifying employers[5] (10 per cent), co-workers (8 per cent) or subordinates (3 per cent) (see Figure 12). This is in stark contrast to unreasonable treatment, and even incivility and disrespect, where the troublemakers were other *employees* of the same organisation, be they managers, co-workers or subordinates. This raises important questions about causal factors as well as about possible policy responses to such problems.

For example, it indicates the importance of understanding the nature of the job and the workplace when attempting to explain workplace violence. It is also methodologically significant as the survey data largely represent non-employee workplace violence, but when people chose to speak to us about their negative experiences at work in the qualitative interviews, violence was rarely recounted. When it was, people tended to tell us stories of recurring problems with certain individuals at work (often including features of unreasonable treatment or incivility and disrespect) which eventually escalated into a violent encounter. Thus, we must remember that the types of data we have on violence may reflect different sorts of experiences. Given the data at our disposal, most of this chapter deals with non-employee workplace violence.

Again, because they were all part of the troubled minority, those who reported violence at work were also asked about the gender and ethnicity of those who perpetrated the violence. Of those reporting violence at work, 48 per cent reported that the perpetrator(s) was/were male, 23 per cent that the perpetrator(s) was/were female, and 25 per cent that they had been victimised by both male and female perpetrators. Furthermore, our analysis showed that violence was mostly male-on-male or female-on-female. Likewise, workplace violence was usually between people of similar ethnicity. The majority of perpetrators were white (76 per cent), with 6 per cent black, 3 per cent Asian, 2 per cent mixed origin, and this is similar to the profile of respondents in the troubled minority. In other words, white respondents were most often victimised by white perpetrators, and BME respondents were usually victimised by people from BME communities. In this regard, violence was similar to other types of ill-treatment at work in that perpetrators tend to match victims in terms of ethnicity and gender. It is also consistent with much criminological research indicating that victims and offenders are socio-demographically similar more often than they are not.

Recognising the importance of considering the type of perpetrator for understanding workplace violence, we wondered whether the significant associations between violence and the other 20 types of ill-treatment (discussed on p. 84) might, in part, be attributable to an especially extreme pattern of abuse and violence amongst those sharing the same workplace. Given what we know about domestic and racist violence, it might be expected that the links between violence and other forms of abusive behaviour might be particularly marked when people were having some form of relationship by virtue of their repeated exposure to each other within a shared work setting. This might include repeated exposure to and/or a close relationship with particular clients/customers.

In fact, our data show that people who experienced violence from other employees had much higher rates of other types of ill-treatment compared to people who had experienced violence from non-employees. Specifically, 12 of the 20 comparisons were statistically significant (e.g. pressure not to claim, having one's views and opinions ignored, constant criticism, being treated unfairly, being excluded from a group, humiliated, gossip and rumours spread about one, hints to quit, teasing, intimidation). Although the number of people reporting violence from other employees was small (only 42), it is clear that these people reported more ill-treatment (including the kind associated with incivility and disrespect) compared to those that had experienced violence from non-employees.

If the closest workplace links between violence and incivility and disrespect are to be found in the relations between fellow employees, this certainly qualifies our conclusion that violence is an aspect of antisocial behaviour that intrudes into the workplace from outside. Moreover, we shall see later in this chapter that this pattern of abusive and violent relationships between employees was more common in the private sector than the public sector.

Employees do indeed suffer violence from the general public, but this is less likely to be combined with other forms of ill-treatment. The links found in our survey between violence and disrespect were not, in the main, the result of alcohol-fuelled excesses on the streets spilling over into police stations, ambulances and accident and emergency departments. There were other reasons for this combination of types of ill-treatment, and we should therefore be very cautious about accepting any argument which suggests that the workplace represents a last bastion of rational behaviour in a 'broken society'.

As mentioned earlier, the qualitative case studies provided few examples of violent behaviour in the workplace, but some of these did illustrate further the contrast between inter-employee violence compared to violence perpetrated by clients, patients or the general public. Violence between employees – as in the survey – was a much rarer event in our case study interviews, but where violent acts were described they appeared to be part of a wider pattern of escalating ill-treatment. It was also sometimes difficult to distinguish the 'tipping point' where verbally aggressive or intimidating behaviour escalated into physically abusive behaviour. One such example came from Westshire (see Chapter 7), where Sarah, a white female consultant in her early forties, described how a deteriorating relationship with another senior colleague finally spilled over into physically intimidating behaviour:

> So he caught me in the office one day, and he said, 'Sarah, I am absolutely f***ing fed up with you, you're a manipulative, snidey cow and I wish I'd bloody well never appointed you.' And he was shouting, and I was just ... I thought consultants shouldn't raise fists, get you against a wall ... He backed me into a corner, you know, literally, physically, and I felt ... I wasn't actually scared that he was going to hit me, but ... he did swear and used lots of nasty words about me. And he stormed out of the room. And I said, 'Derek!' And he said, 'F**k off!' And he stormed out down the corridor!

Another member of staff was repeatedly poked in the chest in an extremely aggressive stand-off with a senior clinician in a dispute over the management of surgical waiting lists. A security officer in the same organisation described how another senior member of staff became so violent and abusive in a dispute over car parking spaces that he assaulted a security guard and had to be physically restrained by other staff.

In the Britscope case study, there were a number of incidents reported to us that could be described as violent. For example, two black female workers told us about incidents in which co-workers had subjected them to aggressive shoving and pushing (another employee was injured quite seriously as a result of a workplace prank). One of the former cases illustrated how, in the context of a mutually hostile workplace relationship, it can be difficult to distinguish between aggressor and victim. One woman in her forties recounted a dispute with a colleague triggered by workplace gossip about an alleged sexual affair. Both parties appeared to see the other as the aggressor, and the incident resulted in a formal investigation. She reported that her co-worker had accused her of sleeping with their manager, who happened to be the boyfriend of the co-worker. This led to a confrontation in front of other staff, in which her co-worker made accusations and approached her aggressively. She described the physical encounter that followed: 'I didn't say a word, all I did was, she was in my face with her hand in my face, so I push her back, I say listen, just get away from me and I didn't say a thing.' This exchange resulted in her being accused of slapping her co-worker in the face, an accusation which was not supported by the formal investigation.

A local line manager in Britscope explained that in his experience physical violence rarely took place between workers in the workplace itself, perhaps unsurprisingly given the potential consequences for those involved in terms of disciplinary procedures and possible dismissal. However, he was aware of cases in which ongoing disputes between workers had resulted in fights 'off site', one of which had been so serious that the police were called, and which had become the focus of an internal Britscope investigation. Britscope also provided further examples of physically abusive behaviour that was part of a broader pattern of serious sexual harassment. Significantly, these examples of inter-employee violent and abusive behaviour all had a 'history'. They occurred in the context of ongoing and deteriorating work relationships, and were preceded and/or accompanied by a range of other ill-treatments such as rudeness, incivility and verbal aggression.

The reported impacts on the interviewees of these damaged working relationships, in almost every case, were severe. A number of these respondents reported psychological problems such as depression. Several had taken substantial periods of sick leave, and a number had moved jobs or even considered quitting the organisation. It is difficult to disentangle the effects of different aspects of the pattern of ill-treatment experienced by these individuals from the violence. We must also bear in mind the results from the FTWS, which suggested that the effects of violence were less pronounced than we might have expected. All the same, it seems clear that, similar to domestic or racist violence, inter-employee violence can have substantial impacts for individuals beyond the immediate physical effects of conflict.

Our survey suggested the links between violence and other forms of ill-treatment were not as pronounced where the perpetrators were not fellow employees. All the examples we had of this kind of violence in the case studies came from Westshire NHS. One interviewee, a security officer (a white male in his early thirties), recounted how his colleague had been spat at by a client while another had been injured trying to physically restrain another member of the public. Saturday nights were particularly difficult, requiring them to deal with between 10 and 12 violent or potentially violent incidents on average. As he said, 'One of my colleagues got punched in the stomach last Saturday by an elderly woman; when another officer tried to help, she got punched too.' Another incident involved a confused patient who struck a member of staff who tried to direct her back to her ward, and the piece of medical equipment strapped to the patient's arm cut the head of the staff member.

Somewhat surprisingly to us, our respondents dealt with these incidents in a relatively matter-of-fact manner. One might argue that security staff, and staff working in high-stress areas such as accident and emergency units, would perhaps expect to experience occasional physical conflict with members of the public or patients. For some staff, it was certainly the case that they saw aggressive and violent encounters as coming 'with the territory' (as one mental health nurse told us). Staff working in front-line roles dealing with the public faced violence, or the potential for it, as part of their everyday working lives. It would be a mistake, however, to think that it was just the members of the blue light services dealing with the extreme end of antisocial behaviour who were in this position.

Whether the violence manifested itself on a daily basis, or was expressed at a relatively minor level, there was the potential for violence in many, if not most, of their interactions with clients/public. For example, confrontation can be a regular feature of working life for those working in health care settings, particularly those dealing with mental health. A further example of this comes from the security officers working in Westshire:

> Well at first it is a bit shocking to see the abuse people have got to take at work. It's not really acceptable, but you do become accustomed to it, and you have a light-hearted approach. It's like I was saying yesterday when we were restraining that male. He took a dislike to my colleague, so I was quite happy he was abusing him, I was okay. I was being let off, but we joke it off between us, so not 'have a laugh', but we do sort of … the boys especially, they do sort of take the light-hearted approach towards it, and they sort of laugh things off.

There is a long tradition of research into how the risk of violence factors into occupational subcultures of certain professions such as the police, often resulting in attributes such as cynicism, burnout, 'us versus them' mentality and so on. But even in less overtly adversarial, but still public-facing, jobs there is an adaptation that has to happen on the part of workers who must come to terms with their (sometimes daily) potential to experience violence. For example, Sheard (2011: 625) found a similar sentiment expressed by female bartenders in her study of violence in the night-time economy:

> Indeed, some of the bar tenders described violence which had been perpetrated against them at work in a matter-of-fact manner as its occurrence (or the threat of it) was or had been frequent enough for them not to be shocked.

On p. 81 we noted that respondents to workplace surveys may feel less tied to formal legal categories when discussing violent behaviours, and this might be one reason why the rates of violence they record exceed those in the annual BCSs. Evidently people are very reluctant to think of violent incidents at work – even those that happen regularly and/or cause injury – as 'crime'. Why might this be the case?

People tend to think of 'crime' as something that happens on the streets, usually between strangers; when bad things happen at work people tend not to think of them as criminal but rather as some negative aspect of the job. Similar to the often-demonstrated and long-standing reluctance of people to acknowledge violence in the domestic sphere as 'crime', our respondents seemed to consider violent incidents within their workday as something other than criminal, particularly when the culprits were known to them. The Westshire security officer provided some clear examples of how quite serious assaults, or attempted assaults, were not criminalised because of the context. Disputes over car parking, both with other staff members and the general public, were a daily problem negotiated by security officers. There was a recent incident when a fellow staff member, with whom there had been ongoing disagreements about car parking, had driven his van deliberately at the parking officer who leapt out of the way to avoid serious injury. This, in theory, was a clear example of attempted criminal assault. However, it was not reported to the police but dealt with internally by the organisation:

> To be honest with you, it's still going on internally. I could have gone via the police because it's something like causing injury by using a vehicle as a weapon, but I didn't pursue that. I should have really, but at the time I didn't feel it necessary, but I wish I had now. It's just being dealt with internally.

Further examples suggested that non-criminalisation was not necessarily a function of lack of severity of the assault, but rather the nature of the assailant and the context of the violence:

> It [the violence] is really bad. It's like this lady that obviously attacked our officer. She was an elderly lady, what do you do? And in the same light we had a 15-year-old girl, no parents there, she was causing absolute mayhem in A and E, but what do you do? She's classed as a minor although she was speaking like she was a bit older, but it's such a sticky situation to be involved in.

Our interviews also found examples of ambiguity about the jurisdiction of workplace procedures to deal with violent incidents between co-workers that happened away from the workplace. In this case, violence ceased to be considered *workplace* violence at the point it became a crime. Thus, the previously mentioned line manager at Britscope reported that a very serious fight between two workers was referred by one of them to the organisational complaints procedures. However, the organisation initially decided that, despite the seriousness of the violence, the fact that it had taken place away from the workplace (and that the police had decided not to take action) meant that it was deemed unsuitable for consideration by the formal Britscope complaints procedures. The victim of the violence had continued to claim that the incident was related to work, however, and pursued it at a higher level in the organisation. At the time of our research, the matter had still to be resolved (although the two men had been put in separate working areas):

> He battered him. It's a bit of iffy one actually, but the bloke who was beat up tried to claim it related from work ... it all stemmed from work with comments made like he was this or that ... But ... there were no hard facts there. The police didn't prosecute so then that made ... actually where do we come in? We're not above the police, we're not above the law. We have our own standards and we can deal with that, and we deemed it that there was no case to answer from his initial complaint because we couldn't see how it stemmed from work. But then he wrote to our chairman ... Then that then comes back down through the porters, personnel and all the rest of it, and it came back that further investigations were done. I don't know what the end result of this one is, but I think it's going to be the same. The police haven't prosecuted so why should we dismiss?

Respondents' answers to questions about perceived 'causes' of violence at work also supported the notion that characteristics of individual victims or perpetrators were less important than understanding the context where the violence occurred. For certain groups of workers, at least, violence emerged from the structures of their working environment. Few respondents reported individuated explanations of violent incidents motivated by particular forms of prejudice, and relatively few respondents identified the cause or motivation for violent incidents as something about themselves (e.g. their ethnic background, sexuality or social class). Substantially larger proportions of the sample identified the causes or motivation for workplace violence to more general features of their working environments. In particular, 'It's just the way things are where you work' was the most commonly chosen factor, selected by 64 per cent of respondents who had experienced violence. Only 14 per cent said it was their position in the organisation, although this was the third most frequently given reason. The second most common reason was the attitude/ personality of the other person (48 per cent). In sum, most victims of workplace violence were more likely to relate these incidents to the wider conditions of their work, or to the general personality dispositions or attitudes of the perpetrator(s), than to any of their own specific demographic characteristics.

Thus far, we have been summarising our interpretations of qualitative data and the bivariate analyses of our survey results. As in Chapters 2 and 3, we now move on to multivariate analysis in order to learn more about the causes of workplace violence. In one important respect, however, we shall be departing from the methods of analysis used at the corresponding point in Chapters 2 and 3. We have only violence and injury to model, rather than the several items of unreasonable treatment and incivility and disrespect. Moreover, we know that there are some causal links between violence and injury. It therefore makes little sense to treat them as a single dependent variable. Instead, we shall refer to the multivariate analysis presented in Jones *et al.* (2011), which not only modelled violence and injury separately but also included some independent variables – for example, occupational variables – which were excluded in the versions of the multivariate models used in Chapters 2 and 3 because they had no role in explaining unreasonable treatment or incivility and disrespect.

What kind of employees experienced workplace violence and injury?

Although experience of violence at work varied between different demographic groups, we did not find much evidence that particular individuals were more prone to violence (independently of where they worked or what jobs they did). We considered gender, sexual orientation, age, ethnicity, religion, education, disability and income, but only one of these was statistically related to workplace violence in our multivariate models, and none were related to injury.

Employees with psychological or emotional conditions, or learning disabilities, were seven times more likely to experience workplace violence. It is easy to jump to the conclusion that this result for a category of disability is, for once, unambiguously pointing towards the health effects of ill-treatment. It is, after all, a common assumption made by clinicians and therapists that someone who has been assaulted at work may subsequently experience some level of psychological trauma. We have also referred to some evidence for health effects in the FTWS (p. 62) and our own case studies (p. 69). There is, however, reason to doubt that all of the association observed here is due to health problems. In the first place, some proportion of the correlation is (probably) with learning disabilities rather than psychological conditions. In the second, we would expect the health effects of violence to be as, if not more, obvious in the case of injury at work. This is not the case, however. Although other health conditions were close to significance for injury, categories of psychological or emotional conditions and learning disabilities were not. Indeed Fevre *et al.* (forthcoming) confirmed that other physical disabilities and other health conditions were significant at the 10 per cent significance level for injury even though psychological or learning disability was not.

Which jobs were more prone to violence and injury?

With the possible exception of health effects, our analyses point us towards more structural explanations of violence and reinforce the importance of context. The data indicated that, on the whole, it was certain types of places rather than certain types of people per se that were especially prone to violence. This underlines, once more, the overwhelming importance of the troubled workplace in predicting all kinds of ill-treatment at work. Once employees find themselves working in one, demographic characteristics make little difference to their chances of experiencing violence.

Multivariate analysis showed that employees were more likely to experience workplace violence if they had managerial or supervisory duties, worked full-time and were trade union members (who were also more at risk of injury as well as violence). It was clearly not the marginalised and peripheral workers who were most at risk of workplace violence but permanent staff in managerial or supervisory positions. Indeed multivariate analyses confirmed that managers/supervisors also were more likely to report witnessing violence, holding everything else constant. Given the predominance of client/public perpetrators, it is reasonable to speculate that such a pattern may arise in part from more junior staff calling in front-line managers to deal with situations of conflict, although it is not possible to explore this further in our survey data.

The other job variable that proved to be significant in multivariable analysis did, however, suggest that some of the most poorly paid workers were also more likely to experience violence in the workplace. Multivariate analysis showed that violence was more likely in personal service occupations. This category includes cooks, waiters, care assistants, child carers, assistant auxiliary nurses, domestic staff and undertakers. As with trade union members, personal service occupations were also significant for injury as well as violence. The fact that personal service occupations were significant suggests something about the kind of workplaces – care homes, private households – where violence took place, and it is to these characteristics that we now turn.

What kinds of workplaces and organisations were more prone to workplace violence?

The multivariate analysis reported in Jones *et al.* (2011) showed that violence was more likely with super-intense work, in the public *and* the third sectors, in health and social work (which also predicted injury as well as violence), and in smaller workplaces. In Chapter 3, we found that the public sector was more likely to produce workplaces troubled by incivility and disrespect, and now we find that the public sector was also more likely to produce workplaces troubled by violence. This clearly lends some credence to the view that incivility often occurred alongside, or led to, violent behaviour and to the notion that it was workers in public services who bore the brunt of this. However, we must be very wary of jumping to the conclusion that these were all blue light employees. Indeed, we know from the fact that personal service occupations were more likely to experience violence that they were not all police officers, firefighters or paramedics. Moreover, public administration (where police officers and others are counted) predicted injury but not violence in the workplace. Another clue is provided by the fact that third sector workplaces were also more likely to exhibit violence. That the third sector featured alongside the public sector probably indicates the degree to which comparable services – for example, care for people with mental illnesses – are provided in both sectors. This may also be why health and social work remained significant even when we controlled for sector: there were sufficient private sector workplaces in this industry to allow us to see its independent effect. We should also note that multivariate analysis showed that violence was less likely in the largest workplaces (with more than 250 employees). This would exclude many hospital facilities but few, if any, care homes.

Other studies have found that intense and heavy workloads, in combination with a lack of opportunities to exercise control over their work, increase employees' risk of violence at work because the stress and pressure under which people are working leads to conflict (Estrada et al. 2010). We found a relationship in our multivariate analysis between violence (but not injury) and super-intense work. Super-intense work is therefore associated with all three types of ill-treatment at work in our multivariate analyses. We did not find a relationship with an increased pace of work or less control, however. In fact, less control predicted less injury. Change in the nature of work was associated with injury, but we suspect that this may, at least in part, have been because the nature of work was modified following the injury.

We know from Figure 7 on p. 53 that both public administration and defence, and health and social work, produced some of the least flattering answers to the FARE questions and to the employers. It is no surprise, therefore, that bivariate analysis showed that these questions were significantly related to the likelihood of experiencing workplace violence. For example, fewer respondents who responded 'where I work, people are treated as individuals' reported workplace assault (4 per cent compared to 7 per cent). Nevertheless, the FARE questions did not predict workplace violence, or injury, in our multivariate analysis with one exception. Injury was less likely where people were treated as individuals. In sum, for violence and injury, conflict over workplace norms is less important than being in a job that entails dealing with the public.

The troubled minority

All those who experienced violence were in the troubled minority, but in the models reported in Jones et al. (2011) we compared them with the sample as a whole. This was why we could see the factors such as sector that characterised (violent) troubled workplaces. Once we have conducted our analyses wholly inside the troubled minority, we should not necessarily expect the same patterns to emerge.[6] In effect, we are comparing those troubled minority members who experienced violence or injury with those who did not. Moreover, since we are only dealing with the troubled minority, we can now bring variables which distinguish the different types of perpetrators into the analysis. In fact, controlling for client or customer perpetrators meant that third sector was no longer significant while public sector remained so, but there were other surprises.

That disability ceased to be significant (at the 5 per cent level, though it remained so at the 10 per cent level) was probably a consequence of not distinguishing those with psychological or emotional problems or learning disabilities from the rest. Controlling for client versus other types of perpetrators did, however, allow a new characteristic of individuals to emerge as significant for violence. Gay or bisexual respondents were five times more likely to report violence at work compared to heterosexual respondents in the multivariate model. (Even simple bivariate analysis showed that 16 per cent of LGB employees reported violence as opposed to 5 per cent of others.) This finding, of course, comes on top of the finding in Chapter 3 that gay and lesbian respondents were significantly more likely to experience feeling threatened and very close to significantly more likely to experience humiliation, hints they should quit, and shouting. Employees who said they were bisexual were significantly more likely to experience hints they should quit, and intimidation, and in both cases the effects were massive. (In multivariate analysis of the FTWS, LGB respondents were substantially more likely to report humiliation.) Finally, Chapter 3 showed that, within the troubled minority, LGB employees were 12 times more likely to receive hints to quit and four times more likely to be threatened. A clear pattern is therefore emerging of serious, and perhaps escalating, ill-treatment of LGB employees.

Given the extent of criminological research which uniformly paints violence as a gendered phenomenon, we expected that gender would play a significant role in our analyses of the troubled minority. Yet, while bivariate analysis showed that women (6 per cent) were significantly more likely to experience violence at work when compared with men (4 per cent), this relationship did not hold up when we controlled for other factors. As we noted above, sector continued to be significant for violence in the analysis of the troubled minority. Public sector workers were more than three times as likely to report violence as those working in other sectors. Public sector therefore predicted troubled workplaces (both violent ones and those featuring incivility and disrespect), but it also helped to predict a violent workplace amongst the wider group of troubled workplaces. Larger workplaces were also more likely to be untroubled, less affected by violence, and with fewer injuries. The same also held true for the FARE question about treating people as individuals but only in respect of injury, not violence. Employees were much less likely to be in a troubled workplace of any kind if they thought people were treated as individuals, but now we find that this variable also separated the violent from the non-violent troubled workplaces.

Finally, employees in workplaces which were more ethnically mixed were more than twice as likely to report violence. This should not, however, be interpreted as an indication of high levels of ethnic conflict at work. Findings on workplace composition probably reflected the ethnic composition of particular kinds of workplaces, rather than higher rates of tension and inter-employee violence in these workplaces. Public sector workplaces had higher rates of 'some BME' compared to 'no BME' employees (and public and third sector workplaces had higher rates of 'some women' compared to 'no women' employees). Overall, then, these findings probably reflect the characteristics of workplaces in particular sectors where the incidence and frequency of physical violence is relatively high, such as health and social work settings which employ relatively high proportions of ethnic minorities. This is supported by the survey findings indicating that more BME-dominated workplaces had higher levels of violence from clients/customers than from fellow employees or managers.

Conclusions

Our statistical models showed that particular occupations and industry sectors were associated with a higher rate of workplace violence. These were sectors and occupations with a high proportion of client-facing jobs, particularly in the public sector, such as policing, nursing and social care. Our work thus suggests that explanations for workplace violence are most likely to be found in the nature of workplaces, rather than in the individual characteristics of victims or perpetrators. Although primed towards individualised explanations by the survey method, respondents rarely identified causal factors relating to their own particular characteristics such as their ethnicity, age or gender. Rather, they were most likely to explain incidents with reference to the general nature of their work.

Although Chapter 3 showed that women in the troubled minority were more likely to report being insulted, the absence of significant results for gender has been a feature of most of our multivariate models of ill-treatment. In other words, holding constant other relevant socio-demographic and workplace variables, men and women were equally likely to experience trouble at work. This indicates, once more, the importance of looking beyond the individual level for explanations of violence. In this respect, it is worth noting that, although women did not necessarily report more ill-treatment at work, they tended to work in places associated with the most extreme types of problems, such as violence and injury. Gender is also interesting when considering witnessing and perpetrating violence. In bivariate analysis, it was men who were significantly more likely than women to report witnessing violence and violence-related injury in the workplace. Perhaps this is because men were more likely to hold positions as managers/supervisors than women, so such incidents were more regularly brought to their attention.

Similar analyses were carried out for workers reporting that they had perpetrated violence or caused injury to other workers during the two years prior to the survey. Perhaps unsurprisingly, reporting rates for these kinds of serious behaviours were very low, and few findings were statistically significant. Men were, however, significantly more likely than women to admit to perpetrating violence at work and to causing injury to others through workplace violence. Interestingly, these findings held at the multivariate level, as men were far more likely to report perpetrating violence and injuries at work compared to women. If nothing else, these findings seem to support the conclusions of some sociological studies of the nature of masculinity and its resistance to change.

With the exception of our findings about LGB employees and those with psychological or emotional problems or a learning disability, exposure to the risk of workplace violence does *not* appear to be experienced disproportionately by certain *workers*, but is rather unevenly spread across certain *workplaces*. This may seem counterintuitive in that it is people, rather than places, that commit acts of violence. We recognise this but what the data have led us to propose is that it is certain workplace contexts which facilitate or even encourage the use of violence. This is not to condone the use of violence in such settings, only to acknowledge that people within these settings might lose self-control sometimes. Indeed, our finding that most of the violence was committed by *non-employees* supports this argument. It is the service users, the clients, customers and other members of the public who tend to 'lose it' rather than employees. The overall effect of the results reported in this chapter is to reinforce what we have said in Chapters 2 and 3 about the importance of sociological studies of workplaces as the key to building useful theories of all types of trouble at work.

As in the previous chapters, we conclude with extensive bivariate analysis of the kind that is most useful to policy-makers and practitioners who need to know where they should concentrate their efforts to make the most effective intervention in this important aspect of ill-treatment in the workplace. In the process, we shall illustrate why, despite what we have just said about the public sector, we think policy-makers would be wrong to think of violence in the workplace as largely the consequence of asking blue light workers to deal with antisocial behaviour.

Our bivariate analyses showed that workplace violence was unevenly distributed across different sectors of the economy. Those working in the public or third sector were significantly more likely to report workplace violence (9 per cent each compared to 3 per cent in the private sector). Rates of workplace violence also varied significantly between different industries. Specifically, we found relatively high levels of violence reported by those working in health and social work (15 per cent or three times the sample average). Workplace violence also had a statistical association with ethnic composition. In workplaces where there were more BME workers, there were higher rates of violence (e.g. when three-quarters were BME, 12 per cent of respondents reported experiencing physical violence at work, compared to only 4 per cent when none were BME).

Another industry sector with apparently elevated risk was public administration and defence (which includes police officers and some other emergency workers), at 10 per cent or twice the sample average. Education was the third riskiest industry, with 6 per cent of those respondents reporting violence. Substantiating these results were the industry classifications of those 25 respondents who reported experiencing violence on a daily basis: five were in public administration, six in education, and 12 in health and social work. Indeed, looking at the industry and occupational classifications (discussed earlier) together shows that most of the violence perpetrated in the three riskiest industries (health/social work, public administration/defence or education) was against those in the associate/professional/technical or personal/service occupations (90 or 70 per cent of 129 respondents).

Another way to illustrate the importance of workplace setting is with Figure 13. Each pie chart represents a different measure of workplace violence – experiencing, witnessing or perpetrating. It is easy to see how the three industries just mentioned – namely, health and social work, public administration/defence, and education – accounted for a substantial majority of each pie. Clearly, these three industries can be considered hotspots for violence at work. This probably comes as no surprise after reading the previous chapters on unreasonable treatment and incivility and disrespect, which also described elevated rates in these industries.

Our survey provided strong evidence of particular places being 'hotspots' of workplace violence. Let us not forget, however, that although most workplace violence is committed by non-employees, a different picture emerges when we distinguish between employee and non-employee perpetrators (see Figures 14 and 15). Work environments in the public sector are troubled and therefore lead clients/customers to be violent. The private sector is where most inter-employee workplace violence takes place.

Figure 16 shows that particular industries were hotspots for *non-employee* workplace violence, but these were *not* the same hotspots where *inter-employee* violence occurred. Specifically, education, health and social work

Experiencing violence (*n* = 156), by industry

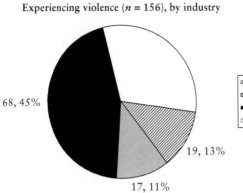

68, 45%

19, 13%

17, 11%

☒ Public administration and defence
▣ Education
■ Health and social work
□ All other industries

Witnessing violence (*n* = 183), by industry

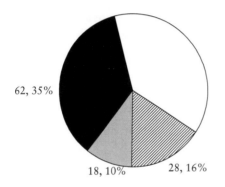

62, 35%

18, 10%   28, 16%

☒ Public administration and defence
▣ Education
■ Health and social work
□ All other industries

Perpetrating violence (*n* = 15), by industry

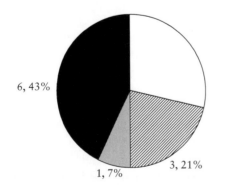

6, 43%

1, 7%   3, 21%

☒ Public administration and defence
▣ Education
■ Health and social work
□ All other industries

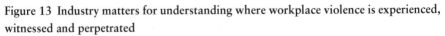

Figure 13 Industry matters for understanding where workplace violence is experienced, witnessed and perpetrated

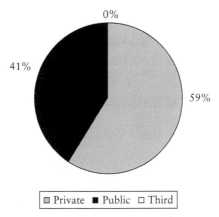

Figure 14 Inter-employee violence tends to happen in the private sector

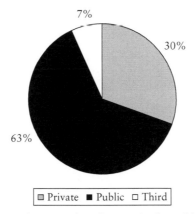

Figure 15 Non-employee violence tends to happen in the public sector

and public administration/defence were hotspots for non-employee violence, whereas more private sector jobs like manufacturing, construction, transport and wholesale/retail trade were the hotspots for inter-employee workplace violence. It is important to note that the numbers were very small, so these differences should be viewed with caution. Specifically, those industries noted with an asterisk (*) had fewer than five respondents each. However, both sector and industry data seem to suggest qualitative differences between violence from clients and customers and violence from anyone else.

With regard to analysis of the workplace characteristics of those who reported witnessing workplace violence, again the picture was similar to those experiencing such violence. Particular troubled workplaces, such as those in the

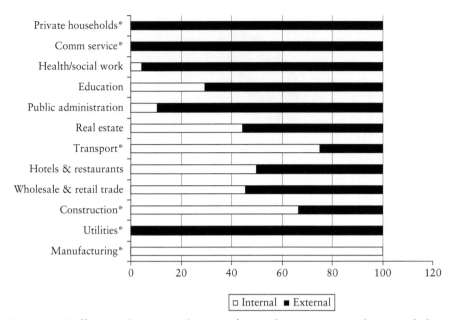

Figure 16 Different industries are hotspots for employee vs non-employee workplace violence

public sector, were associated with a greater likelihood of witnessing violence, and the type of industries associated with higher risk of *experiencing* violence was unsurprisingly also associated with greater likelihood of *witnessing* violence. With regard to perpetrators of workplace violence, those working in the health and social welfare sector were most likely to admit to perpetrating violence themselves in the workplace. Thus, public administration/defence and health/social work can be considered true hotspots as they have high rates of unreasonable treatment, incivility and disrespect *and* violence. Workers in these industries were more likely to report witnessing and perpetrating the full range of ill-treatment in the workplace.

PART THREE

The process of selecting and recruiting organisations for the case studies discussed in Part Three was exhaustive and lasted for two years. In some cases, we spent several months building relationships with potential partner organisations but were not able to proceed. For example, we spent significant effort negotiating with a government agency but were unable to meet their requirements for data control without compromising the confidentiality of our interviewees. The search for potential partners led us to spend several months travelling the length and breadth of the United Kingdom to undertake meetings with organisations in the public, private and third sectors. These meetings typically involved HR directors and sometimes trade union representatives. Several national and international companies pulled out of the project at the final stage, often when the approval of a CEO, or equivalent, was required. Our search for organisation partners was taking place at the height of the credit crunch in 2008 when the UK economy was entering recession and organisations were particularly sensitive to employment relations issues. We were often told our project did not fit an organisational agenda, or that there were concerns that findings might influence negotiations with trade unions on things like redundancy and pay.

Each participating organisation was offered a report on the results of the research we undertook with their employees, presentations of the results to an audience of their choice, bespoke training sessions based on our findings, and critical reviews of organisation literature, policies and processes. Nevertheless, given the difficulties we had in securing the partnerships, it is well worth asking why those organisations which did take part were willing to cooperate. Britscope had particular reasons to be concerned about the ill-treatment of its female staff (see Chapter 5) and was keen to have the assistance of independent researchers to help them understand the problem and whether company efforts to improve matters were working. As part of our partnership with Banco (Chapter 6), we undertook a confidential survey of 2,700 employees which provided a range of information on ill-treatment. Banco used our report from this survey to inform policy and practice improvements and drew on our data to evaluate their HR strategies on dignity and fairness at work. Although we did not undertake surveys in Britscope or Westshire NHS (Chapter 7), these organisations used the reports we produced for them on the qualitative research we undertook in their organisations in the same way. Westshire had already instigated significant developments on fairness, dignity, bullying and harassment but judged from staff engagement surveys that there remained significant problems to address.

Our engagement with their specialist health and well-being team was seen as a critical next step. With resources within the NHS at breaking point, the no-cost option of working with us was seen as a prudent way of accessing independent research.

Our gatekeeper at Strand Global Systems (Chapter 8) was particularly interested in the experiences of BME staff and hoped to use our research to understand better the company's difficulties in recruiting BME employees. It was often the input of such individuals that drove the successful negotiations and subsequent final approval. They also provided us with unrestricted access to organisational literature where policies, procedures and processes were described. Our research could not have been undertaken without such champions, but we also relied heavily on the support of Acas and the Equality and Human Rights Commission (EHRC) in brokering meetings and introducing us to key decision-makers. General ethical approval for the qualitative stage of the research was provided by the Cardiff University research ethics process, although we also had to negotiate the protracted NHS research ethics procedure in order to undertake the research at Westshire.

Our eventual engagement with over 100 interviewees and key informants was achieved in different ways in each case study organisation. At Banco, the survey of 2,700 staff allowed us to ask for volunteers whom we then sifted and screened. At Westshire NHS, we used an intranet and poster campaign distributed via the health and well-being team, followed by telephone interviews, to select participants in the face-to-face interviewing programme. At Britscope we were given unrestricted access to the responses from the company's own very large survey of female employees. We were then able to screen a very large number of respondents to reach our target audience of women who had disabilities or long-term health conditions, or who were from ethnic minority backgrounds, and who had reported exposure to workplace ill-treatment. Potential volunteers who had indicated their willingness to take part in further research were then asked by the survey organisation that had gathered the original data if they would be interviewed. At Strand Global Systems, we used a series of briefing meetings with employees to publicise the research and encourage employees to volunteer for the interviewing programme.

We knew from our previous work with people who had suffered workplace ill-treatment that the interviews would require careful management. We spent considerable time and effort informing the employees who were selected for interview (usually in an initial telephone call) in order to make sure they understood the nature of the research they were committing themselves to. We followed principles of good practice by seeking written consent and providing participant information sheets, contact information and the telephone numbers of agencies such as Acas, the EHRC and anti-bullying charities should someone feel upset by disclosure of their experiences. We also provided specialist training with a workplace counselling team for Martyn Rogers, our researcher who conducted a significant number of our interviews, to prepare him for dealing with sensitive topics. Some of our interviews took place at the workplace but the majority did not. Interviews were often conducted at home and at times that were always convenient for our interviewees. Sometimes this meant our researcher travelled hundreds of miles only to be told the interview was not possible and to come back on another day. We are, of course, extremely grateful to Martyn Rogers for his invaluable contribution to this phase of the research.

The accounts of ill-treatment presented in the following chapters illustrate the brutal, unpleasant and downright miserable experiences that some employees face when they have a bad day at work. We also present the thoughts and observations of a number of key informants who, by the nature of their roles, were likely to have indirect experience of ill-treatment and direct experience of company policies and processes. These included HR officers, trade union representatives and managers.

Our case studies are intended to help us answer better the questions raised by the BWBS, in particular why some workplaces are more troubled than others and what can be done to reduce trouble at work. To this end, we explore the leads which the BWBS has given us, particularly the importance of sector, loss of control, super-intense work and the characteristics of organisational culture as measured by the FARE questions. For example, Westshire NHS was dogged by political interference in the form of patient waiting times, referral processes and constant budgetary pressures which sometimes placed intolerable pressures on managers and staff in a way which seemed neither logical nor sensible. The other three case studies also had their share of reduced autonomy, super-intense work and cultural shifts. Banco seemed to have undertaken a strategic change of direction away from customer relationships built on trust and respect. Britscope had been engaged in a long battle with the trade union over its efforts to change working practices. Strand was making the transition from a UK champion to a global corporation with significant implications for its future relations with its UK employees.

In all four case studies, we saw people coping with the demands of intensive work demands whilst maintaining what they saw as fair and decent treatment. For many managers, troubles at work were rooted in a constant struggle to cope with super-intense work. For managers and others, productivity ultimatums from their superiors might be coupled with systems and processes which placed excessive demands on them. We saw these pressures in all our case studies; for example, sickness absence monitoring, management returns using online systems, customer call-waiting times in call centres and excessive checking and monitoring were all leading to problems. We also saw how workplaces seemed most troubled when people felt they were not treated as individuals and where people felt they had to compromise their principles. By the same token, our study of Strand Global Systems suggested that organisations that were able to maintain some sense of fairness and respect were better able to cope with situations which might lead to escalating trouble at work elsewhere.

Not very long ago, it would have been far-fetched to consider any of the organisations we researched to be candidates for troubled workplaces. All four of the organisations had been able to rely upon an extraordinarily high level of commitment from their employees and had enviable public reputations. Banco and Strand have not suffered the decline in commitment and damage to reputation that had occurred in Britscope and Westshire. We do, however, wonder whether the sense of malaise in Britscope and Westshire would be quite so strong if they had not been held up to be exemplary employers alongside the likes of Banco and Strand not so long ago.

In each of our case studies, it was possible to observe a range of trigger points for both virtuous and vicious spiralling effects. In many cases, managers were involved and they were often at the heart of troubled workplaces. Problems with poor communication, lack of awareness of employment rights as well as ignorance of management responsibilities were implicated in a pattern of actions and reactions that often led to prolonged absences, and periods of sustained ill-health, as well as fractured workplace relations. In some cases, these appeared to be exacerbated by the very policies designed to help rid the workplace of these kinds of troubles. For some managers there was an appeal for common sense and a genuine fear that policies and practices often made things worse rather than better. Trade union representatives often explained their frustrations with the way relatively minor troubles could escalate leaving organisational damage that often became irreparable. This could lead to protracted trench warfare where individuals refused to see the right or wrong in their own and others' actions. This, in turn, led to frustrations for HR and trade union representatives, as well as managers who were charged with finding amicable and acceptable solutions. The ultimate effects of these troubles could mean retraining, relocating and reorganising individuals, teams and structures in an attempt to return to harmonious working.

Our case studies also revisited those who might be most at risk of trouble at work, for example, younger workers. Our interviews with a number of ethnic minority employees revealed how racial abuse, and workplace practices, left them feeling isolated outside the work team. In Britscope, managers apparently favoured their own ethnic groups to the detriment of other minorities. Our interviews also revealed how many people with disabilities and long-term health conditions suffered appalling treatment at work, often because of the ignorance of their line managers and supervisors. Simply speaking out was itself a major emotional challenge for many of these employees. For some, recounting their experiences was upsetting and brought back unhappy memories; yet they still chose to speak to us. As one interviewee told us,

> I'm glad I did this because … I don't think I've told maybe two people what I've told you today, out of 20 years. So it's just nice for somebody else to come in from outside and listen to it, and just me babble on for an hour.

As we noted at the beginning of this book, the contributions of our interviewees afforded us an opportunity to better understand the nature and causes of trouble at work, and we are also extremely grateful to them.

5

The Briar Patch

This case study was based in a major business unit of a large public limited company, to which we have given the pseudonym 'Britscope'. At the time of the research, the organisation employed over 100,000 workers across the United Kingdom and had a history of turbulent industrial relations. The organisation had faced substantial external pressures in recent years and responded with a significant programme of 'modernisation' which included organisational restructuring, substantial reductions in the labour force and the introduction of new technologies to bring about efficiency gains. Senior management acknowledged that bullying and harassment, particularly the sexual harassment of women employees, was a particular problem for the organisation.

Britscope employed people in various locations across the United Kingdom in a number of different workplace types, and the employees we interviewed worked in sites scattered across the United Kingdom, but all were employed in workplaces with between 50 and 400 people. Aside from the managers and union representatives we talked to, all interviewees were working in semi-skilled manual jobs that often required a demanding level of physical work. They worked in small teams, overseen by line managers, in distribution centres, and often undertook shift work. The rhythms of the working week could vary substantially, depending on the day and the time, with highly frenetic and pressurised periods separated by periods of relative calm. In some workplaces, there was a considerable amount of noise and dust from the machinery used in the job, and during the summer especially, temperatures could be quite hot.

As mentioned in the introduction, the organisation had a long history of industrial relations problems. A single national union represented a high proportion of its manual employees, and another union represented managerial and administrative staff. There had been periodic industrial action during the past decade, with major episodes during 2007 and then again in 2009. Conversations with management and union representatives suggested these periods of industrial unrest were related to attempts by the organisation to 'modernise' in the face of declining revenues relating to growing external competition and falling market demand more generally. Union officials also referred to an established organisational culture of suspicion between management and workforce, and problems in communication and management style. One union representative reported to us that until relatively recently, the union was more or less on constant 'war footing'. Both employee and management representatives were keen to point to improvements in this situation and highlighted attempts to develop a more constructive partnership between management and unions.

Both sides agreed that the external pressures faced by the organisation had played a significant part in triggering the industrial disputes of recent years. The organisation faced the twin problem of a general fall in demand across the board for its products and services and increasing competition from other providers within this reduced market. Lower cost, smaller competitors could significantly undercut Britscope, and during the early years of the new millennium it was reported to be making huge losses. The organisation was seen to be relatively strongly reliant on old-fashioned manual methods of work organisation, offered relatively generous sickness and pension benefits, and was highly unionised compared to some of its market rivals. In addition to days lost to industrial action, it had a major problem with relatively high levels of sickness absence and staff turnover. The major programme of modernisation that was introduced included a substantial package of labour shedding through a combination of natural wastage and voluntary severance. Many thousands of jobs had been lost in the six years running up to our interview programme. Substantial investment in automated technology had taken place in order to improve efficiency and productivity levels. These changes seemed to be having some effects with the organisation as a whole moving into profit by the time we undertook the interviews in 2009/10.

Britscope remains distinctive in its relatively low proportion (15 per cent) of female employees and relatively high proportion of older workers (almost half the workforce at the time of our interviews was in the 40–55 age range). At the time of the research, the proportion of BME workers, at almost 9 per cent, was comparable to that in the working population as a whole, although it varied very considerably by region and by workplaces within a region. In recent years, the organisation had invested a significant degree of effort and resources in addressing problems of bullying and harassment, and in particular, the sexual harassment of female employees. The formal policies that arose from this official concern are considered below, but in general, this concern was sparked by a number of developments. Most important of these was the fact that the organisation was subject to a formal investigation following a high number of reports of sexual harassment by women employees. In addition, the arrival of a new chairperson for the company as a whole, and a major organisational restructuring, provided new impetus to attempts to improve employee relations with a particular focus on 'diversity' issues. The policies discussed below were, in part, agreed as part of a three-year 'action plan' that led to the suspension of the formal investigation into sexual harassment in Britscope.

Britscope's formal approach to trouble at work

In late 2003, Britscope and its sister 'business units' had reviewed existing policies and practices in the light of problems raised by the investigation and organised employee focus groups across the organisation. The review and the focus groups had highlighted a number of findings about existing policies and practices: low levels of awareness of formal policies amongst both management and staff, different policies and practices in different business units across the organisation, a general desire for informal resolution where possible, confusion about what precisely was meant by the terms 'bullying' and 'harassment', and the problems of including bullying/harassment under the generic set of grievance procedures.

This led to the establishment in 2004 of a distinct bullying and harassment policy – reviewed and refined in 2005 – that covered all business units in the organisation. This 21-page document included formal definitions of 'bullying' and 'harassment', along with details of a '12-step' investigation process to be followed in cases of reported bullying or harassment. Further documentation and policy initiatives included an independently operated bullying and harassment 24-hour helpline (to which employees could make anonymous reports of bullying/harassment and seek advice and support); a national programme of 'diversity training' which was compulsory for every member of the workforce and a programme of workplace discussion groups (with specially trained facilitators operating according to a detailed set of guidance notes) aimed at discussing issues relating to 'dignity and respect' in the workplace. Britscope also commissioned an independent survey company to undertake a quantitative survey of women employees to explore their workplace experiences which led to a detailed report on women employees. All this formed part of a wider package of publicity and training materials, which, on the surface at least, suggested a very impressive level of commitment on the part of the organisation, not least in terms of the investment of management time and resources.

As part of the many formal policy statements relating to this push on respect at work, the management, unions and other employee representatives agreed a general statement of principles that was intended to reflect the core 'business values' of the organisation. The moral tone of this statement was echoed in interviews with senior managers who stressed the importance of the business ethos of the organisation and deployed the metaphor of a family to capture what they wanted working relationships in the organisation to be like. The following statement, from a senior HR manager, was a specimen of this kind of discourse:

> We're all people. We all work together. We're here every day ... we need to have a framework against which to behave so that we all know what we're supposed to be doing so that there's a common understanding of, in a very broad sense, what's right and what's wrong ... We have a framework, we have a common theme, and it's about respect and it's about dignity.

The formal policy defined 'harassment' as 'inappropriate and unwanted behaviour that could reasonably be perceived by the recipient, or any other person, as affecting their dignity' and noted that such behaviour could be based on age, creed, disability, race, sex and sexual orientation. 'Bullying' was defined as 'intimidation on a regular and persistent basis or as a one-off which serves to undermine the competence, effectiveness, confidence and integrity of the person on the receiving end'. A number of specific examples of harassment were provided, including such things as suggestive remarks, graffiti, offensive comments or jokes and so on. Part of the motivation for a concrete definition was to clarify for staff that reasonable requests by managers – regarding performance issues, for example – should not necessarily be defined as harassment, and that managers should retain the 'right to manage'.

The 12-step investigation included the exhortation to the complainant to resolve the issue informally if possible with, at each stage, opportunities for informal resolution to the satisfaction of the complainant. There was a clear statement of time limits for response and action on the part of the company (response to formal complaint within one working day; if the case proceeded to a higher level of formality, the complaint to be interviewed within three working days). Key management personnel were given responsibility for different levels of investigation in the formal process. For example, regional 'case managers' were to lead the initial investigation once the case was formally processed and, should they be unable to resolve the case, it would be referred to an 'investigating manager' if the complainant wished to press their case. The latter steps set out the process and timescales for interviewing the complainant, alleged perpetrator and witnesses; the basis on which the decision should be made about whether the complaint should be substantiated ('reasonable belief'); and finally, the communication of the outcome to all involved parties. Various 'remedies' were to be deployed in the case of substantiated complaints, ranging from informal mediation/conciliation (such as informal apology and 'air clearing' meetings), formal written apology, redeployment to different section or workplaces, and formal disciplinary action up to and including dismissal for gross misconduct. In the case of formal disciplinary action, the case would be handed to another manager to deal with the conduct code case.

The central HR department of Britscope coordinated and monitored the operation of this formal policy, recording the nature and outcome of cases reported via the formal process. Formal complaints of bullying and harassment in the organisation had fallen in recent years, from an annual total of over 1,000 in 2004 when the new policy was introduced to something like two-thirds of this level four years later. The proportion of complaints that were substantiated grew over this period, from 60 per cent in 2006/7 to 77 per cent in 2007/8. These trends were interpreted by management as some indication of the success of encouraging the informal resolution of relatively minor incidents at an early stage and the concentration of the formal system on the more serious complaints.

However, falling numbers of complaints might signal a lack of awareness of, and confidence in the organisation's formal procedures, rather than a reduction of problem behaviour. One objective of our employee interviews was to assess levels of awareness of and confidence in these formal procedures.

In practice, it was organisational policies regarding sickness absence, rather than bullying and harassment, which were the focus of many of our employee interviews. Following consultation with the unions, the company had implemented a disciplinary system for sickness absences (self-certified or certified by a doctor) deemed too frequent or lengthy by the company. Employees whose absences exceeded the allowable levels set by the company were subject to two warnings (Stages 1 and 2) and then dismissal (Stage 3). This needs to be borne in mind in the discussion that follows.

Ill-treatment

Figure 2 on p. 33 confirms the overlap between the constituent factors of ill-treatment – unreasonable treatment, incivility and disrespect, and violence – in the BWBS. Analysis of interviews with Britscope employees suggested that the most widespread type of ill-treatment in Britscope would come under the general category of unreasonable treatment, although there were also a striking number of reports of behaviour that constituted incivility and disrespect. Reports of violence were rare, although this was by no means unheard of in the organisation. There was little difference in the ill-treatment experienced directly by the interviewees and the ill-treatment of other employees that they witnessed.

Unreasonable treatment

The most frequently reported forms of ill-treatment experienced by our sample of employees concerned the perceived failure of employers to follow proper procedures, employers ignoring staff views and opinions, and being treated unfairly by the organisation. Less frequently reported, but still of interest, were employee reports of being given unreasonable workloads and a perceived lack of communication from the organisation.

The interviews suggested that disputes over sickness and injury were a major source of tension between management and staff, and it was complaints of this sort that constituted almost all the reports of employers failing to follow proper procedures. Other disputes surrounding procedures concerned attempts to change shift patterns, requests for annual leave (or other forms of special leave relating, for example, to family caring duties), and requests for reasonable adjustments relating to disability or illness. We noted above the perception of the high sickness rates within the organisation and the stated determination of management to address what it saw as a culture of absenteeism among some staff. Our interviews reported some very heavy-handed approaches to illness or injury to employees. For example, during one shift some months prior to the research, a worker suffered crushed fingers on one hand (resulting in considerable bleeding, swelling, bruising and pain). Although employed on manual work requiring both hands, her manager ordered her to continue working with one hand only:

> So I struggled for three, four hours and ... another first aider ... said well I should have gone to the hospital, which I should have done anyway. And then after work I went to the hospital, and they had to drain the blood because there was a lot of damage to the finger.

When this employee subsequently developed a back problem and had to take time off work, she was repeatedly ordered to return to work by her shift manager who refused to recognise the (diagnosed) back problem and continually accused her of taking time off on grounds of her injured finger. During her eight-week period of sick leave, she experienced a number of contacts from managers, including telephone calls and letters, which requested her to make herself available for an interview to help her return to work. This was experienced by the employee not as help but 'more like harassment'.

There seemed to be a considerable degree of discretion open to local managers about the implementation of the sickness policy, in particular, regarding the circumstances when an employee should be placed on a formal 'stage' of the policy. As one employee (who had been placed on a Stage 2) told us, she was informed by a union representative that the manager who had taken this decision was known for not being 'lenient' in his application of the company sickness procedure. Local managers' implementation of the company sickness procedures was also a particular feature of the interviews with employees covered under the Disability Discrimination Act (DDA). Their accounts underlined the arbitrary nature of managers' interpretations of the rules, particularly regarding what constituted 'justifiable' absenteeism. Although still recorded, absences which were considered to be related to a disability recognised under the legislation could be excluded from the count of absences triggering staged warnings if the manager concerned thought this justifiable. In fact, interviewee transcripts provide evidence of managers placing employees covered by the DDA on the disciplinary system, resulting in the disciplined employee experiencing anxiety and a sense of victimisation. For example, one employee was placed on the disciplinary stages after several illnesses resulting from a damaged immune system, following radiotherapy for cancer. She remarked,

> They issue them, they just issue them and I just think it is *totally* wrong. You live in fear; you're frightened to be ill ... [The managers] are most definitely under pressure to issue the warnings. I'm quite friendly with some of the managers and they tell me about it.

Rather than applying objective criteria as to what constitutes justified disability-related absenteeism, it would seem that their own subjective viewpoint was guiding managers' assessments. Several interviewees suggested that local managers often lacked the skills necessary for the job, typically because many had no prior managerial experience. Another employee observed,

> In the past I've had incidences when I've been in a stage interview and issued with a stage [disciplinary warning] for things that come under DDA. The company's own DDA helpline gave me advice, but the managers [saw] fit to overrule this.

A further example of problems with the management of DDA issues occurred with regard to one employee who had a history of serious breathing problems relating to asthma aggravated by dusty working conditions or being in the vicinity of cigarette smoke. She reported this to management 'on numerous occasions' and requested that the working area be cleaned more frequently and thoroughly. The response from management was that there was no significant dust problem in the building, and therefore no need to clean more frequently. Furthermore, the employee was told by her manager that asthma was not a recognised condition under the DDA, even though the opposite was later confirmed by the organisation's own occupational health department.

Another relatively common type of unreasonable treatment reported by staff concerned excessive monitoring or surveillance of particular employees. A number of employees felt that they were singled out by managers, for example, querying them about the time taken for a toilet break or accusing them of not working quickly enough. This was perceived as particularly upsetting when the employees concerned felt that other workers who were not pulling their weight remained unchallenged by managers. As one employee told us,

> To say, 'well why aren't you working harder', when there's people, two, three or four, just chattering through the shift and not doing a lot of work at all and they are never questioned. Where is the, you know, fairness in that?

Sometimes this inconsistency was perceived as being influenced by racial bias. This particular employee (who was white) felt that line management did not intervene where Asian workers were chatting or away from their workstation for a while.

Incivility and disrespect

One of the striking themes that emerged within this category of behaviour concerned quite extensive accounts of perceived sexual harassment and discrimination, ranging from inappropriate sexualised 'jokes' directed at female employees to more serious forms such as unwanted touching. Seven of the interviews (two white and five BME) reported examples of such behaviour which they felt were clearly discriminatory. The perpetrators were male colleagues or managers, and often the victims reported that they were in a minority of women in their workplaces. Examples of comments that exuded casual sexism included the following:

> I got in the lift, they were like 'oh, you're not so glamorous now are you?' ... I never used to wear make-up or anything but it was that sort of comment – they hated women being there.

> He started on me outside the manager's office about something, and that was when it was harassment because he was going on about females, time of the month, that kind of thing, and I thought 'okay, I've had enough now.'

The behaviour some interviewees experienced was more overtly sexual, in the form of sexual comments and suggestions, and sometimes rumours being spread around about them. The following example was typical:

> He used to say to me 'oh, them thighs' and he used to always rub his hands and that ... he once said to me 'oh, whip out your tits ... oh let me bite that bum of yours, let me squeeze it, I really want to smack it hard'.

Whilst these comments came from one male colleague in particular, this employee reported that other male managers followed suit, making comments about her breasts and on one occasion touching her inappropriately whilst she was working.

Other forms of inappropriate behaviour included sexual gossip and rumours, such as the following:

> And later on, one of the girls came to me and said ... the manager is going around showing people that I've sent him a text message that I'm desperate for him, I want him to sleep with me ... I want sex with him ... It was a nasty text message.

One interviewee had to take sick leave to undergo surgery and post-operational convalescence. During her absence, her manager decided to pension her off against her wishes. While convalescing, she learned from her sister, also working for the same employer, that the manager had a meeting with her sister to discuss the details of her illness. Not only did the interviewee rightly consider this a breach of her privacy, but also she discovered later that the manager had made a sexist comment about her illness. She explained,

> I had to have an emergency operation because they found this cyst growing, and he said, 'oh well, if she was not having so much *jiggy jiggy*' – that is slang for sex – 'then, she wouldn't need an operation like that'.

Another set of issues relating to disrespect and denigration related to tensions between different ethnic groups. A (bare) majority of interviewees reported ethnic tensions and conflicts in the workplace. The majority of these reports came from BME interviewees, although four white interviewees also reported ethnic tensions. One black former union representative painted a stark picture of the ethnic tensions between the various groups in her workplace:

> [White East European workers] get resentments from the Asians, because Asians don't like them because they see them as immigrants but they are going to be better off than the blacks and the Asians because they are white. So it's a lot of, I can't explain it, put it this way, I used to have a chip on my shoulder before I became a union rep, now I've become a union rep I'm like, oh the world has gone mad because everybody has got a problem with somebody and really comes down to culture, tribalism, we've got tribalism in [Britscope]. 'I'm Asian, you're white, I'm black' – that is what we have got.

The seven BME interviewees who did report such tensions came from a range of backgrounds, including employees of Indian, Afro-Caribbean and African origin. The Indian interviewees cited poor workplace relations between themselves and white British workers. The majority of the black interviewees cited poor relationships between black workers (regardless of origin) and British South Asians, particularly, British Pakistanis. Where workplace conflicts existed between black and South Asian workers, the number of white workers employed was few with the exception of some East European contract workers. In these contexts, mainly in the South-East, the majority of the local management was South Asian, typically, British Pakistani. It is important to note, therefore, that the ethnic dynamics of inter-group animosities within Britscope were complex and multi-directional. In many cases, it seemed that, rather than reflecting generalised animosity between different ethnic communities, underlying workplace tensions (job insecurity or rapid workplace transformation, for example) played themselves out in terms of competition between different groups in particular workplaces. In particular, there appeared to be strong perceptions amongst some employees that one particular ethnic group acts as the gatekeeper to the accessing of workplace privileges and benefits.

Despite these tensions, only a few interviewees reported experiencing disrespectful language or comments relating to ethnicity. However, those that did report hearing such language reported some quite extreme cases. Both black and white employees cited as a focal point of workplace friction South Asian co-workers (particularly, British Pakistanis) conversing with each other in their first language. Non-South Asian employees feared, whether correctly or not, that Pakistani workers conversed in Urdu in order to speak derogatively about co-workers without their knowledge. An extreme example reported by a black respondent (a husband of an interviewee, working in the same workplace) highlighted these fears. He was shocked to discover that the nickname given to him by male Pakistani co-workers – which he had assumed was a harmless nickname – was in fact the Urdu equivalent of the word 'nigger'.

As noted previously, some white interviewees alleged that local management facilitated inter-group animosity by ignoring misdemeanours by BME workers, for fear of being accused of racism. The following quote summed up this viewpoint:

> They can do what they like, they can come and go as they like, [and] they don't get pulled. If they get pulled it's racial – you are pulling them because they are Asian. 'I am going to have you in the office, (and) tell the management; I'll have you fired.' That's how it goes, [so] management leaves them alone.

One employee who made a formal grievance against her manager reported that the escalation of her complaint resulted in her husband – who was also a co-worker – becoming the target of strong verbal, racial abuse in the workplace from white workers whose sympathies lay with the nightshift manager against whom the complaint had been lodged.

Aside from disrespect and denigration relating to sex and ethnicity, the interviews also provided examples of more generalised behaviour of this kind, usually delivered by immediate line managers. The majority of these reports came from white employees and referred to such things as 'snide comments', sarcasm and being spoken to, and looked at, 'as if I was a piece of dirt on the bottom of their foot'. There was no clear indication of what lay behind this kind of behaviour beyond poor personal relationships with particular managers. A particular subset of disrespectful behaviour involved supervisors losing their temper and shouting at employees. Eight of the interviewees reported experience of such behaviour, which was most usually perpetrated by managers and usually revolved around work-related disputes. The behaviours reported included shouting and swearing, and sometimes physical intimidation as well. The following example was particularly striking:

> He [the manager] starts following me to the toilet, he would have a go at me on the floor, like screaming at me on the floor … he came screaming at me, and I could feel his saliva spraying into my face.

A substantial proportion of the interviewees reported experiencing intimidating behaviour from people at work. In general, the more serious forms of threats and intimidation involved co-workers. Some notable examples revolved around workers who had not supported the union in the recent industrial actions. One interviewee reported feeling intimidated by a union representative when she did not participate in the most recent strike: 'You get heckled anyway, but if you are in the union and you don't go on strike, you get heckled even more … I had someone follow me around one day, that was while I was in the union.' Other examples of threats and intimidation were connected to particular workplace disputes. The employee mentioned earlier, who suffered from asthma, heard indirectly about a vague threat against her relating to her reporting the presence of cigarette smoke in the ladies' toilets, which had resulted in a colleague being spoken to by a manager (who identified to her the source of the complaint): 'I had heard through a third party that she ... had told me to watch my back, and I felt intimidated.'

Violence and injury

Three interviewees reported experiencing actual physical violence or injury in the workplace as a result of the behaviour of male co-workers. One reported that she fell into a machine after a white male co-worker rubbed his groin up against her – apparently as a joke – resulting in her hospitalisation and prolonged absence from work. Another interviewee reported an attack by a co-worker who jostled her in a workplace argument and pushed her to the ground. A third interviewee reported that her shoulder had been dislocated as an accidental result of some workplace high jinks. Reports of violence to others (witnessed or heard about) were more common in the interviews than direct accounts. For example, a local branch manager reported to us that workplace grievances occasionally 'spill over' into physical violence outside the immediate work area. Two male co-workers who had become involved in a dispute at work had recently arranged to meet for a fight in the car park. The case was still being considered by the company, but the assault was relatively serious: 'He beat the other bloke up in a nutshell. He battered him' (local branch manager). Two other interviewees claimed that they had heard about violent incidents in their workplaces, but they had not directly witnessed them.

Factors influencing ill-treatment

There was clearly a wide pattern of ill-treatment experienced by employees in Britscope workplaces, which were likely to be the product of a range of factors. We shall discuss the most important explanatory factors discussed by interviewees.

Poor management

As noted above, the bulk of the negative treatment discussed in the interviews could be broadly categorised as unreasonable treatment, with the perpetrators mainly being managers or supervisors. There were numerous complaints of unprofessional, under-confident, poorly informed management that resulted in managers ill-treating employees. In cases where bad behaviour was between co-workers, managers were criticised for being either too afraid or unconcerned to intervene. There was a perception that local line managers did not have the skills required to do the job. The majority of the interview discussions of the individual characteristics of management perpetrators therefore focused on incompetence of various kinds, rather than personal maliciousness. Indeed, a number of interviewees expressed some sympathy for managers because of the pressures that they understood them to be under from their superiors. For example, there was a clear perception that the tough enforcement of the company sickness policies was a result of edicts from the most senior management in the company. Some accounts emphasised perceptions of the pathological personalities of the perpetrators, which highlighted deviousness, a lust for power, rudeness and aggression, amongst various other unsavoury personal characteristics, but these were in the minority.

Discrimination

Many of the interviewees reported that they felt the ill-treatment they experienced amounted to discrimination. The discussion so far included a number of incidences of quite serious sexual harassment, and, despite the considerable efforts devoted by the organisation towards addressing this problem, it seemed that there was, in some workplaces at least, an entrenched culture of sexist behaviour. A number of the examples reported to us appeared to be unlawful, including clear examples of sexual harassment and, in one or two cases, sexual assault. A number of interviewees discussed the sexualised nature of workplace relations with reference to the historical dominance of older males in most workplaces, with women (especially ethnic minority women) considerably outnumbered. A union representative accepted that the employment of women, and growing proportions of ethnic minority workers, had challenged the previous dominance of older white men in the organisation, and was experienced as threatening by some more established staff.

In terms of ethnic tensions, our analysis suggested that inter-group animosity often revolved around disputes about workplace favouritism and the perception of unequal treatment. This favouritism manifested either as racial discrimination, actual racist behaviours or favouritism to co-ethnics from particular managers. One white employee reporting inter-group conflict alleged that the white management ignored or downgraded the workplace misdemeanours of young 'Asian' workers for fear of the offending workers branding them racists. Another white worker at a different site alleged quite the opposite, asserting that the disciplining of young 'Asian' workers by the management led to inter-group conflict. It is important to note at this point that these claims of favouritism are wholly reliant on interviewees' personal accounts, and we cannot verify the claims. Nonetheless, the high level of reports of inter-group animosity by interviewees does point to significant levels of workplace conflict and resentment within the organisation.

Workplace reform and modernisation

It is impossible to understand the sometimes fraught workplace relationships discussed here without reference to the broader challenges faced by the organisation. The already difficult historical climate of industrial relations was exacerbated further by major workplace changes, including performance pressures, job losses, mechanisation and work restructuring. Past disputes had left a bitter legacy of mistrust between workforce and management, but also simmering resentment between workers who supported the strikes and those who did not. The increased pressure to reduce costs and improve productivity had led to an experience of work intensification, which almost certainly fed into the wider climate of social relations in the workplace. As one employee told us,

> It was a much more sociable time when I first started. You had time to chat to people; there was a social club which now there isn't because nobody wants to do it. But now, you go in at quarter to eight, and you hit the door running and you have got to keep going for most of the time because you have got to get the work done and there is no time for hello, what did you see on TV last night or anything like that anymore.

Linked to this process of work intensification in the organisation is increasing job insecurity. Interviewees covered by the DDA were particularly worried about employment insecurity, feeling managers would single them out for redundancy, especially as the physical tasks they could perform were limited. Even long-serving employees on full-contracts reported that they felt insecure, a feeling justified by the significant programme of job cuts referred to earlier. This insecurity appeared to have had a knock-on effect on the official reporting of negative workplace behaviours via the formal bullying and harassment procedures, especially against managers, as will be discussed further below.

The characteristics of our interviewees

Although, in a few cases, the interviewees reported that they felt some responsibility for what happened to them, the clearest theme of the interviews was their self-perception as strong personalities. Most of the employees interviewed made reference to themselves in such terms as 'fighter', 'strong' and so on, and many of them prided themselves on being able to speak out and stand up for themselves, and presented their self-image as relatively robust. Some suggested that without such strength of character they would not have survived as long as they had within the organisation. Another striking feature of the interviews concerned the expression of positive commitment to their work, which was somewhat surprising given the nature of some of the workplace experiences that they were reporting. One reported that she was extremely positive about the actual work, but it was the workplace 'atmosphere' that she found difficult. Other employees described themselves as hard working and conscientious, and a number of them reported a strong reluctance to take time off work. It was interesting that several complaints about poor management related to managerial reluctance to tackle fellow workers who were not pulling their weight. The following quotes are indicative of this positive attitude to work:

> I still give my 100% because as I said I am from the old school and we go in and we work.

> All I wanted to do was a good job.

> I'm that sort of person, that will go to work regardless, whereas somebody would say, 'oh I've got the flu I'm staying home' and it might only be a cold. So I've always been used to going to work.

Most interviewees reported that they enjoyed their jobs, and some went so far as to say that they loved the work and felt 'proud' to work for the organisation. Indeed, interviewees recounting the most awful episodes of harassment or discrimination continued to enjoy their jobs. For example, one employee, who reported that she had been bullied by a manager, was asked if she would consider leaving her job or pursuing constructive dismissal. Her answer was unequivocal: 'I wouldn't, no. I love my job, I do. I love the people. No, I think [the perpetrator] would feel that he had won. I don't want him to feel that, because he would only get stronger.' Her comments encapsulate the sentiments expressed by most of the interviewees. They had a strong sense of working-class pride in their work and comradeship. This set of values seemed to act as something of bulwark against negative workplace behaviours, even though co-worker relationships were often strained and confrontational. According to our interviewees, however, this sense of affiliation is increasingly under threat from poor management and the constant rationalisation of the business. Despite continuing to enjoy their jobs, interviewees also commonly expressed the feeling that a golden age of employment security and job benefits had long passed.

Responses to ill-treatment

Complaints procedures

Only three interviewees had not filed a grievance of some kind, whether formal or informal, with the management of the company. Even though two of these three told us they had experienced negative workplace behaviours in some form or other, they had been able to negotiate satisfactory changes in their working environments without recourse to procedural solutions. Four interviewees pursued informal grievances, making an unofficial complaint to the local management, three of which had satisfactory outcomes in the viewpoint of the interviewee. What the three successful informal grievances did have in common was the fact that a third party was able to negotiate the positive outcome. In two of these cases, this third party was a union representative, and, in one case, it was an enlightened manager. What is not known is whether the perpetrators actually reformed their behaviour as a result of the informality of the complaint. With regard to the unsuccessful informal grievance, the BME respondent concerned felt her complaint was merely 'brushed under the carpet'. This is hardly surprising given her complaint was made to the local management about their own discriminatory practices.

Of the 12 interviewees pursuing formal grievances, four respondents considered that their complaint resulted in a positive outcome; however, only two of the positive outcomes were a direct result of the company investigation procedures. The other positive outcomes were actually the result of the complainants leveraging the outcome using supplementary actions of some kind. In the one case, the complainant successfully organised a petition among BME co-workers and, in the other, the complainant threatened to take her case to the Equalities and Human Rights Commission if her case did not get a positive outcome. She subsequently took the company to an employment tribunal. However, the tribunal was cancelled when the company finally acquiesced to her demands. Three other formal grievances were ongoing at the time of the interviews. In one case, the complainant had taken her grievance against a manager's bullying to appeal and, in the second case, the complainant was taking the company to an employment tribunal for racial discrimination. In the third case, the complainant was still awaiting the outcome of the grievance investigation.

The remaining complainants either failed to have their grievances upheld or the company offered a solution that the complainant considered unsatisfactory, such as reconciliation with the perpetrator of the ill-treatment. A number of the interviewees who had submitted formal complaints via the organisation's bullying and harassment procedures reported that they found the process of getting involved in the complaints system stressful in itself, and many complained about the length of time that the investigation took to be completed. Twelve interviewees who had raised a complaint of some form reported that the organisation had not responded satisfactorily, and they suggested that the issue had been swept under the carpet. Three complainants expressed a level of distrust in the formal procedures, arguing that their cases had been undermined by management collusion with the alleged perpetrator or the appointment of a person who was insufficiently independent to investigate the case. For example, one complainant reported that a 'friend' of the perpetrator was appointed as investigating manager.

We outlined above the very significant amount of organisational effort that had gone into developing and promoting formal policies at work to improve awareness and behaviour surrounding diversity issues and, in particular, to address perceived problems of bullying and harassment (of which sexual harassment was a key issue for the organisation). Overall, there was a mixed response about the effects of such policies. Some employees reported that things had improved since the policy drive and acknowledged that Britscope was making a real effort to improve things at the policy level. Less positive was the fact that few of the interviewees reported experience of the workplace discussion groups that had supposedly been introduced across the organisation, and a number of respondents clearly felt that the policies were, at best, window dressing. The following comment was typical of such respondents: 'They put all these leaflets or whatever, these big plaques up and say "stamp out bullying and racism" – load of rubbish.' One union representative that we interviewed accepted that the company had put all employees through its 'diversity training', but he questioned the impact of such approaches, dismissing the training, in particular, as 'sheep dipping'.

Trade union support

In general terms, interviewees were positive about the support they received from their trade union regarding bullying and harassment complaints, though some interviewees had problems with grievance claims when the perpetrator was a union official or a close colleague of a union official. The study found no evidence that union officials in regional offices or HQ were complicit in subverting grievance claims, however. Rather, it would seem that, when the union command became aware of these problems, they disciplined the troublesome representative. In one case, for example, the union removed from post a union representative accused of bullying, even though the management's investigation of the grievance proved inconclusive. This outcome appeared to have been the result of an accumulation of similar complaints against the representative over a number of years.

Despite the history of poor labour relations in Britscope, there was little evidence that the union had politicised the issue of bullying and harassment. Rather, the interviews suggested the union's response to the issue was generally measured. Employees' ideas about what actually constituted bullying and the labelling of negative workplace behaviour had more to do with the company's communication of equality issues to its employees, and pre-existing public discourses about bullying in society, than overt union activism on the issues.

While the union generally seemed supportive of women's grievances, some interviewees felt that, at the grass roots, union representatives often fail to take into consideration women's viewpoints. As mentioned previously, this would seem to be the consequence of the male-dominated gender cliques in many of the company's workplaces. For example, one interviewee, a black, former union representative, reported that she gave up her union work because the local union often failed to understand the difficulty that women had balancing family commitments with the demands of the job. One point of issue was recent industrial action, when she upset local union organisers by supporting black and Asian single mothers who remained at work throughout the strike. As she argued,

> I am not going to tell a single mother to strike, right! Or someone who is divorced from an Asian husband ... The single mothers walked across the picket line. Now, the men – because the union, obviously, it's very male, very white; old angry white men, right! – [claimed I was] telling people to walk across the picket line. [Her co-workers] stuck up for me and they said I did not.

This employee obviously took her union work seriously. Unlike the other union representatives, she attended college in order to learn how to do the work professionally, but the way the male union representatives treated her eventually convinced her to give up her official union work. She told us, 'because I am professional and they are unprofessional, they don't like me. That's all I can put it down to, and I'm a woman, and I am black and mouthy.' Although she had given up her union work, female workers continued to ask her for advice rather than consulting the male union representatives.

Other interviewees provided similar evidence of tense relationships with union representative arising from their working through the strike action. One Asian single mother recounted the treatment she received after the strike finished: 'They gave me dirty looks, they just kept blanking me; it was horrible and there were so many whispers about me. I just ended up in tears.' From the other side of the fence, a regional HR manager had a mixed perception of union representatives' role in grievance processes, sometimes being supportive of management and at other times being perceived as antagonistic:

> I mean, union reps are sort of funny things. Doing an investigation, they can be your best friend or your worst enemy. They can be a complete nightmare and make your life really difficult, or they can be fabulous and really help with the process and help everybody involved in the process. It just depends on what the personalities are, realistically.

Occupational health

The majority of our interviewees reported some contact with occupational health during their experiences of ill-treatment. The majority of these contacts concerned seeking advice about medical conditions relating to the provisions of the DDA. Occupational health professionals sometimes gave advice that contradicted the position of local management, for example, on which conditions or illnesses came under the DDA. One interviewee, who suffered from chronic asthma, reported that, although her line manager rejected the argument that asthma came under the provisions of the DDA, the occupational health department of Britscope had provided clear advice to the contrary. A small number of employees had been examined by occupational health specialists with regard to physical problems, such as back strain or shoulder problems, which restricted their abilities to perform some kinds of manual work such as heavy lifting. Occupational health representatives were able to support employees' requests to be put on light duties due to such health conditions.

The consequences of ill-treatment at work

Representatives of management were clearly concerned about some of the negative impacts of such behaviours on the organisation, including increased staff turnover, sickness absence, lower productivity and the opportunity costs of tying up employees, union and management representatives engaged in formal investigations. From the viewpoint of our individual interviewees, the personal costs of ill-treatment in the workplace were considerable. There was substantial evidence of strong emotional responses on the part of employees to their experiences of ill-treatment, and self-reported levels of mental illness were high among the sample of people interviewed. Several of the interviewees appeared to be visibly upset when discussing their workplace experiences. A number of the respondents had received some form of counselling and/or antidepressant medication directly following ill-treatment at work. Some of the interviewees were still receiving antidepressant medication at the time of interview.

Interviewees reporting a strong emotional or psychological response divided into two broad groups based on the specific causes of the stress. One group of respondents clearly experienced strong emotional responses, or indeed mental illness, as a direct result of the ill-treatment they experienced at work. The second group reported experiencing stress or mental illness due to a toxic combination of workplace situations and factors outside work which were difficult to disentangle.

In the first group, two interviewees experienced mental illness which was, in their view, a direct result of co-worker or manager bullying and harassment. For a third employee the mental illness was the result of exposure to harassment from customers, although the company was not seen as without blame. Not only had they demonstrably failed to uphold a duty of care for their employees, they also seriously contravened health and safety legislation. In this case, the interviewee worked in a public liaison role which often involved dealing with annoyed and frustrated customers who were complaining about the service they had received. These customers were often confrontational and abusive; yet, despite a health and safety report advising the company to protect employees through the use of protective counter screens and barriers, and cautioning them against making employees work alone in such roles increasing their vulnerability to attack, this interviewee continued to work on her own in a relatively unprotected office. After a number of confrontational encounters, she began to suffer from panic attacks. Recounting her experiences, she noted,

> I wondered what the hell they were. I had this shaking. I just went to the doctor, eventually, and she said they were panic attacks. She put me on beta blockers and I stood it for a few more weeks. But, then, that was it: one morning, I had the keys in my hand to open the [office] door and I just broke down. I said, 'I can't go in, I can't do it, I cannot do this on my own anymore' ... It was just a build-up, a build-up for asking for help and not getting it. And not being listened to at all by anybody; it was horrid.

Diagnosed with stress and anxiety, the employee took six weeks' sick leave and on return to work, she took up a different work role. The company continued to make her replacements work solo.

In the second group, six interviewees reported experiences of stress and depression. As noted above, these experiences were concurrent with either a physical disability or a pre-existing mental illness that was exacerbated by workplace ill-treatment. For example, two of the respondents were experiencing depression following the death of a close relative, and this became compounded by ill-treatment in the workplace; one respondent became the victim of serious sexual harassment, and following a dispute over working hours, the other respondent filed a grievance against a manager for harassment.

One employee claimed her stress was work related and the company disputed this, fearing widespread compensation claims. Nevertheless, 26 years of physical labour had taken its toll on this employee's body, and she suffered from osteoarthritis and a hernia. Yet, despite these disabilities and advice from her GP to give up work, she continued to work in a physically demanding manual job. She struggled to keep up with the demands of the job, and the management increasingly criticised her performance. Following her husband's advice, she went on a sick leave for a week. As the company allows self-certification for illness of up to seven days, the employee submitted a sick note, writing that the illness was due to 'stress from the management'. On return to work, the sick note triggered a tirade of abuse from her manager:

> When I went back to work after a week, he was waiting for me. He came out, threw it down. He says, 'how, f***ing hell, f***ing, do that.' He was swearing; he was using the F word and everything. He said, 'you can't put stress on there.' I said, 'you caused my stress, that is what's on the form, that's what I've got to go with.' He blew his top, everyone around me was listening, f'ing and blinding he was ... Everybody around me said, 'well I don't know how you really just stood up to him, and stood your ground, and said what you said without swearing.' Because I don't use the F word; it's not a word I like using. And they said have him for sexual harassment.

This employee filed a grievance against the manager and the company censured him for using abusive language in the workplace, though not for sexual harassment. The manager himself reported that he was suffering from stress and took sick leave, eventually leaving the organisation after being offered voluntary redundancy.

Conclusions

In this chapter, we have learnt much more about what lay behind some of the main findings of the BWBS, but we only have space to pick out a handful of examples here. We now understand the way in which health conditions became the cause of conflicts over workplace norms, leading to both unreasonable treatment and incivility and disrespect. In addition, we have found out how psychological or emotional conditions featured as both causes (where conditions were affected by events beyond the workplace) and effects of ill-treatment. We have also learnt more about the causes of incivility and disrespect between employees. The reports of sexual harassment, and even sexual assault, by co-workers, supervisors and managers confirm our expectation that it was within inter-employee incivility and disrespect that we would be more likely to find repeated, perhaps escalating, ill-treatment. This kind of ill-treatment may have a great deal to do with why the analysis of the troubled minority in the BWBS suggested that women in troubled workplaces were particularly likely to be insulted.

In some cases, incivility and disrespect between employees appeared to have been caused, or at least exacerbated, by the legacy of bitter and repeated industrial disputes. The disputes were part of the wider context of the case study which featured the company's attempts to respond to external pressures. Throughout the chapter, we made mention of the changes which the company was trying to introduce to this end, but the reports of associated ill-treatment, and particularly unreasonable treatment, do not appear to have been the result of conflict over change per se. Rather, change was related to ill-treatment where employees experienced a loss of control and super-intense work. Was conflict the fault of the trade union which was urging its members to hang on to outdated practices, thereby forcing managers to assert their right to manage, and demand higher productivity, which were then interpreted as ill-treatment?

This interpretation sits uneasily with what we heard about the pride employees expressed in their work. Moreover, their complaints about unfairness often centred on managers' failure to act consistently to address problems of *under*-performance. Some of these complaints were indeed wrapped up in perceptions of ethnic conflict in the workplace, but the employees we talked to were deeply concerned with issues of fairness and respect (as measured by the FARE questions asked in the BWBS). If Britscope could be described as a troubled workplace, the major causes of its problems were not the behaviour of the public to whom the organisation provided face-to-face services. They were, rather, employees' lack of faith in the reasonable behaviour of their employer and, sometimes, their fellow employees.

The employees we talked to were not at all sure that Britscope would not, without good reason, dismiss them, or make them redundant, or demand more work of them than was humanly possible. Nor could they count on fellow employees to treat them fairly and respectfully. Britscope's attempts to deal with these latter problems were well-meaning, but our interviewees did not seem to have much faith in their efficacy. In Chapter 9, we shall return to some of the things Britscope might have done to turn this situation around. For now, it is enough to conclude that the considerable effort that had been put into the policy drive on dignity at work did not appear to have (yet) wrought the changes in day-to-day behaviour which were desired. As for remedies for ill-treatment, the policies designed to deal with ill-treatment by managers seemed particularly ineffective, and there was reason for some scepticism about the complaints procedure. In particular, what counted as success at the conclusion of such a procedure might be debatable, and falling numbers of complaints might have been influenced by employees' perceptions of heightened job insecurity.

6

The Office

This chapter discusses research carried out within an organisation we have called 'Banco Finance'. As with many organisations in the financial sector, Banco had experienced growing market pressures in recent years, with increasing competition and related moves to expand sales and reduce costs. The organisation appeared to have maintained its tradition of relatively harmonious relationships between management and workforce, at least in terms of formal industrial relations. The workforce of Banco had a high level of union membership, which accounted for over 70 per cent of the workforce. Whilst it would not be accurate to describe senior management as complacent, there was a strong perception at this level that the organisation had no major problems with diversity issues or major concerns about negative workplace behaviour in general. Nevertheless, although Banco was not a troubled workplace, our research found that beneath the surface there were problems, in particular relating to performance pressures.

Banco operated throughout the United Kingdom, providing a range of services including current accounts, loans and mortgages, credit cards, savings, investments and insurance. In recent years, as was the case for many of its competitors, the organisation had experienced significant restructuring relating to the incorporation of new business units, with the result that the organisational culture was perceived by several of the employees we interviewed as in a state of flux. As with many other private sector organisations, Banco had experienced job losses in recent years and shed about 5,000 jobs between 2005 and 2009. This was achieved in partnership with union and other staff representatives, mainly via a programme of natural wastage, redeployment and voluntary redundancy. Indeed, rather than industrial action or other measures of management–workforce tensions, these changes had if anything led to some tensions between the union leadership – whose strategy focused on avoiding redundancies, both voluntary and compulsory – and union members who were redeployed into other jobs within the organisation and not, therefore, offered favourable leaving terms.

Organisational change was an important theme in some of the interviews, and is discussed in more detail below. Whilst most of our interviewees expressed positive views of the organisation and a general sense of job satisfaction, many interviews conveyed the impression that the culture of the organisation was becoming harsher as a result of wider economic pressures. In particular, it was felt by some staff whose job involved a sales function that the pressure to make quick sales – sometimes at the expense of developing long-term relationships with customers – was undermining what they remembered as a more ethical and customer-oriented approach that had traditionally been encouraged by the organisation.

The organisation employed staff in a range of functions working primarily in skilled or semi-skilled white-collar occupations. There were 'professional' staff working on specialist tasks associated with banking and finance, and various other staff working in sales, administrative support and management. These employees worked in a variety of settings, including high-street bank branches, large office buildings and telephone call centres, with a field force of financial advisors working mainly from home. Senior managers and union officials reported that there was significant variation in 'workplace cultures' between different functional specialisms and geographical locations. For example, they reported that they were aware of particular concentrations of problems relating to call centres in particular locations and to specific parts of the business, such as the financial advisors field force.

At the time of the research, Banco reported that 6.4 per cent of its total workforce was BME, although clearly this varied substantially according to geographical location. The organisation appeared to employ roughly equal numbers of men and women but was unable to provide reliable records on the percentage of its total staff who had a disability.

Banco's formal approach to trouble at work

As at Britscope, union officials had been involved fully in the development of Banco's formal policies, including the discipline and grievance procedures, the sickness absence procedures, the diversity policy and its formal dignity at work policy. The dignity at work policy had a number of distinctive features: it was relatively short, amounting to only four pages in total, and primarily focused on exhortation and definition, rather than setting out detailed policies and procedures. It set out in general terms the responsibilities of colleagues and managers in promoting dignity and respect at work, and stated that bullying and harassment would not be tolerated. 'Bullying' was defined as a particular kind of harassment, one not undertaken on grounds of membership of a particular group. It was 'offensive, intimidating, malicious or insulting behaviour' that 'may be an abuse or misuse of power or authority through means that undermine or humiliate an individual or group of individuals'. 'Harassment' was often associated with sex or race and defined as 'unwanted and unreasonable conduct that affects the dignity of men and women in the workplace or any other work-related environment or situation'.

The policy stated that bullying and harassment should not be confused with legitimate criticism of work performance or behaviour at work. It included a legal definition of direct and indirect discrimination as well as 'victimisation' (ill-treatment at work as a result of making a complaint about bullying or harassment). The procedures to be followed to deal with ill-treatment under the dignity at work policy were summarised in one paragraph which suggested that the employee should first attempt to deal with the situation himself or herself, either via an informal discussion with the alleged perpetrator or via a union representative or line manager. In cases where the employee's line manager was the person about whom they wished to complain, a telephone contact number for an HR advice point was provided along with a number for the organisation's independent counselling service.

Ill-treatment

Unlike the other case study organisations, we undertook an employee survey at Banco before undertaking qualitative interviews with staff. This was a method of recruiting participants for the interview stage, although it also allowed us to collect a wider range of contextual data relating to ill-treatment across the organisation. The response rate to the survey was low, and response bias was almost certainly an issue in inflating reported incidence rates for various forms of ill-treatment, but the data were useful in enabling us to ensure that our interview sample included an appropriate range of respondents. During 2008–9, we interviewed 10 white non-disabled employees, six BME non-disabled employees and four white disabled employees. The sample included six women and 14 men from age groups varying between late teens and late fifties. The interview sample included employees from different levels in the organisation and from various areas of the business. We also undertook a number of 'key informant' interviews with senior managers in HR, union officials and a call-centre line manager.

Many of our interviewees gave us detailed accounts in order to impress on us that Banco was a good place to work. Several praised the positive flexible working arrangements at Banco that had helped people with young children. One employee explained how this flexibility had helped him while he was struggling with major mental health difficulties following a divorce. It was also the work itself that they prized, particularly the opportunity that Banco gave them to work in a team. There were, however, accounts of ill-treatment in the interviews and, as in Chapter 5, most ill-treatment recalled in the interviews was unreasonable treatment, usually from managers. Fewer employees discussed incivility and disrespect, although there were some interesting variations here relating to ethnicity and religion. Finally, there were no direct reports of violence and intimidation. However, there were some second-hand reports of such forms of behaviour.

Unreasonable treatment

At Banco complaints of unreasonable treatment often appeared to be related to managers' attempts at performance management. For example, the interview data revealed poor communication from line managers and the organisation in general. The most frequently mentioned types of ill-treatment were being ignored in matters relating to work, pressures to undertake work below the employee's level of competence, withholding important work-related information, impossible workloads or unmanageable deadlines, persistent criticism of employees' work performance, management failing to follow proper procedures, and being treated unfairly compared to others.

As in the BWBS, the most frequently discussed theme in the interview data related to perceptions of being given unmanageable workloads or impossible deadlines. Some interviewees talked about mounting workloads with very tight deadlines imposed by financial regulatory authorities, but unmanageable workloads were a particular feature of the interviews with financial advisors and staff working in call centres, and almost all of these related to pressures to improve sales performance. There was no apparent variation between the accounts of men and women or between white and BME staff – all were feeling the pressure to increase sales and many were uncomfortable with this. Customer service advisors working in call centres referred to the major pressure to make sales and improve efficiency, for example, by reducing the average time spent on a call. In their view, this resulted, at best, in a reduced emphasis on customer service and, at worst, the promotion of a purely instrumental view of customer interactions. Several staff used the term 'wham bam and thank you ma'am' to refer to this approach towards customer relationships. One of these staff members felt that he had been persistently criticised unfairly about his work by a manager who felt that he was taking too long with customer calls and not focusing on making 'quick sales'. This member of staff referred to what he called a 'Thatcherite' ethos emerging in the company, one which he felt contrasted starkly with his previous experience of the organisational culture. A general advisor working in a retail bank branch complained about branch managers being brought in from other industries, with no experience or knowledge about the banking sector, but simply employed because of their background as sales managers:

> And the main complaint would be about the new manager … it's been over six months. He won't even tell us to do like our procedures and stuff like. We have online training that we have to do every month for specific things and it's like there, brushed under the carpet. Yeah, have you got sales today? Have you done this, have you done that? Have you got this, have you got that? It's always sales, sales, sales. What about the procedure side of it?

Financial advisors were also prominent in the complaints about workload pressures. The ways in which managers approached performance in this part of the business is dealt with below under the more serious forms of ill-treatment. Irrespective of the manner in which these issues were managed, however, the existence of the performance pressures in themselves were experienced as very problematic for this group of employees. For example, one told us, 'there's the pressure of "you must do 10 appointments" – I'm not saying it's not possible to do 10 appointments … but I'm finding that it's not as easy as I thought it would be because a lot of these people I don't know, I'm calling cold.' Another employee reported that the pressure to perform was related to the 'service level agreements' that were put in place with the company: 'That's how it manifests itself you see. They say, "well you haven't met your SLA, and we say "well we've not met our SLA because we haven't got time to do it".' Another employee reported, 'it piles up, and they say, "what are you gonna do about it?" … they say "well you can come in on the weekend", but I don't want to come in on the weekend, I've got family.'

The feeling of being ignored or by passed was a relatively common complaint amongst the employees we interviewed. Again, many of these matters related to problems with heavy workloads or short staffing, when employees who had raised these issues felt that their views had not been taken account of. These complaints also concerned the failure of managers to respond with concerns about sickness policy and about racial abuse from customers reported by a BME call-centre employee (who was told he should not end such calls). Perceptions of unfair treatment involved a range of specific issues, including perceptions of favouritism amongst managers making decisions about promotion decisions, allowing employees special leave and reprimanding an employee for taking a personal telephone call during working time (when such behaviour, according to this employee at least, had been overlooked in the case of other colleagues).

One respondent, who worked in a relatively senior management position, had an ongoing problem with one manager who he felt constantly criticised his work performance unfairly. In this example, as in some others, disrespectful and uncivil personal behaviour overlapped with unreasonable treatment. This employee had experienced problems in his personal life, and these also became entangled in the work problems. As he explained, the manager who he felt unfairly criticised him went to see

> my executive director … making complaints and insinuations about my behaviour, my work, saying that I wasn't fit to be in work because of what I was going through … in my divorce.

One employee working in retail banking also felt unfairly criticised over her work, telling us that 'I really, really do get picked on sometimes.' This concern dovetailed with a wider concern about lack of communication and training, in that she was required to make decisions, for example, about granting overdrafts, but had received little or no guidance from the company.

Incivility and disrespect

Not only were complaints of incivility and disrespect few and far between, but complaints of any ill-treatment perpetrated by co-workers were rare, with most interviewees emphasising the good working relationships that existed between colleagues in their workplace. Compared with the frequency with which unreasonable treatment was raised in the interviews, relatively few employees raised examples of being subject to gossip or rumours, being treated insensitively, being excluded from a social group, feeling isolated, being shouted at or being the subject of teasing or mocking.

This is not to say, however, that such behaviours were completely absent in our interview accounts, and those examples that were provided concerned two groups of employees in particular. First, those employees from a BME background raised some interesting issues about respect and civility, which related more to their religious beliefs rather than their ethnicity per se. These employees gave us examples of situations in which they were aware of gossip, had felt socially excluded from their colleagues, and (in a very small number of cases) had heard about or experienced disrespectful language relating to their ethnicity or religious belief. Bearing in mind our earlier caveats about sampling bias in the internal survey, it is also worth reporting here that the survey found that BME employees were significantly more likely to report incivility and disrespect. The BME employees that we interviewed all provided examples of this kind of behaviour, for example,

> I did notice a difference [from last job] in that if you spoke to someone in confidence it would stay there, but I have noticed a big difference [in this job] ... you say something to someone whether it is gossip basically, just you have to be careful of who you speak to. (Customer advisor, call centre)

The only example of personal experience of explicitly racist language was provided by a call-centre customer services adviser, already referred to, who explained that he occasionally had to deal with angry customers who used racially offensive language. Another call-centre employee was annoyed that callers occasionally asked to be put through to an 'English person', which he found offensive as he defined himself as British and clearly spoke English fluently. Although never having personally (to their knowledge) experienced racial discrimination from colleagues, two employees had observed or heard of such cases in the organisation. One reported that a female Muslim colleague had told him that her (white) managers had made derogatory remarks about her faith during a difficult work meeting, which had reduced her to tears. Another described the 'bullying' of the only Asian working in a team of white people; although racist language was not used, our interviewee believed the ill-treatment stemmed from the fact that the man was Asian, and that he was better qualified than his colleagues, which led to them feeling threatened by him.

There were a number of cases where the ethnic background – but more particularly the religious beliefs – of BME employees was a factor in ill-treatment and raised notions of cultural insensitivity on the part of white workers and managers. Perhaps the most striking example was the discomfort reported by all Muslim interviewees about the emphasis on drinking alcohol during out-of-hours socialising of their work colleagues (often including managers). This led to a sense of social isolation and exclusion from the main group, and may have contributed to the greater levels of concern expressed in both survey and interview data by BME employees about gossip and rumour. All the BME employees reported that they saw themselves as good friends, as well as colleagues, with their workmates. This made their sense of exclusion more acute in relation to these out-of-work activities. The following excerpt from a product analyst typifies this feeling:

> Sometimes after work we tend to meet up on occasions. In fact, every other week they go to pubs and stuff and because of my religion and beliefs unfortunately I am not able to go there. I still try my best to go, so for instance they are just going for a dinner after work then I'll take part in it because obviously it's okay for me to eat. But because I can't drink alcohol and stuff … when they go to the pub I try to refrain … maybe they are better friends because of that, I don't really know.

Another BME interviewee, a customer service advisor, reported that, although he did not drink because of his religion, he wanted to make an effort to attend post-work functions, even those that happened in the pub. He wanted to try to 'blend in' and be part of the group. However, he said that he had Muslim friends who did not feel so comfortable about this and always avoided social occasions involving alcohol. He noted that, on occasion, what amounted to informal 'business meetings' occurred in the pub, at which work-related information was shared and plans of action discussed. This respondent explained that a Muslim colleague of his felt left out by this practice: 'So automatically it is excluding him in these meetings; often they had little celebrations then it would be in a pub.' One other Muslim Asian interviewee reported that he had suggested alternative social activities that did not necessarily involve alcohol, such as tenpin bowling or going for a meal. He found that his white colleagues were not enthusiastic because 'they only seem interested in drinking'. The other aspect of religious belief that was mentioned in the interviews was the special provision for prayer requirements during Muslim festivals. Employees were grateful that Banco had provided a prayer room, and felt that this accorded religious beliefs a proper degree of respect from the organisation, but some problems were reported because the prayer room was rather small for its purposes. During Ramadan, for example, Muslim employees were often waiting outside to use the facility. Pressure on the resource was exacerbated by the room's status as a multi-faith prayer room and, indeed, a 'quiet room' for employees who just wanted some time out.

The financial advisors that we interviewed were unusual in that none of them made positive remarks about working for Banco. Indeed, many were strongly critical of the company and expressed significant anxiety about their future within Banco. Unlike the others, this group of employees reported extensive experience of more serious forms of negative workplace behaviours, including verbal aggression, deliberate humiliation and bullying. The perpetrators were in every case regional or district managers who were attempting to improve sales performance, so these behaviours overlap with unreasonable treatment. Reports of highly aggressive behaviour from managers were common, including shouting and swearing, being publicly humiliated in meetings, and receiving offensive and aggressive emails and mobile telephone texts relating to their performance. Several financial advisors referred to the practice of ritual shaming by regional managers intended not only to punish but also to publicly humiliate financial advisors who had not made their sales targets. One example of this was the practice of requiring financial advisors who usually worked from home to report daily to regional head office in order to make phone calls to clients. For example, one employee told us,

> But that's the old-fashioned way of managing … to threaten and pressurise: 'you will do this and you will come to this office at nine o'clock in the morning and you will be in here all day and you will phone customers, and you will do what we tell you because I'm in a position above you and I say so.' … As time goes by and business gets more and more difficult to obtain, the old-fashioned way comes to the fore again, which is a shame because it shouldn't be that way.

Given the location of regional offices, this demand often required long commuting distances during heavy traffic times, resulting in financial advisors spending 'dead' time in the car rather than contacting or visiting clients. Not only was this practice seen as overly harsh and punitive, it was also counterproductive.

A number of financial advisors told us that they felt anxious and beleaguered to the extent of feeling victimised by Banco. Several reported that they felt the company had a deliberate policy of 'managing out' people via aggressive performance management, so that the 'failing' employee would leave voluntarily rather than have to be made redundant. Although one financial advisor reported that this kind of behaviour was associated with one manager in particular, most presented the problem as systemic, arising from what one referred to as a 'bullying culture' in management. Another used the term 'organisational bullying' to describe what he saw as attempts by the company to reduce the number of financial advisors and move more sales business to call centres. He argued that the head office did not encourage clients who telephone call centres to make appointments with financial advisors, and felt that they were often put in a position of being in competition with telephone sales advisors, who could offer products more cheaply over the telephone but were not qualified to give advice. Many expressed great regret at what they saw as a devaluation of the skill of developing personal relationships with clients over their life course (a central part of the financial advisor job), which was being replaced by an emphasis on short-term volume sales. This approach was underpinned by a primarily commission-based pay scheme, in which a very low basic salary was paid along with 'advanced commission' to make up the salary. If financial advisors failed to meet their sales targets, then they could end up 'in debt' to the company. Most reported very dramatic falls in their total earnings over the past few years.

Without exception, the financial advisors saw the aggressive style of management as counterproductive and demotivating, and compared them unfavourably with what they saw as more effective management styles in other companies they had worked for. Several expressed a desire to leave Banco but knew that alternative job opportunities would be few and far between given the current climate in the financial markets. Only one reported that he had considered raising a formal grievance and, in the end had not done so. Even more than was the case amongst other employees, there was a sense of distrust of the formal procedures and that making a complaint would simply exacerbate the problem or attract future trouble.

Violence and injury

The interviews provided very few examples of the most serious forms of negative workplace behaviour. One customer services team manager observed that the young age of many of the employees he dealt with sometimes led to what he termed 'playground'-type behaviour. On one occasion, a dispute between two employees which bordered on the farcical threatened to boil over into physical violence. The dispute concerned a well-known video game, with one employee claiming that her boyfriend had obtained a much higher score than her colleague (also a fan of the game) was able to achieve. When her colleague expressed disbelief at the alleged score obtained by her boyfriend, she became enraged, and the argument escalated to the extent that she physically threatened her colleague. The team manager reported this to us, humorously substituting the word 'classroom' for 'office':

> From there on she was saying, 'you're saying my boyfriend is a liar', and at which point then she was being dragged out of the classroom threatening to get her boyfriend to come in and kick his head in.

There were just two other examples of serious disputes between staff, both involving mid-level managers who experienced very difficult meetings with their own line managers. One of these respondents said that he felt so angry after one confrontation with his manager that he almost used physical violence against him. Following the incident, the interviewee stormed off to his car in the car park in order to fetch something with which to hit the manager. However, he had calmed down by the time he reached the car park. Another interviewee, after a dispute with a manager, reported that he was 'absolutely fuming', but the verbal support and reassurance of colleagues helped to calm his anger. To reiterate, these incidents were isolated examples of behaviours perpetrated between work colleagues at a similar level. The vast majority of behaviours described in the interviews involved work-related disputes involving managers, rather than colleagues or the general public.

The characteristics of troublemakers

It was unreasonable treatment of financial advisors by their managers that suggested that Banco might be, in any way, a troubled workplace. As with our other case studies, interviewees offered a range of opinions about the characteristics of the troublemakers. Managers were sometimes described as impulsive and unpredictable, despicable, spreading falsehoods, covetous, moody, driven and ambitious as well as bumbling and inept. There were several interviewees who felt their managers were incapable of management or at least managing 'properly' as they saw it. Positive opinions were more common outside the Financial Advisor section where the generic workplace tensions of an organisation that was increasingly being driven by performance measures were not quite so extreme. Managers were more likely to be held in high regard if the interviewee was older or the manager being spoken about was very experienced.

In describing some of the troublemakers, interviewees acknowledged that some managers were 'top performers' and that subordinates could learn from them. However, several of our interviewees felt that their own good performances were held up as proof of their manager's sales drives when their manager should have credited the team as a whole. Terms such as 'steal', 'trample over' and 'exploit' were used to describe this striving for higher performance. Interviewees told us how some managers deliberately aimed for higher targets than other managers, as this was the vehicle by which managers could be promoted or rewarded with financial bonuses. Managers who fell into this category were reported to 'scream and shout' and do whatever was needed for them to advance their careers.

In respect of managers who were described as weak or inept, our interviewees mentioned poor people management and poor understanding of processes and procedures, leaving employees to sort out customer disputes or procedural difficulties. This left some employees feeling unsupported or forced to seek support or assistance from co-workers or managers in other parts of the organisation, which they felt was unfair. For many of our interviewees, their troubles were the product of managers who were simply incompetent, lacked financial knowledge of processes and procedures and who were employed purely on the basis of sales performance rather than a proper understanding of the needs of the customer and the organisation.

Perceived poor performance of employees by their managers was an issue interviewees felt was badly handled, even though they accepted that poor performance needed managing. Swearing, shouting, screaming and 'given a kicking' or 'being given a public bollocking' were some of the behaviours heard about. One employee used an analogy of going into the head teacher's office: 'You might as well stuff magazines down your trousers as you knew you were going to get six of the best.' One or two interviewees felt that poor performance rarely involved dismissing people because Banco deployed a range of pressures through tools and performance techniques which meant employees had a fair chance of rectifying problems before they became dismissible. Nonetheless, many felt that the deployment of these performance tools was leveraging undue stress and pressure as managers and the organisation sought ever-increasing performance targets.

Aside from the pressured performance environment at Banco, some managers were reported as simply unpleasant and nasty. Nitpicking, finding fault, power hungry and 'complete bastard' were used to describe some managers' behaviour. Others were portrayed as 'point scoring' in order to demonstrate their power over their subordinates or described as 'clever' or 'manipulative' and able to cover their backs so their deficiencies could not leave them exposed to criticism. As in the BWBS, the troublemakers' attitudes or personality was often cited as the reason with interviewees saying, 'I think that's just the way she is' or even, 'he is not right in the head'.

The characteristics of our interviewees

As we reported earlier, two-thirds of our interviewees were men and most were white with some of these classifying themselves as having a disability or long-term health condition. A smaller number (six) would be classified as from an ethnic minority, but overall they represented a cross section of Banco employees who had a range of lengths of service and ages.

As with our Westshire case study (Chapter 7), many employees we spoke to had worked for Banco for a number of years, leaving them able to reflect on how their work and the organisation had changed. We have already described how the financial sector, and Banco with it, had become more performance and sales driven, and this was a difficult adjustment for some employees. The increasingly pressured sales-driven and marketing-led operations at Banco caused some people to feel picked upon. A feature of several interviews was the conviction of employees that customers should come first, not sales to customers. These employees saw themselves as having to have a strong personality.

When they said, 'I'm a fighter' and 'I am not scared of anyone', they showed their sense of moral indignation at the injustice of the position they found themselves in. Many used analogies of having their backs to the wall or retreating but still fighting, and as one interviewee summed up, 'I have vowed that they are not going to push me out of the door, and I will stay and I will be the last one standing and I will be on the beach with a machine gun.'

This sense of defiance reflected employees' commitment to their principles, and possibly to 'old Banco', rather than the new pressured sales-led operation. Along with knowledge of products and the financial sector generally, excellence in customer service was seen by these employees to be the key measure of their value to the company. Their convictions led some employees to question why they continued to put up with ill-treatment from managers and supervisors. While some staff told us they found it challenging and difficult, others felt that complaining was not an appropriate course of action. Others still felt that the benefits of working for Banco outweighed the negatives, and some weighed up the number of good days against the number of bad ones and tried to take a balanced view of their work lives. Yet, despite this measured view, several of our interviewees described themselves as 'drained' or 'disillusioned', even while describing their love for Banco, or the sense of self-worth achieved from doing what they saw as important tasks in serving customers.

Factors influencing ill-treatment

As with the other case studies, interviewees outlined many different triggers for their workplace troubles, including relationships, illness, disability, understaffing, work pressures, performance issues and pay and reward. Salaries and pay in general were a recurring feature of the interviews. Because pay was often linked to performance, employees might not be guaranteed a regular monthly income. This was particularly common amongst the financial advisors, who were employed on relatively low baseline salaries. This was a substantial issue for many of them, which became much more pronounced if they encountered difficulties with managers. This resulted in some finding they were placed in lower pay bands or were working in teams that were short-staffed. This made making a sale even more critical, resulting in them being unable to manage and maintain a reasonable workload.

Those interviewees who told us they had a disability felt that this was a reason for their workplace troubles. Repetitive strain injury – which affected one sales person's ability to drive lengthy distances – irritable bowel syndrome, asthma and partial sight were all cited as disabilities that were poorly understood by Banco and its managers and triggers for ill-treatment. For some of our interviewees with disabilities, the fact that they worked remotely and away from conventional HR and occupational health teams left them feeling that

Banco had abandoned them and their disability. Other interviewees felt that managers interpreted the DDA differently, so that some applied the minimum adjustments to take account of an employee's disability whereas others were more generous.

Some staff told us about their perceptions of inequality issues. One Asian male explained how he would love to attain the grade of manager, but he had not seen one Asian manager in his time at Banco. Without a role model, and the reduction of manager positions, he was beginning to question what he was working towards. Another Asian female interviewee questioned the appropriateness of having a prayer room doubling up as a 'quiet room' when people required a space to pray for up to five times per day in a building occupied by a few thousand people.

Some of our interviewees mentioned understaffing as well as performance-driven management, and performance issues were a common trigger for ill-treatment. Several saw business as getting more difficult and staffing levels, including management staff, being scaled down leading to a cultural change at Banco. This cultural change was described in terms such as 'kicked', 'booted' and 'pushed' and retained little of the more traditional ways of working. This change is very effectively captured by this account from a white male aged around 40:

> The rumours began to spread that between 16 and 20 managers had come in that morning. Some had not been able to get into the building; some had had their access rights taken away from them to the computer network. Some were physically escorted from the building and told they were no longer in employment. That for Banco, culturally wise, was absolutely unbelievable. The transitional step there, the reverberation, was unbelievable and it was like – what was coming next?

With management layers being removed, and the pressure to perform and drive new business in an increasingly competitive financial services sector, all employees were under pressure. If that pressure manifested itself in the take-home pay of all staff, many of whom were low-paid and on unpredictable salaries, it produced a tense and fragile workplace.

Managers, and management style, were the trigger our interviews cited most often, and this was again closely related to their perception of change in the cultural roots of Banco's operations. Most of the complaints about management referred to target-driven cultures, often mentioning that teams and manager salaries were linked to performance. We were told that managers earning as little as £18,000 per annum were driving their teams as much as those managers who were on six-figure salaries. The ability of managers to de-authorise sales agents meant a significant impact on take-home pay if a sales agent made a minor error, such as forgetting to leave an instruction sheet with a client, for example. Other managers were referred to as bullies, using shouting, fear and intimidation to control their teams. One interviewee talked of bully-boy tactics, which was part of the culture of several manager grades. The culture was referred to as 'you will do as you're told because I am telling you to', and staff who questioned this would have a miserable and unpleasant relationship with their manager.

Some of our interviewees recognised that managers had a very difficult task driving increased value for Banco and its stakeholders. One experienced male interviewee in his late fifties talked with deep reverence for his manager whom he saw as a mentor and friend. This interviewee had many years' experience at Banco and could observe at first-hand how managers were changing around him with less time to spend with their teams and less time to develop management skills of coaching and mentoring. He thought managers were bullied from above, and this is how they thought managers should behave, and they replicated their own ill-treatment. Other interviewees talked about a form of ill-treatment where poor performance was blamed along the chain of command so that those at the bottom were constantly being blamed for generic failures of organisational targets, but because they were lowest in the hierarchy there was no one left to blame.

The managerial blame culture also appeared to have a direct bearing on those employees who worked in teams. Some referred to team-working as 'dog eats dog' with managers encouraging a competitive culture. Other interviewees thought managers treated their teams as colleagues rather than subordinates. It is important to also point out that some teams and work groups deployed a range of social activities in order to cope with the pressure of work but that these caused problems for some members of the groups. For example, some groups were mainly women with male members rarely invited to join in social events. As we have already seen, for some Asian interviewees social events that involved alcohol meant they could not take part, leaving them feeling isolated. They understood how alcohol could be a central part of after-work socialising and were not trying to change this radically. All they wanted was for an occasional social event to be alcohol free so that they could take part and feel some membership of the team.

The processes and consequences of dealing with ill-treatment

We wanted to understand from our interviews how policies and processes had been deployed to help overcome employees' workplace difficulties, along with what support they had found to be most helpful. Although many employees felt that Banco had moved away from its traditional values, no one told us that they felt they had to blow the whistle on how the organisation was conducting its business. Overall, the interviews demonstrated a good level of awareness of the formal Banco policies on dignity at work and the formal grievance procedures, but this did not mean they were willing to use the complaints procedures set out in these policies. Most interviewees reported that – despite their various experiences of negative workplace behaviours – they were extremely reluctant to take any formal action to have grievances redressed. Only a small minority of 20 interviewees reported that they had taken out a formal grievance or considered doing so. There was a general lack of confidence in the fairness of the process, with most interviewees not wanting to 'rock the boat' and some stating explicitly that they were concerned about the future consequences for them personally if they took out a grievance. Some actually expressed concern that such a course of action would lead to them losing their jobs. For example, one product analyst, who felt that that he was repeatedly given less challenging work by his manager (and not valued in other ways), reported that he would not consider making any kind of formal complaint under the Banco policy:

> I didn't make a complaint or anything because I don't really want to lose my job. That's what I'm scared of … And that bad feeling, I don't really want that at work you see. So therefore I resisted from making a complaint.

Another quotation, from a customer service advisor working in a call centre, was typical of this attitude: 'The thing is that you know that if you cause ripples you won't last long within your role. That is definitely known to everyone.'

Other interviewees felt the process of raising grievances was not as confidential as they had hoped. The complainants felt that witnesses who had been cited were either unable to keep matters confidential or that they had close friendships with those who were being complained about. Some interviewees felt the procedure would be very time consuming (sometimes several months), resulting in it being more difficult to contain and keep confidential. Others felt that managers stuck together and were unlikely to act against each other in providing evidence or testimony. Some interviewees felt they were being singled out for taking a grievance and were made to feel as if they were troublemakers even though they were only (in their eyes) standing up for what they felt was right or what they were entitled to. One interviewee felt that the grievance procedure had made her feel like a criminal with her personal computer being subjected to extreme levels of scrutiny and monitoring of her work being taken to an exceptional level. We should say, however, that this was an isolated case amongst the range of interviews conducted.

Although most of the interviewees were union members, only a few had actually taken their problems to the union to get support. A substantial minority were not union members, reporting that they felt the union was not likely to help them and was perceived as 'too close' to the company. A typical quote from this group was the customer service advisor, who said that the union had 'little power' because it was 'in bed with the company'. Very few employees reported that they had considered leaving the company due to negative experiences, although some had moved jobs within Banco to escape from the particular situation they had found themselves in. Several interviewees talked of their preference for informal resolution of problematic situations at work, having drawn on the support of colleagues or other managers. In two of the most serious conflicts with individual managers, the manager in question eventually moved to another section or department which resolved the problem.

Some employees deployed more informal tactics such as 'having a quiet word' with management. A few interviewees felt that disputes and grievances were commonplace but that they took a long time to resolve, often over several months. One disabled staff member with impaired eyesight complained that it had taken four months to obtain the right type of screen that could display large typeface. By contrast, another interviewee felt that younger employees got themselves into hot water with poor absence records and timekeeping difficulties, which exacerbated the grievance system because these employees felt put upon leading to grievance claims.

Some of those interviewees who had taken out grievances, or considered doing so, had been encouraged by their trade union whilst others took it upon themselves. The sources of grievances were many and varied, but it seems that it was a last resort for most employees. Entitlement and unfairness seemed to lie at the heart of many complaints, with interviewees feeling they were being unfairly treated regarding pay, promotion, access to training/personal development or if they were absent because of sickness. We should also report that we were presented with no detailed accounts of any employment tribunal claims or legal actions having been taken against Banco by these employees.

Apart from the grievance procedure, those who had been on longer sickness absences found that their engagement with Banco's occupational health team had been a poor experience, with some citing that it was unstructured, haphazard or piecemeal. By contrast, one interviewee who had been reprimanded for poor performance was very supportive of his personal development plan, which he saw as now helping him attain his targets. One or two other interviewees felt that the processes they had been involved with were unstructured and very informal, leaving them to question why policies existed in the first place. The believed managers lacked the competence to help them work through processes, which led to increased frustration and anger. Other employees also felt frustrated with the outcome of their grievance or complaint because they felt the systems favoured managers. Proving bullying, for example, was extremely difficult, primarily because of the subtleties of manager behaviour which were not often demonstrated in public workspaces. Those interviewees who had engaged with the HR department felt that, whilst HR were good at listening, they were much less effective at reaching acceptable outcomes. Some said they felt HR's 'hands were tied' or that it was impossible for them to arbitrate between employees. These frustrations with HR, management and general organisational processes are summed up succinctly by a white female disabled employee aged around 50 who was trying to find a resolution to her disabled situation:

> It is really beyond line managers. I don't know what HR's responsibilities are, and I don't know what my line manager's responsibilities are, but I do have a feeling that things haven't worked the best that they could have done, and I do think that from an organisational and a human point of view nothing is set up to deal with it.

The consequences of ill-treatment at work

Our interviewees showed a range of physical, psychological and emotional consequences of their workplace troubles. Interviewees reported stress, including clinically recorded stress, which resulted in a number of physical symptoms, including anxiety, depression and chest pains. Some interviewees told us they had been prescribed antidepressants, beta blockers, migraine tablets, steroids and other medicines to help them cope with what they were encountering at work. Ill-treatment resulted in periods of sick leave, some of them prolonged and lasting several months, where in one case, the employee had run up several thousands of pounds worth of debt that she was now struggling to repay. Regular short-term absences of two–three days also seemed to be a common feature with the resulting impact of increased workloads for teams. Some staff reported how their work would mount up whilst they were on sick leave, which resulted in further stress and complications in relationships with customers and senior managers, as one woman in her twenties told us, 'You just think, God, why am I doing this sometimes.'

Employees with a disability recognised that Banco's practice of following up absences with back-to-work interviews was dictated by policy. They were embarrassed at having to provide details of their illnesses or long-term health conditions. Some felt that the process of being interviewed was making an issue of their disability or long-term health condition, which caused unpleasant emotions and feelings including making them feel vulnerable or liable to be selected for redundancy. This seemed to be particularly pertinent for those whose illnesses or disabilities were hidden and not obvious.

Some Banco employees told us how they dreaded going to work on a Monday, and the tension and anxiety of preparing for work meant their weekends were shortened as pressure began to build on a Sunday. Some talked about how their morale was affected, whilst others felt they were on a treadmill they could not get off. Sickness meant sales were not made, post built up leading to further lost business, which in turn resulted in management pressure and reduced earnings. Some talked about earning 25 per cent less than they did three or four years previously, while others had seen their income halve with the economic and competitive pressures of the industry. We were told by a significant number of our interviewees how Banco's core business had changed in recent years.

Some no longer had client contacts and were trying to build these from scratch. Others felt their telephone allowances for cold-calling were paltry, and others owed Banco money because they had been paid at a salary level that was not commensurate with the business they were actually generating.

These reactions to a pressured work environment were particularly acute in some parts of the business, and several of the financial advisors interviewed were actively seeking alternative employment. They felt undervalued and their qualifications were not commensurate with how Banco now saw them. Many were contemplating simply walking away from Banco regardless of the financial implications or their 'love' for the company. By contrast, one or two were trying to take on extra work to impress Banco management or trying to develop new skills that they were paying for themselves by attending local colleges.

Whilst the implications of troubled work are clear to see for our interviewees, there are also very obvious implications for Banco. The loss of productivity during sickness absence and the time taken for back-to-work interviews appeared to be considerable. There was also diminishing goodwill towards the company from employees who appeared to have a genuine love of working for Banco and obvious business consequences from these episodes where customers were not dealt with effectively. Training a sales-based employee to minimum standards was estimated by one interviewee to cost circa £9,000. With increasing levels of labour turnover, and the desire of many employees to leave Banco, the financial implications of ill-treatment were considerable, particularly as the majority of our interviewees had at least a minimum of three years service and some had over 20 years' employment experience with Banco. Many who were contemplating leaving had built a significant customer base, and some spoke of how they would attempt to take their customers with them to competitor organisations.

Conclusions

If we were to sum up those we interviewed at Banco, we would describe them as strong-willed, principled with a sound work ethic. Most liked working for Banco for the flexibility it gave them, and the benefits they received, but many hankered for old Banco and felt the organisation has lost its moral compass. We shall take up this point in shortly, but first it is worth mentioning that Banco also remained the kind of employer young Asians, especially young Asian women, might find attractive because they would imagine it offered a safe and friendly working environment. For the most part, this expectation was borne out. Banco provided a better environment than many workplaces, but that did not mean the Asian employees had the same experience as any others. They told us that they felt excluded from social events and from decision-making and sometimes wondered if their ethnicity might be a barrier to their building a career in the company.

What the Banco employees told us helps us to understand the relationship between ill-treatment and answers to the FARE questions in the BWBS. They described a company that seemed no longer capable of putting people, especially customers, first, and they felt that they were frequently asked to compromise the principles that they had once shared with their employer. It may not have been quite as obvious as the other FARE questions, but the organisation's increasing inability to treat people as individuals was also a theme of the interviewees. We could see this in the way that employees told us they received no recognition for special contributions they made to the success of the company and no recognition, still less support, for the efforts they made to add to their skills. Most importantly, those who felt they had accumulated knowledge and skills once invaluable to their employer now found that these assets were discounted. Indeed, these employees' only value lay in the degree to which they could divest themselves of this knowledge and skills and adapt to alien ways of working. This was a more general theme, of course; Banco appeared to have dismissed many of the old managerial guard and substituted a smaller number of replacements who had little knowledge of, and no commitment to, the Banco way of working.

As in Chapter 5, it was not change per se that employees associated with ill-treatment but change that jeopardised the culture of fairness and respect they had associated with the company. This was not simply a matter of the new managers setting little store by the procedures Banco had put in place, although this cavalier attitude to procedure has caused several financial services companies to fall foul of their regulator and, indeed, the courts. It also extended to the language they used to convey their wishes and the manner in which they treated their subordinates. None of this makes sense, however, without the information our interviewees gave us about their falling incomes and their fears for their jobs. It was their fear for their jobs that led so many to tell us they would be too terrified to complain of ill-treatment, but then job losses, falling incomes and intense working all appeared to be part of the same pattern. It was an assault against which the trade union appeared to be unable to offer Banco workers protection. This is the other side of the coin to the protracted industrial relations disputes over modernisation at Britscope. In the interviewees' eyes, they did not feel they could trust their union to protect their collective interests and redress their individual ill-treatment.

Our judgement is that Banco was not yet the kind of troubled workplace discussed in Chapters 5 and 7, but the way in which Banco's strong reputational capital amongst its own employees was being frittered away suggested that this might only be a matter of time. Were leaders in the organisation unaware of the risk they were running, or did they simply not care? The appalling treatment of financial advisors suggested that, in that part of the business at least, senior management had decided that the loss of good will and reputation was a price worth paying, and it was far better to have employees fear for their jobs or salaries and better still, perhaps, to see them leave the company.

7

Permanent White Water

Located in the health and social care sector, Westshire NHS had 7,000 employees working in a mix of urban and regional settings at the time of the interviews. As with many organisations delivering public services in the United Kingdom, it was beset with constant organisational change, often driven by external political decision-making, budgetary constraints and the widespread adoption of management practices from the private sector. 'Permanent white water' is a term coined by Peter Vaill (1989), an American writer on organisation development, and is often used to describe the turbulence of organisations and society, and it certainly fits the situation we found at Westshire.

Westshire was wholly dependent on government for the funding to deliver its services. It was increasingly dependent on expensive technologies to deliver these services and for the functioning of its administrative and support functions. The working environment ranged from small individual buildings housing less than 10 employees, often located in community settings, through to large purpose-built behemoths housing several thousand employees. Some operational units were effectively running as semi-autonomous operations run by professionals, while others were more conventionally organised with spans of control and managerial hierarchies. The majority of the physical working environment was best described as dated, and it was questionable if it was 'fit-for-purpose', although there was a programme of investment in new purpose-built buildings. The spread and complexity of the organisation meant that some staff never came into contact with some of their colleagues because of the specialised nature of the services offered or because of the geographic dispersal of services. Other staff located in centralised services were required to travel to service those functions in more rural locations.

Occupations at Westshire ranged from well-paid, highly skilled professionals through to low-skilled employees. The workforce was predominantly female, which was typical of other organisations in the sector and which was, in part, a product of the occupations that made up the organisation. Westshire had been forced to go outside its traditional recruitment areas to find the staff it needed to function effectively. Employment relations in the sector could be described as good. There was a long tradition of no-strike agreements amongst the professionals who delivered the services for which Westshire was responsible. These professionals could belong to a trade union if they wished, and many, if not all, would be required to have professional affiliation to their own professional body in order to practise. There was also a standard expectation that continual professional development would be a feature of these professionals' careers as they tried to maintain high levels of competence to stay at the forefront of their professions. The management, administration and support functions were also able to join trade unions if they wished. There was less of an expectation to follow a no-strike tradition for these employees, although employment relations for them were also good. Westshire had been through a significant job evaluation process in the recent past as part of a wider attempt to rebalance grades and salaries and to recognise the skills, knowledge and competencies of all of those working in the sector. The process was also deemed important in helping to attract potential new employees from within the United Kingdom to overcome an increasing reliance on overseas recruitment.

Westshire, like other NHS organisations, appeared to have experienced a protracted struggle between the professionals whose expertise provided the foundation for the organisation's existence and the managers of the organisation who were charged with meeting government policy and stringent targets set by politicians. The tensions of meeting externally imposed targets appeared to have changed the culture of the organisation from one of professionals delivering expert services to a machine-like bureaucracy that counted, measured and evaluated all aspects of performance. This approach had meant a shift in control away from the professionals who decided what was to be done and when to managers who now shuffled resources to ensure government targets were met in return for annual increases in budget of approximately 4 per cent in 2010 across the sector.

The performance-driven environment of Westshire had seen the establishment of a structure that reflected the pressures externally imposed and internally driven. Directors existed for performance improvement, operations and planning and for a range of other services. The organisation was led by a chief executive and supported by a board that was externally chaired. The language of management, such as audit, performance, governance and stakeholders, suffused internal and external communications. At the time of our interviews, Westshire was running with an in-year deficit of many millions of pounds.

Westshire's formal approach to trouble at work

Like many large organisations, Westshire has no shortage of formal procedures and policies relating to employment relations and people management, and in many ways Westshire could be regarded as an employer of good practice. Policies and procedures existed for dignity at work, grievance and disputes, equality and diversity, flexible working, sickness absence and so on. Many, if not all, of the policies and procedures were available via the organisation's intranet for employees to download. There were clear indications in these policies that trade unions and staff associations had been consulted and that the advice and guidance of specialist agencies such as the EHRC and the Acas had been sought.

Like many policies in organisations delivering public services, Westshire's policies appeared to be written as a process of good governance rather than as user-friendly guides for managers and employees. Most policies were made available in formal documents which represented an employer's statement of intent, but they did not offer a procedural toolkit to handle grievances and disputes and often failed to give guidance on the prevention of trouble at work. The 22 pages of Westshire's dignity at work policy contained many of the classic elements one might expect to see in a policy of this kind. Definitions of dignity, bullying and harassment were presented in order to help employees reach a judgement about whether they had been ill-treated. The definitions differed quite markedly from an almost identical policy on Workplace Respect written by the government and the trade unions for the NHS. While there was no contradiction between the policies, the language, definitions and processes were different. As a result, employees of Westshire could legitimately seek out either their organisation's policy on Dignity at Work or the very same policy meant to describe ill-treatment in the sector as a whole, and find completely different definitions as to what dignity at work or bullying or harassment meant. This caused difficulties not only for individual employees experiencing trouble at work but also for managers. If a manager followed the official policy of the organisation, he or she might be faced with a diligent lawyer or trade union representative who could exploit these policy differences.

A generally good feature of Westshire's dignity at work policy was their self-analysis series of short questions that allowed employees to evaluate for themselves if they were, or had, experiencing problems such as bullying and harassment. The approach was sound but made some far-fetched assumptions about the information available to employees who were trying to answer the questions. For example, the criteria meant to enable an employee to reach a judgement on whether his or her dignity had been infringed included, 'was the behaviour intended to belittle or harm you or strengthen the other person's power base?' Most employees who are ill-treated have no idea what a troublemaker intends by their actions. Another problem exemplified by Westshire's policies and procedures was the adoption of legal and quasi-legal terminology. While policies and procedures have to take into account the legal implications and mitigation of risk to the organisation, the language in which they are written could inhibit employees who might be afraid of the consequences of their actions, thus defeating the drive for dignity at work that the organisation seeks.

Interviewee characteristics

Most of the men and women we spoke to would be regarded as professionals with specialised skills, knowledge and experiences of working in the health and social care sector, and some were extremely well qualified. The majority of the people we spoke to were women. Many were career-long employees and most had between 20 and 40 years of service with very few young, newly qualified staff featuring amongst our interviewees.

The fact that many of the people we spoke to had served a number of years in the NHS allowed them to take a longer view on how work and the nature of the sector had changed. One man we spoke to described it as a 'privilege' to have worked for clients and how working 'almost all the hours that God sends' was a historical part of ensuring clients were the priority. As in the previous chapter, we needed to understand this sense of commitment to the sector and its clients that interviewees had if we were to properly grasp the nature of their current troubles. Some talked about how things 'used to be' or how their relationships with those who were now ill-treating them used to be good. As one woman told us, 'She was fantastic, we got on really well but things changed.' Others talked about how they loved their jobs, describing them as 'my dream job', and some talked about being desperate to keep their role because they 'loved it' and could not bear to part company with their friends and colleagues. There was a sense of frustration about what was happening to some interviewees with statements such as 'I liked my work, why couldn't I be left to do that', and the phrase 'I like my job' or 'I like my work' reflected the fact that the work that people did was not the cause of their problems.

Indeed, many Westshire employees told us they felt they were good at what they did, describing themselves as committed, enthusiastic and loyal. Some felt they were doing the best work they had ever done and, even though many were stressed and busy and being pushed to go the 'extra mile', they were happy to serve the needs of their clients and organisation. Their commitment, loyalty and enthusiasm seemed to stem from a sense of moral purpose, which was sufficient to make an employee proud to tell us he or she 'worked my butt off' or to describe themselves as a 'solution finder' in dealing with their workloads. Some described their working experiences as a 'pleasure' or that their 'conscience' could not allow them to fail the needs of their clients. It was clear that many men and women felt themselves to be principled professionals who would go beyond the call of duty to get the job done. Yet, many were honest enough to admit that they themselves had occasionally treated people badly in Westshire. Some described how they had lost their tempers or shouted or used bad language because they were so annoyed about what was happening around them.

A number of those we interviewed might be described as having a strong personality, describing themselves as 'assertive'. Several said they felt the reason they found themselves where they did was because they would readily voice their opinion: as one woman stated, she had a strong sense of 'what's right and what's wrong'. Many felt that this assertiveness or willingness to give their opinions had got them into trouble at work, despite the fact that many described themselves as being 'strong'. Yet, alongside their assertive personalities, several described themselves as 'emotional', 'sensitive' or said that they cried a lot. It seemed that their moral convictions made them incapable of turning a blind eye, but they also felt injustice quite keenly, being cursed, as well as blessed, with a highly developed ethic of care.

Ill-treatment

Unreasonable treatment

The 'permanent white water' described earlier is most clearly represented through the actions of managers and those charged with leading the organisation. The target culture of achieving more output with fewer resources appeared a central feature of the working lives of many employees we interviewed. Irrational and punitive management manifested itself in many different ways and had an impact on managers as much as it affected non-management grades. We begin by describing how employees perceived their workloads as pressured and how deadlines were increasingly seen as a source of workplace pressure.

Health and social services are significant destinations for public spending and, like other branches of public expenditure, subject to increasing levels of scrutiny and performance evaluation. Employees at Westshire were subject to internal and external targets that emanated from government and were then passed down through layers of organisational bureaucracy to be delivered by front-line services. Employees saw these pressures as unfair; as one female employee in her forties said, 'They are bullying us to do more work and not listening to us, and just cracking the whip all the time.' It is worth noting that most employees did not use the word 'bullying', and this employee used the word in the context of '*institutional* bullying'. Our interviewees told us that their managers were overbooking clinics in order to meet stringent targets, and some staff were working every Saturday morning for several months in order to meet targets and clear waiting lists. In some cases staff were regularly doing 3–4 hours of additional work per week simply to keep up. Several said their workload had increased not because they were seeing extra clients but because they were covering for colleagues who were on leave, away from work because of illness or had left and not been replaced. Others told us how they were frequently having to train others who had come from a non-medical background.

Some staff at Westshire had complained about the pressures of increased workloads and understaffing, but they viewed this as largely a waste of time. Meanwhile, they were 'struggling' to cope with workloads and becoming 'more and more stressed'. These pressures and feelings of stress were felt at all levels and grades, including managers. One manager felt that there was very little organisational support for him in his role, and he referred to being constantly audited: 'what am I doing about sickness, what I am doing about this, and HR will say, "How many KSFs (knowledge skills frameworks) have you done"?' This frustration from front-line managers with Westshire's senior managers came through in many of the interviews. Some referred to feeling bullied because of the stresses and pressures they faced, and one told us he felt he was being asked to 'climb Everest with a six-foot stepladder'. Other managers felt that the targets and measures imposed on them were passed down by senior managers who did not understand the clinical needs of patients. Some of those we interviewed felt that managers did not understand variations in the needs of clients or patients but categorised them into standard, homogenous groups when estimating how many resources they required. For example, one employee who dealt with children with learning disorders knew that a child with autism had very different needs from one with less severe learning difficulties. To apply targets to their treatment without reference to the individual child's needs afforded no recognition of the time and effort actually expended by staff in order to meet individual client needs, many of whom would be in the 'system' for many years.

Some managers told us how their own workloads had doubled because fellow managers who had left Westshire were not replaced. Others told us how their operational domains had increased to take on more locations and operational areas with no extra resources. One manager said, 'I have been budgeted for five staff when in reality I need 20', and another manager felt that budgetary control was over simplified with blanket cuts in his department of 3 per cent: 'I don't feel that there's much fat in the system anymore.' Some of the managers felt that cutting budgets and expecting similar or even enhanced performance was futile; yet it felt for many that financial resources were diminishing but everything else was a constant. It is not surprising then that some felt they were 'being set up to fail' because their targets were unachievable. Others were struggling to comply with procedures and processes because they had no PC or IT access and all targets, budgets and staff procedures were completed or downloaded online. Another talked about how emails were bombarding him 'left, right and centre' but that he had 'no computer or laptop in my departments. I have to travel 20–30 miles away, which doesn't help when I am trying to do budgets'.

Poor communications between managers and employees was also a central feature of perceptions of ill-treatment. Some employees reported that they knew about things at the last minute or were specifically kept out of the loop;

for example, jobs were advertised 'quietly' leaving very little time for them to apply. Others told us how important meetings were organised on days when they could not attend. Email communications was problematic for different staff in different ways. Several employees told us how email was used with an expectation of an almost immediate response. As one staff member told us, 'She even rang me up at the clinic, and I said, "Well I haven't seen your email, I have just come back from holiday ... and I need time to think about what you are proposing".' Others told us email was used as an alternative for face-to-face communications; with managers using it as a 'catch all' for informing staff of changes to workloads and working practices. Some employees felt that communication used to be a fairly straightforward process, where they could go and talk through difficulties and sort them out, but now that email was the preferred communication vehicle, appointment calendars ruled availability, and it was almost impossible to have a conventional conversation. A few employees reported feeling left out of communications and 'disconnected' or 'kept away from decisions' or 'cut off', while others told us how their emails were conveniently ignored or a manager response was 'I am looking into it' but that nothing ever happened.

Other communication difficulties lead to feelings of frustration. Getting a 'straight answer' was a real frustration because the chain of bureaucracy and the external imposition of targets meant that blaming others for targets was a feature of communicating decisions. One member of staff reported how they had not had a team meeting in over a year, which resulted in gossip and rumour being the primary mechanism for communicating. We were also told by some staff how a lack of human interaction about returning to work from sickness, poor levels of general concern with staff well-being and poor human engagement were representative of weak communication with managers.

The move to electronic communication had led to managers struggling to keep everyone informed and non-managers feeling isolated. The tensions between professions caused by communication with one group but not with other groups resulted in chaotic operational activity, which in turn led to behaviours employees found inappropriate. Words such as 'screaming like a banshee' were used by one employee to describe the behaviour of her supervisor who wanted her to work a particular shift pattern. In fact, several interviewees reported being frustrated that their views were not taken into account over issues such as working patterns. Given that Westshire had a female majority in its workforce, flexible working arrangement such as annualised hours, part-time flexible working, job sharing, working term-time only to fit with the needs of parenting were commonplace. These aspects of employment contracts contributed to tensions between managers, supervisors and employees. We heard from senior consultants how they were pressured to work additional sessions even though their employment contracts stipulated a set number. Insisting on their contracts did not seem to be an option, and here as elsewhere employees told us that their objections 'fell on deaf ears', that they were instructed 'without discussing, asking, negotiating' and 'talked over' by managers.

Frustration with the effect of management demands and ever-increasing targets on their own working lives was coupled with concern over the effect of these demands and targets on patients and clients. Employees told us on several occasions how they would be under pressure to function with unqualified and inexperienced colleagues and how the stress of being 'the only qualified person' left them anxious about the legal implications if something went wrong. Others talked about their 'neck being on the line' if things went wrong and struggling to be in more than one place. These pressured environments meant that being shouted at, told to shut up and even 'screamed at' were regular features of work for some of our interviewees. A small number of people told us that they felt they were being excessively monitored in their work, with one male employee reporting that it was 'obsessional' to the point that he was moved seven miles to be relocated to the office of his manager.

These situations led many people we interviewed to feel they were being treated unfairly compared to others at work. Employees from a broad spectrum of roles and occupations reported how they felt they were overlooked for training sessions or development opportunities. Most of the issues where bias was perceived were fairly minor in nature but still rankled with those we interviewed. For some, this was because they could not move forward with their development because they needed something that was being denied to them. Others felt that they were being passed over in favour of younger, less experienced colleagues, and the key issue was the lack of recognition which they felt should have come with more experience. Failure to recognise status distinctions was a common feature of perceptions of unfairness, as was the notion that the unfairness they experienced was capricious. Many of those we interviewed talked of 'change of attitude' or a 'switch' from being well regarded as an employee to one who was no longer seen positively, and they could not understand why this change had taken place and were left puzzled and upset.

One of the challenges of working in a professional services organisation such as Westshire is the large number of experts in different fields who, by nature of the services being offered, come into regular contact with other professionals. It is therefore not surprising that many employees had professional disagreements which sometimes centred on the use of proper procedures. Examples ranged from disagreements on a course of action taken, such as drug dosage or treatments, to claims that statutory processes were being bypassed. Others thought the following were unreasonable: internal processes such as jobs being advertised at short notice, incorrect short-listing procedures, irregular personal development reviews (PDRs), training opportunities, annual leave entitlements, shift patterns and so on. Sickness absence and entitlement to reduced hours when returning to work were seen as unreasonable by some staff because processes and procedures were either not explained properly or were being overlooked. Interviewees told us how they felt policies were not adhered to covering areas such as discipline, returning to work and complaints.

This range of perceptions of unreasonable management caused a great deal of consternation with some feeling that managers were increasingly behaving like demagogues who were unaccountable for their actions. We now turn our attention to the behaviours we describe as incivility and disrespect where it is not only manager behaviours that left Westshire employees feeling ill-treated at work.

Incivility and disrespect

We have already seen that Westshire employees negotiated a complex web of interactions between professionals, many of whom were highly specialised and very well qualified, and the joint pressures of client expectations and political interference. The working environment appeared to function as a 'pressure cooker' where managerial and political targets meant that tempers could fray and behaviours could become fraught with insults and intimidation. Employees of all ages and backgrounds appeared to be on the receiving end of incivility and disrespect with aggressive acts being seen as commonplace. It may, indeed, be too easy to excuse such bad behaviour in workplaces which are supposedly shaped by both professional ethics and an ethic of care.

Shouting and loss of temper were widely reported by those we interviewed, and swearing, screaming and aggressive gestures seemed to be quite a common occurrence for many staff both in face-to-face meeting and on the phone. Most of the perpetrators of these behaviours were co-workers, although managers were also known to have recourse to bad language or shouting. Very senior and highly paid professionals reported being sworn at by their senior colleagues. Rarely were our interviewees able to pinpoint why the ill-treatment occurred. Some staff also told us that they were subject to bad behaviour from clients and patients but that these were broadly accepted as 'part of the job'.

Many staff did not seem to be unduly affected by being shouted or sworn at by their colleagues, although a smaller number reported it as 'stressful' and 'unprofessional'. Swearing and shouting was reported by some as a form of intimidation and threat. In one interview with a member of the estates team, we were told how a very senior professional was swearing at an elderly member of the public, who had asked him to moderate his language, because he could not find a car parking space. In another example, a newly promoted manager was yelled at across a desk because his budget was overspent. These situations left people feeling too intimidated to respond, and in some cases the physical size of the perpetrator meant that the staff member was intimidated.

As one employee told us, 'He walked me into the corner and his face was literally 5–6 inches from mine.'

Insulting behaviour ranged from junior staff ridiculing the decision of a senior colleague through to trading insults when a colleague was asked to undertake a task that they perceived as beneath them. Again, insults usually took the form of bad language and swearing but also manifested as public ridicule and professional humiliation. For some staff, the professional humiliation by their peers was particularly hurtful and was seen as unacceptable, which was in contrast to behaviours received from members of the public, which were seen as an unfortunate inevitability. In most of the situations described to us, employees found it difficult to understand why they were receiving insults and threats but simply described the perpetrator as 'rude', 'bristling', 'nasty' and 'unpleasant'.

Several of our interviewees had similar experiences of incivility at Westshire: their emails and calls were ignored, and normal courtesies abandoned leaving them isolated and ignored. Again, in most cases interviewees could not explain why they were now isolated by colleagues or a manager. Some felt it was because they had moved into management grades and were ostracised for doing so by their former colleagues whilst at the same time they were at too low a management grade to be accepted by existing managers. Feelings of exclusion manifested themselves in many different ways. One employee told us how he worked in a team of five or six but was the only one to be moved out into an office on his own. A manager told us how he was excluded from senior management meetings discussing the department he was running. Other more petty behaviours included being excluded from social events, not being included when someone made tea or coffee in group meetings and not being spoken to in team meetings. One woman told us how whenever she entered the staff room, some colleagues got up and left. Another was never included in a cash collection for birthdays, leavers or other events. These behaviours left people feeling more bemused than angry or upset. Many people we interviewed simply resigned themselves and reached the conclusion that this was just the way things were at work.

The very nature of Westshire's operations meant that employees were encountering ill-health and difficult emotional challenges on a daily basis, and some told us this made insensitive treatment of employees' health problems from managers and peers more difficult to accept. Several interviewees told us how their own ill-health or family circumstances were poorly handled, particularly from managers and support services such as occupational health departments. One interviewee who was recently bereaved talked about being shouted at after her return to work and saw this as undignified, given the very recent death of her father. Others talked about being put in insensitive situations when they themselves faced personal dilemmas. For example, one woman who was receiving fertility treatment was placed in a children's disability unit, while another worker whose partner had miscarried was told, 'It's only a miscarriage.' Another employee who was on sick leave was sent texts which went to all members of the team saying 'due to excessive sick leave, I (the manager) have had to once again reorganise shift patterns', leaving the individual to feel ostracised and humiliated amongst her peers. Small numbers of employees perceived discriminatory behaviour as one factor behind their negative experiences. These issues concerned discrimination over ill-health and disability but also part-time working and sexual orientation. For example, a lesbian employee felt that people were whispering that she should have nothing to do with children, even though her job was not related to children in any way.

The work that people undertook was also a source of feelings of unfairness and ill-treatment. Several told us how they were encouraged to 'look for something else' or told outright, 'You ought to be sacked.' Sometimes behaviour was a little more subtle with statements such as 'I do not think this is for you.' Others were less fortunate and received what they perceived as threats about their performance, resulting in their department being formally investigated but without the opportunity to give their side of events. One manager felt that when budgetary pressures were being imposed, they were not thanked for saving money but continued to be 'kicked'.

Violence and injury

Violence can manifest itself in a number of ways, and some might think being 'poked in the chest' or 'backed into a corner' were sufficiently violent acts in their own right. Besides the swearing and aggressive posturing described earlier, we did not come across significant numbers of stories of violence or injury at Westshire. We were told about one instance of violent behaviour where a very senior professional ended up having to be restrained by a member of Westshire's security team who had little choice but to 'take him down in a head lock'. Such situations between colleagues appeared to be rare occurrences, and the few instances of violence that were reported to us normally involved clients or users of Westshire's service. One interviewee recounted how his colleague had been spat at by a member of the public while another had been injured trying to physically restrain another member of the public. One respondent told us there were between 10 and 12 violent incidents every Saturday night, and 'One of my colleagues got punched in the stomach last Saturday by an elderly woman; when another colleague tried to help, she got punched too.'

Car parking problems were a regular source of conflict. One male member of staff told us how he had to 'jump out of the way' because a delivery driver from an associated professional organisation refused to slow down when asked. Other traffic-based problems resulted in face-to-face confrontations which required a telephone call to the police. As in other cases studies, conflict and confrontation extended beyond working hours and the workplace. One manager who was forced to dismiss a member of staff for falsifying an application form was subsequently threatened by the partner of this former employee at a local supermarket. 'I bumped into her and her husband ... and her husband actually threatened me, my house and everything else. I had never come across this; it shook me up.'

Witnessing ill-treatment

A number of men and women we interviewed spoke of witnessing ill-treatment to demonstrate that they were not the only ones who had experienced unreasonable treatment or incivility and disrespect. An interesting feature of witness accounts is how interviewees were more willing to use phrases such as 'bullied' and 'harassed'. Both men and women told us how they believed colleagues were both being bullied and were bullies, and they seemed much less reticent about applying this label to others than they were to themselves or their situations. This reflects research findings on bullying (see, for example, Einarsen *et al.* 2011 for prevalence rates and historical discussion). Some of the uses of terms such as 'bullied' or 'harassed' were in a caring context where there was sympathy for a colleague because of what was happening to them; for example 'he was singled out' or 'you can see her picking on her' or 'she picks on vulnerable people.' Some witness experiences were used to create a context for particular episodes of ill-treatment: 'she was bullied in another department', and 'she was also bullied by a different staff member.' Occasionally, men and women appeared to be using their observations of others in a systematic way, such as making mental notes or keeping 'a diary', as evidence to indicate they were not alone in suffering ill-treatment.

Discriminatory behaviour also appeared to be more readily reported as something people witnessed rather than personally experienced. Like bullying, interviewees seemed more willing to offer us their own opinions about whether someone was being discriminated against, and this seemed to be particularly likely from employees who were themselves members of minorities. A lesbian interviewee told us how a male employee with a long-standing health condition was mocked and teased because of his condition and how racist comments were dismissed as 'general humour'. One woman told us how she felt sorry for a male colleague because 'he was from the same background as me.' Elsewhere, incivility and disrespect in relation to visual impairments, physical health conditions and psychological or emotional problems, racist comments about Irish/Welsh/English/Scottish colleagues, and homophobic remarks were frequently reported as observations of Westshire's workplace.

Some of the men and women we interviewed appeared to use their observations to build timelines to show how long episodes of ill-treatment had been going on, while others were using their witness experiences to show up 'poor management', 'bad practices' or a 'lack of professionalism', thus allowing them to reach a reasoned judgement about what was taking place around them. In some cases, the judgement they reached from their observation of unfairness and injustice and cronyism was of an organisation which was operating at moral hazard.

The characteristics of troublemakers

The characteristics of those deemed responsible for causing trouble at work ranged from classifying perpetrators as ambitious, corrupted by power, incompetent, bumbling, unprepared and overstretched through to feeling sorry because the person(s) concerned had outside pressures and stresses. In fact, when interviewees were willing to attribute characteristics to perpetrators they rarely focused on a single perpetrator attribute. For example, a woman described as 'ambitious' was regarded so because she 'didn't have a family' and 'resented' those that did. Similarly, another female perpetrator was described as powerful but 'lacked experience' resulting in 'aggressive and unreasonable behaviour'. Interviewees also appeared to try to corroborate their experiences by bringing in other colleagues and co-workers. Phrasing such as 'we always think' and 'other people have noticed' were used. 'We', 'us' and 'the team' seemed to be helpful to people as they tried to come to terms with a situation that they were constructing as not being their 'fault'.

Men and women also told us that troublemakers often lacked knowledge or confidence or were 'battling' against a tide of change. On one or two occasions troublemakers were reported as being very competent and talented, and these talents had been recognised when they had been promoted through the ranks. At this point they had become detached and aloof from their former colleagues or were making changes that were universally disliked. There were, of course, other interviews in which employees described troublemakers in a variety of highly personal and pejorative ways, for example, as 'manipulative', 'malicious', 'lying', 'deceiving', 'forceful' and so on. Others were described a being mentally deficient, lacking sexual prowess at home, being bullied by their partners, lacking an education and being 'thick'. It was clear that some interviewees had no respect at all for those they regarded as responsible for what was happening to them.

Given the female majority in the workforce, it is no surprise that the vast majority of troublemakers who were described to us were women. Female perpetrators were described as bullies and confrontational but could also be described as charming and capable. One of the most frequently reported traits of female perpetrators was controlling and authoritative. Occasionally, interviewees described these types of perpetrators as enjoying this style of behaviour and liking situations where they could keep people 'under their thumb'. Some even talked about a type of stalking perpetrator who went 'for the kill' or 'manipulated people's fears and anxieties'. Interviewees also talked about past histories and described how someone is 'well known for' or 'has a history'.

The processes and consequences of dealing with ill-treatment

We spent much time asking men and women about their experiences of support systems and whom they turned to in dealing with their workplace troubles. As we described earlier, Westshire had a set of policies to deal with workplace disputes, and like most organisations, these were the responsibility of the HR department. In fact, our interviewees did not report HR becoming involved until a long time after they decided to do something about their ill-treatment, perhaps after several months. Most people we spoke to did not mention the involvement of HR but told us they took their complaints to line managers or senior managers (one employee told us that HR represented the interests of management, which is why she chose not to involve them). Several doubted that managers had the skills to resolve disputes and felt that if only things could be resolved at an early stage most of the policies and procedures would be irrelevant (chiming with the principles of the Gibbons Review for better workplace dispute resolution).

Although they did not consult HR, employees were indirectly engaging with them through policies and procedures such as grievances and complaints. Several spoke about how they felt formal policies and procedures had taken over events, with some feeling that they were detrimental to satisfactory workplace resolutions. One very senior professional felt that, in the past, they would have sat down over a cup of coffee to settle differences, but once a complaint had been made, the organisation was duty-bound to let procedures and policies take over. A particular feature of Westshire's systems was an 'incident report form' which several interviewees thought hampered resolutions to workplace troubles. The form had been designed for reporting critical incidents where clients were put at risk, but had mutated into a process for complaining about colleagues and co-workers. A similar process seemed to have occurred throughout the organisations processes: their language focused on complaints, investigations and discipline; all phrases associated with formality and a quasi-legal environment.

In many cases, the process, once initiated, seemed to have dragged on for an inordinate amount of time. Some employees told us it was 'too much hassle' and others said it was a 'waste of time', not meaning the outcome but referring to time wasted in a process that involved so many people being distracted from what they were paid to do. Others talked about the costs of processes, including reports, letters, meetings and investigative costs. One male professional told us how it took 15 months from the first formal notification of a dispute to reach a final outcome. This resulted in him leaving work for this duration with stress. Two women talked about a nine-month process and a five-month process. In most of these accounts, our interviewees were absent from work on stress-related health grounds.

The outcomes of organisational processes also left many of our interviewees feeling frustrated. There were interviewees who felt that accessing formal complaints procedures made them look like 'whingers', but other interviewees felt that speaking to managers about their ill-treatment had actually made things worse. One told us how a manager had mishandled things so badly that she was forced to move departments, while another felt the grievance process had made things '10 times worse'. Several employees spoke of the dangers of being tarred as 'troublemakers'. Relationships appeared rarely to get back to normality with some describing communications as 'we slowly got back to grunting at each other.' Some talked about their preference to have received an apology, although this rarely seems to have happened. It was clear from the interviews we conducted that there was a significant period of readjustment for many staff with some having lengthy return to work adjustments, meaning they were not operating at normal capacities for some time. Several staff ended up moving to other departments and to other roles adding to retraining and redeployment costs as well as the costs of having to recruit replacements. There was also some evidence of a tit-for-tat approach in individual disputes. Claims and counterclaims were mentioned and interviewees sometimes referred to detailed logs to explain the chain of events to us. Some retaliatory activities from troublemakers included ostracising complainants, and one woman told us how she was telephoned by her manager to be told she was not getting an invitation to her daughter's wedding. Another was not invited to make a donation for a collection for the birth of a colleague's daughter.

Some employees used the services of Westshire's occupational health unit with most of them self-referring because they felt they were not getting the support of managers. It seems that those who self-referred did so under periods of stress with several talking about being 'very unwell' or 'not fit to go in'. For many, the occupational health service was a very positive experience in terms of helping them to get well or feel better. One of the most positive features of the way in which Westshire's processes and procedures were organised was that the health and well-being team located in the occupational health unit had responsibilities for the dignity at work procedure. The unit was also linked to Westshire's staff counselling service.

Contact between those with workplace troubles and their trade union seemed to be rare. This might be because many of those we spoke to were professionals and relied on professional bodies and networks in Westshire.

Those who did use their trade unions seemed to be happy with the service they received, and trade union representatives seemed able to bypass formal procedures wherever possible to reach outcomes that served the best interests of their members. Terms such as had 'a quiet word with senior management' or 'worked the system' were used. However, this approach also left some frustrated that things had been 'swept under the carpet' or 'pushed to one side', and one even referred to the informal approach of their union rep as 'collusion' and 'working hand in glove with management'.

Several men and women spoke of the informal support they received from co-workers and, in some cases, managers in other departments. Some used their colleagues in affirming ways, showing that they were not alone in trying to understand what was happening, while others sought solace amongst a group of colleagues for a collective 'moan' about the behaviour of an individual. These reassurances seemed to be important to our interviewees, and in some cases their colleagues offered strategies and advice on how to deal with whatever situation was being faced.

The consequences of ill-treatment at work

Our interviewees told us that they felt there were significant consequences for them and for Westshire. Besides the financial costs of processes and procedures described above, and the inability of many staff to get back to a civilised and normal working climate, many women and men we spoke to talked of the impact of the episodes associated with their trouble at work. It is not too dramatic to state that one or two interviewees were 'shattered' by their experiences and were suffering many months or even years after episodes had ended or the person they were having troubles with had left Westshire. One male employee produced notes and diaries going back several years suggesting he could not let go of this experience. Many of the men and women we spoke to had received counselling, medical treatment, psychological and psychiatric support. Psychosocial symptoms reported to us included crying and emotional outbursts, stress and its associated symptoms, feelings of vulnerability and insecurity, lack of confidence, feelings of foolishness, feelings of guilt, low self-esteem, outbursts of fury and anger, feelings of paranoia, work-phobia, feelings of powerlessness, going mad, irritability, frustration, becoming distant and remote with friends and family, impaired social life, demoralisation and so on. Symptoms such as nausea, back pain, tension, sleep disruption, clinical depression, chest pains, headaches, weight loss, upset stomach, drowsiness because of prescribed drugs and so on were reported by a wide range of our interviewees. During interviews when people were talking about the impact of their experiences, they referred to feeling like 'a punchbag' 'kicked' 'assaulted' and 'battered'. People talked about 'having the stuffing knocked out of me' and 'you knew it was coming but you didn't know where or when'.

Of course, there were also organisational effects from these workplace experiences. Apart from the expense of carrying out investigations and the production of reports and other documentation, a considerable loss of workplace productivity could be expected. Organisational costs could be significant resulting from redeployment, loss of staff who had left the organisation, long and protracted absences, adjusted workloads after periods of stress and other productivity reductions. In addition to accumulating costs, Westshire's troubles were shaping the organisation. For example, employees were increasingly wary of the very processes and procedures which had been designed to protect them. Grievances, disciplinary procedures and mediation had all affected people in ways they were not expecting, with some feeling that simply going through a process was itself an ordeal, regardless of any outcome. Goodwill and positive workplace attitudes, traditional features of the health and social care sector, also appeared to have been damaged by the events to which they have been exposed. This was summed up well by one of our male respondents, who said,

> And I think how it has affected me and I know, speaking to colleagues, how it has affected them, is you now have in our workforce, people who have been the epitome of consummate professionals, doing more than their contracted hours, going home late, going into work early, taking sheaves of work home at weekends and evenings. Professionalism. And they've gone into 37.5 hours mode instead.

Conclusions

Our in-depth interviews at Westshire revealed a complex organisation facing continual change, most of it externally imposed through government targets and budgetary pressures. These pressures left managers and employees struggling with working arrangements which were strained and often fractured. For the professionals in Westshire's workforce, these pressures and tensions provoked an existential crisis. Exposure to a troubled workplace was experienced as a threat to their identity and purpose. Assuming managerial responsibilities did little to recover that identity and purpose; indeed it might make matters worse.

On the surface at least, our analysis of the BWBS data did not lead us to anticipate such problems within an organisation in the health and social work sector. Indeed, we expected that organisations like this one would be more prone to ill-treatment than other organisations solely because of the amount of contact employees had with the general public. There are fairly obvious reasons why professionals and others in health and social care might come across clients or patients who are disrespectful and even violent. Yet, although a few interviewees mentioned such things, they generally reassured us that they took them in their stride and were far less affected by them than they were by ill-treatment from managers and co-workers.

On deeper reflection, we can see, however, how the BWBS analysis revealed the problems which preoccupied employees at Westshire (and at Britscope). It was the questions about decreased autonomy, super-intense work and, above all, the FARE questions that predicted troubled workplaces in our national survey. Employees in health and social care organisations were more prone to unreasonable treatment, and incivility and disrespect, from managers or colleagues, but this was entirely explained by their greater exposure to these predictors of the troubled workplace, for example, the feeling that they had to compromise their principles (see Figure 7). It was not providing a service in the health and social care sector that predisposed employees to this kind of ill-treatment (although it did predispose them to ill-treatment from clients and other members of the public). Instead it was reduced autonomy, super-intense work and the failure to allow them to act on their principles. We have seen how badly Westshire fared on all of these counts. For example, we heard a great deal about the shift in authority and control from managers to professionals and the way that Westshire's use of IT disempowered many of its employees. We heard just as much about employees struggling to cope with providing cover for colleagues who were not replaced and the deadlines and workloads imposed by managers who were under pressure to meet government targets.

8

Keeping the Faith

The organisation of the chapter on Strand Global Systems differs from the preceding three because we want to make it easier to explain how organisations can get things right as well as wrong. We have already learnt about some of these things in Chapters 5–7 but, from this point, we want to adopt a more focused approach. Rather than concentrating on what our employee respondents told us about themselves, the troublemakers and the consequences of ill-treatment, we shall make space for more analysis of those features of the organisation – and not simply the policies explicitly concerned with dignity at work – that might help to reduce and manage trouble at work. Aspects like leadership and workplace culture benefit from a more narrative structure. We hope this structure allows readers to understand that, whether senior managers realise this or not, Strand is actively engaged in a process of managing trouble at work.

We interviewed a senior HR director who worked at Strand's global headquarters, who knew the company she came to work for in 2009 had a global reputation in sophisticated engineering design and manufacture. What surprised her was how loyal the workforce was to the company and how proud they were of its reputation. The way these employees felt about their employer could not have been further from the disillusion expressed by Westshire employees in Chapter 7. As we shall see, Strand was just as complex an organisation – with internal markets, many divisions, worldwide locations, complex multidisciplinary teams and a huge array of products and services – but it had a unified culture that the trust lacked. The first employee engagement survey she had seen was done shortly after the new director arrived, when our interviews with Strand employees at the company's Longstretton location were under way. She found 'the pride that individuals feel in working for Strand is quite extraordinary', and engagement levels far exceeded those in the Fortune 500 and FTSE 100 companies they liked to compare themselves to. The director believed that the employees considered themselves to be uniquely fortunate to work for such a company. No other business had the same reputation or offered the same opportunities for challenge and fulfilment, but the key to it all seemed to be the belief employees had in what Strand did, a 'belief in what we produce, that it's worthwhile, that it's of high quality and that it's something that they want to be personally associated with'. We found the same thing in our interviews with employees.

In the United Kingdom, this belief in Strand made them an employer of choice for engineering and science graduates, and it was very highly regarded in the day-to-day work lives of their employees. The director said that it provided not only motivation but also compensation for the things people did not like about their work:

> [It] gets them up in the morning and that rises above some of the ups and downs that you would otherwise experience quite normally in 'are you feeling motivated today, what's annoyed you at work, what's motivated you at work'. It seems to give a sort of balancing effect that says, well, 'okay I go up and down but do I absolutely believe in this company and want to remain part of it and feel excited about the sort of work that I'm involved in?' That has been an overwhelming 'yes', despite some of the things that we know we need to do better.

This all-powerful assent went a long way towards explaining why Strand employees were less likely to experience ill-treatment or, at the least, less likely to dwell on trouble at work when it did occur.

We found it hard to find employees who would talk to us about ill-treatment at Strand despite our own, the employers' and the trade unions' best efforts, and we decided to increase the proportion of interviews with managers and union representatives in order to find out why there might be less trouble at work. Management practices and policies are therefore given more attention in this chapter than the others in Part Three, but let us begin by exploring the relationship between employee commitment, or belief, and the apparent dearth of trouble at work.

How Strand employees minimise trouble at work

Strand employees tended not to sow or cultivate the seeds of ill-treatment because this would have prevented them from aligning their behaviour with their belief in Strand. In the first place, that belief committed them to collaboration and there were hardly any jobs in Strand which could be managed without it. An engineering team leader and a technician in manufacturing engineering explained that this meant colleagues would give whatever help was needed. The technician also made the point that the way work was organised in Strand around projects meant that collaborations were continually renewed because everyone moved around the company and worked in a succession of different teams. We noted that this arrangement provided fairly frequent points at which people would naturally exit from difficult situations if trouble at work was brewing.

For employees to do their jobs and act on this belief in Strand, they had to get on with people. This engendered mutual respect and care not to give offence. In interviews with all levels of employees, we found people were keen to explain the importance of humour to good working relations and the sensitivity needed to make sure that colleagues were not offended. Collaboration also required openness and the atmosphere at Strand was described as both open and relaxed. The team leader believed, 'you can tell your manager nearly anything, I think.' From the point of view of senior managers we talked to, openness had to be constantly nurtured because time pressures sometimes made it difficult to give consideration to everyone's opinions. Openness also helped to ensure that if the seeds of discontent were sown, they did not get watered. A project accountant described her PDR as a very open process. For example, she had the opportunity to comment on any judgements made in the PDR which she did not think fair. The importance of fairness was one of the recurring themes in our interviews and we shall return to it.

We have already seen that one threat to openness and collaboration was shortage of time, and the trade union convenor for salaried workers at Longstretton told us how some people might be so overloaded with work that they would not 'see your priority as their priority'. Our interviewees mentioned other threats including organisational politics, power struggles and competition for roles. For the most part, these threats did not damage openness and collaboration because, our interviewees told us, people protected good working relationships by exercising self-control, compromising, not holding grudges, keeping things in perspective and, in an oft-repeated phrase, treating each other as adults. The self-control of Strand employees was also evident in their dealings with corporate customers, some of whom could be very rude and disrespectful, 'but you're kind of up for it, it's customers and it's not something that you take personally', according to a chief programme executive. This was no mean achievement since the executive was referring to a customer who repeatedly humiliated him in public. The situation was made all the more difficult because the customer was also a competitor. Moreover, like other global corporations, Strand ended up in litigation with customers and suppliers now and then, and it might have been that the underlying problems in this case were very serious ones.

Most Strand employees seemed to know, however, that they were required to keep their cool with customers, however difficult the situation – indeed there was Strand training to help them do this. A commercial development manager was scandalised when her boss upset a customer-competitor. She described herself as 'much more of a people person' – a sociologist would say, someone who was good at 'emotional labour' – and the distinction between this and technical competence suffused our interviews. The manufacturing technician introduced earlier was prepared to forgive the dreadful behaviour of 'a team leader who was renowned for probably being very technical but a real crap people person' because of his expertise. Sometimes that team leader might not suffer fools gladly, but that was only because he cared so much about his work, 'but I have to work with him, so I want a reasonably good relationship.

So instead of knocking him every five seconds, I just swallowed the fact that he's quite good at his job and all the rest.'

How workplace minorities cope with ill-treatment

We came across evidence that it was more junior employees, and particularly young women, who had to exercise this kind of forbearance, and there might have been a structural reason for this. As we shall see later in the chapter, strategic thinkers in Strand now felt that promotion solely on technical competence had been a mistake made in the past but which they would have to deal with for some time to come. Strand had also been very slow to recruit women and it was therefore likely that many of them would be in junior positions at the mercy of the poor people-managers. Most of the young women we talked to – like the project accountant we have already mentioned and a specialist illustrator in her twenties with a graphic design degree – were prepared to take this ill-treatment on the chin. The accountant explained to us that she had one rule for work and another for life outside Strand. She would not put up with ill-treatment outside but at work she was worried that if she seemed 'too upfront, too forward or direct, people may see me as being too rude' and her working relations and promotion prospects might be affected. She was aware that there were fine judgements to be made, however, since she had observed that assertive people did quite well in Strand.

A woman logistics manager confirmed it was not just the more junior women who did not make an issue of ill-treatment; other employees would 'take the flak throughout their working life … I just think they just don't want to make it worse, because then you could be snubbed.' The (male) technician we have already quoted thought that many people would put up with bullying in social situations in Strand and was worried about the long-term consequences for them. We gently probed the young woman accountant to tell us what sort of ill-treatment she been required to put up with. It included bad language in written and verbal communication and jesting which was offensive and which she would certainly object to outside the workplace. As the programme executive, himself with a mixed Asian background, said, it was not 'an overtly PC organisation', and not being a white, British male might entail putting up with an awful lot. For the accountant, with a white father and a Nigerian mother, the offensive jests included disparaging references to her background. If she took offence she would be told it was only a joke, and she should not be oversensitive, and she was learning that the only way to respond was to give as good as she got. Most women in Strand knew this, but most still found it hard to do because, no matter how sharp they might make their responses, they were giving tacit legitimacy to the offensive opinion.

The one woman who was capable of humiliating her tormentors was becoming something of a local legend. As the logistics manager said, 'she is a one-off, where she will be very abusive and verbally intimidating to the guys.' This was one of a tiny handful of woman fitters on the shop floor, who told us, 'there is a lot of banter that goes around and some of it's a bit inappropriate, I suppose, but it depends on your sense of humour I guess. I find it funny.' The older fitters with 'daughters your age and stuff' did not get involved though they, like the younger men, were unlikely to ask for her help. In her opinion, 'Male fitters and people like that don't like to admit that you could probably come up with a better idea than them.'

The young woman fitter said she did not mind fairly constant sexual banter and innuendo because she had 'quite a male sense of humour anyway, so I'm not really bothered by anything. I'm quite hard to wind up, whereas Danielle, the other girl, finds things a bit harder to take sometimes, and she gets a bit upset about stuff'. She might be better 'at taking it' than Danielle, another fitter, but she did not complain for the same reason others at Strand put up with ill-treatment: she wanted to 'fit in'. 'If you want to work here with men you could not ask for special treatment.' That also ruled out joining one of the special support groups that existed for Strand's women employees. She thought such groups undermined the demand that women should be 'treated equally'. If women had problems, they should complain to the manager just as the men had to. The logistics manager, a woman with long service in Strand and experience in more senior jobs, thought that managers might be blind to the fact that women in Strand were not treated equally. A male line manager on the shop floor, where the young woman fitter worked, assured us that white-collar female employees had no problems walking through the shop floor even if they were 'extremely attractive', but some women told us how 'very uncomfortable' it was for women to do this. As for the young female fitters, the line manager had noticed their 'quite courteous' treatment from the older fitters but not the looks and remarks that made Danielle rush to the ladies to change out of a specially issued blouse that Strand had asked its female employees to wear for a VIP visit.

To be fair to the line manager, he thought that women white-collar workers put up with 'absolutely disgusting' things said to them away from the shop floor where there was more of a gender balance. However, the young woman illustrator, who worked on the staff side with one other woman in a group of 25, preferred a 'very, very male-orientated workplace ... because you don't get half as much bitchiness as you do when you work with a bunch of women. It is so good, it really is, it's a chilled out atmosphere and everybody just gets on with it'. The male technician thought there was not enough respect shown to women in his office: 'They think oh great I can talk about sex to a woman at work and she's quite nice looking. So they're getting a bit of a kick out of that, which as a bloke, for me I understand that, but sometimes, they can take it too far.' Indeed, he wondered if this might explain why, at the meeting he attended at which we explained our project to Strand employees, two-thirds of the employees were women. This was the first time in his career at Strand he had been in a room where the majority were female: 'Maybe it's all to do with ill-treatment being towards people's feelings and all things like that. Blokes aren't so open about it, so maybe they don't want to bother with that.'

Thus far, there has been no suggestion of people's careers being affected by their gender – as long as they turned the other cheek – but the engineering team leader we have referred to thought her manager wanted her out of her job, and she did not know whether it was because she was a woman or because she was Greek. The (female) commercial development manager thought women were not always valued in Strand, and her manager had told her he would not employ women if he had a choice 'because of maternity leave'. He also thought 'women are just too emotional'. Like the project accountant, she did not know how much of this was teasing since he was one of the younger, more enlightened men in the organisation. She had heard racist comments made in a similar way: 'they think it's okay to say something like that to you and that you just agree with them basically … I don't know if it's because they're a manager and you're not going to question them or whatever.'

In her experience at Strand, sometimes with 40 people reporting to her, the logistics manager had found 'some of them didn't like having a woman being their boss', and they would 'blank' her and 'they would actually say as soon as I'd left the office, I'm not taking that from a woman. I don't take it from my wife at home and "I'm not taking it from that bloody jumped" … what was it, "jumped up little cow" or something'. These days she was more likely to be treated, to her face at least, with schoolboy ridicule. These men were graduates yet 'it's just like kids, where you get two, then they do the little whispering, and then they look at you and they start giggling. And you're thinking you're grown men, for God's sake. And then, there can be a couple of them firing stupid comments at you'. These comments, made when she was making presentations at large meetings, undermined her confidence in her grasp of technical information and, like other women, she felt she had to be 110 per cent on top of her brief, not 70 per cent like the men. If she reacted to the comments, she would be told she was 'hormonal' and at times felt she simply had to walk away. In this case, it is clear that good working relationships were sometimes strained to the limit, and she had seen other women, including the women fitters, keeping quiet in meetings perhaps because they felt intimidated.

BME employees were even rarer than women at Strand, and the proportion of BME employees may even have fallen over the years (despite Strand's much admired community outreach programme) with successive reductions in the blue-collar jobs where there had been a BME presence. Those BME employees we interviewed generally had a tale to tell about the racist treatment they had received over the years. An engineer who had been there for over 25 years told us he had put up with exclusion and disrespect, the company telling him his ill-treatment was all in his mind, and subsequent mental illness for which he was then stigmatised. The persecution was aggravated because it was from close colleagues and because his family felt similarly isolated and persecuted in the all-white community where they lived and where they had been subject to violent attacks. (The blue-collar convenor confirmed that National Front and British National Party (BNP) members had worked for Strand; indeed he had very recently forced a steward who made it known he was in the BNP to hand in his card.)

Another BME employee, again with very long service, had worked his way up as an apprentice but was now leading a team of white-collar staff. He had endured lots of racial abuse when he was a supervisor on the shop floor, and 'clearly I think the responsibility lay with Strand, and not with those individuals, to sort these things out, and that didn't happen.' He also suffered persistent and repeated racial discrimination in promotion, which others were too weak to challenge and where the 'right to manage' was used to head off union intervention and sideline 'morality' and 'honesty'. He thought that Strand 'need to manage the managers, and they haven't been able to do that, and they still can't do that, because it still exists now' rather than waiting for individuals to change their ideas. All the same, he thought things had got better in the past 20 years. This was partly because he was now well-established (and had greater confidence) and because those he now worked with had better attitudes. Abuse, including racial abuse, still went on, however, even though the company has tried to improve things over the years, and he would agree with the woman logistics manager that 'you've got to be a little bit better than the others'.

How Strand risks creating trouble at work

To recap, the belief in the product, and loyalty to Strand, and engagement in the work, encouraged people to behave well, to sort out any unpleasantness that did arise and put up with ill-treatment when it did occur. This might not simply mean laughing off offensive remarks but also putting up with unfairness and possibly detrimental impacts on one's career. We discovered that there were reasons why the company had to reinforce the original belief, loyalty and engagement because they were threatened by organisational politics, power games, bullying, misogyny and racism. But we should now add to this list of threats some things that the company itself wanted to do which might put it all at risk.

Insecurity

The senior HR director knew that reputational capital people had when they entered the company could not be relied upon: 'It gives you, sort of ironically, is it all there for the losing? So you have a good start but there are a number of other factors that come into play that will mean individuals feel engaged and motivated in the endeavours of the corporation.' And nothing could be better proof of this than that, when the 2009 employee engagement survey was being undertaken, and we were starting our interview programme at Strand's Longstretton location, the company was in the process of making lots of its employees redundant, creating plenty of opportunity for squandering reputational capital. However, we had several employees telling us that made them *less* likely to complain and more likely to want to prove how engaged they were for fear of losing their jobs.

Even in the most uncertain times, however, most of our interviewees thought that Strand compared well with other employers they knew from their own experience or had heard about from family or friends (the NHS, a firm in the same sector as the organisation in Chapter 6, a government body, for example). They were 'thankful to be working here because they do look after their staff, despite what anybody says' (specialist illustrator). And 'you're protected by lots of rules and things' at Strand (technician in Manufacturing Engineering). As the chief programme executive said of the NHS, 'you hear the stories and all the strife coming out of there. I really just don't recognise much of that in here.' The logistics manager was pretty typical when she said there were few employers who compared in terms of facilities, working patterns and the chance to work around the world. A project officer, who had similar feelings, told us Strand was 'a great company to work for and over the years I'd never had a problem, never, ever had a problem. They've always supported me, whether it's in training, higher education, they've always been there. Great people and obviously great experiences, you can travel the world and there are different roles'. There were plenty of hints here as to how Strand built on the initial reputational capital, and we shall be coming back to them, but we need to know more about the threats to the belief and commitment.

Performance and rewards

At the same time as the redundancies, though not necessarily directly related to them, there were all sorts of changes to reward structures. It was in this area that the chief programme executive thought most trouble at work was likely to happen: 'I mean the main issues are sort of corporately driven issues.' One of the most fraught of these issues was Strand's intention to move blue-collar workers over to some sort of performance management that was individually based (as on the white-collar side) and not done via collective deals. But the issue was not just one of the company risking blue-collar workers complaining of ill-treatment, if collective deals were scrapped, because white-collar workers were already complaining it was unfair. This was what the senior HR director said came through loud and clear in the 2008 engagement survey. We certainly heard white-collar complaints that some people were still getting something for nothing a year or more later, although the director was proud of the way this problem had been addressed subsequent to the redundancy programme.

The project accountant felt, for example, that real performance was not rewarded (with promotion, for example), whereas Strand rewarded 'pretending to be good' and getting on well socially. She did not think this at all fair, though, of course, we have seen how such a pattern might work well to keep the lid on ill-treatment. The chief programme executive thought that, in an attempt to be scrupulously fair, and give poor performers time to improve, the slow and deliberate way in which poor performers were handled could disrupt team-working and nurture a sense of unfairness. The technician said failing to deal with poor performers on the shop floor could lead to lower productivity amongst their colleagues but suggested that management did not act because they feared 'they'll all drop tools and then they haven't got anybody building anything. Management walk on eggshells with the shop floor'. While it was right that Strand should aim to be a more understanding employer than most, it was not too much to ask for 'an honest day's work'.

In 2009 the process of addressing individual blue-collar performance had stalled. The white-collar convenor explained they were presently stuck with a local agreement for performance pay which was specific to Longstretton and which was far too blunt to discriminate between the performance of individual blue-collar employees. Instead, the bonus was paid to 80 per cent and sometimes 100 per cent of the shop-floor workforce. The lower end of the staff, the ones closest to the shop floor, looked at their tiny bonuses and thought this very unfair when the workers on the shop floor did not seem to be doing much for their bonuses and did not have much responsibility. This perception of unfairness could be exacerbated by the shift-working premiums that works people got (but very few staff worked shifts). He now had members who had shifted from blue-collar to white-collar roles wondering why they had done something so silly.

A specialist employee relations consultant with Strand described a similar 'difficult managing situation' in which the plethora of local agreements at Strand meant that different categories of workers doing the very same job could be 'rewarded on different bases'. This would be an increasing problem because mixing up different categories of workers was exactly what Strand wanted to do as part of its push for more flexibility from the workforce. The old bargaining structure was now creaking because things changed so fast that agreements were very soon out of date: 'The nature of the business now is that people have to be far more flexible, whatever role that they are in.' We shall return to this issue later, but we need to note here that the trade unionists at Longstretton thought that Strand was trying to get more for less out of the workforce by circumventing binding agreements that were still in place.

The blue-collar convenor told us Strand turned a blind eye to individual managers breaking a 40-year-old agreement in which a pay rise had been moderated in return for time off, say to attend the dentist, at the discretion of the manager but without having to make the time up. They were taking advantage of employees' lack of knowledge or reluctance to complain. He thought this happened when managers were 'feeling a pressure always to get the hours out, if they don't get the hours out. But there is a system to use and they should be using the system'. He told us that when members complained to them they put an end to it, and one of our shop-floor interviewees confirmed it happened to her and she got her half day back which she missed because of snow. Not least because of her no-nonsense approach, the story she told us had the clear potential for trouble at work: she believed her manager refused her the half day's paid leave as a way of 'getting back' at her or 'making a point' to show he was in charge, 'It's like you don't have any control and I can screw you whenever I want, basically. So I got the union involved in that and got half a day off.'

The blue-collar convenor gave other examples of Strand taking advantage of its employees. He had members who worked extra hours at management request, to meet a deadline for example, and did not bother to claim the time off in lieu that they had earned. This was extra hours on top of the annual 100 hours' flexibility agreed (for extra pay) in the 'new working arrangements' agreement in order to get new factories sited at Longstretton. The other Longstretton convenor, representing the staff, confirmed all of this. In particular, managers were using the new working arrangements agreement to try to bamboozle the workers and the union into letting them get away with the extra hours. For him, the biggest issue with the company they were facing at the time was when 'the members get pressured when they're trying to claim back extra hours that they've worked'. It was important because he was not prepared to 'allow additional hours to mask inefficiencies or lack of staff'.

The senior HR director explained the company's point of view. The 'new working arrangements' were 'a particular collective agreement that was struck with a number of unions across the United Kingdom, not all of them, and it was struck in different ways site by site. So you had very little similarities', and Strand now wanted standardisation and not just across the United Kingdom. Strand wanted UK blue-collar employees, in particular, to realise they needed to measure what they offered for performance management and rewards against what Strand could get outside the United Kingdom in its increasingly global operation. The key thing was the 'individual comparability' between shop-floor workers, which the 'collective mindset' saw as inappropriate. The director also talked about new manufacturing techniques, which offered massive improvements in productivity, being perceived as a threat by long-serving blue-collar workers who grew up in a UK-only company which prized 'artisan skills'. For the works convenor, the move away from such skills, to training for a task and not the craft, was short-sighted and would prove damaging to his members' job security and the company's long-term prospects. He thought Strand was being ruined by short-termism, centralisation and rule by accountants (not engineers).

Industrial relations

There was a lot more than rewards at stake here and there were therefore multiple risks to the conditions which minimised trouble at work inside Strand. For one thing, we found Strand a relatively untroubled place to work, due to local agreements and local discretion. They underpinned a partnership in which the union cooperated with management to make sure that ill-treatment did not occur or did not fester into trouble. As the works convenor said, 'usually what I'll say to them is, talk to your manager and if you don't get any success from your manager, come back to us. And nine times out of ten, they never come back.' If they did come back, still unhappy 'we'll have a meeting with the manager and see what's going on.' This sorted it out one way or the other; there was never a need for an employment tribunal. This view was confirmed by a line manager.

The company was risking a lot when it ran into – albeit mild – trade union resistance to organisational change, especially in relation to flexibility, because the unions frequently helped to pour oil on troubled waters. The works convenor summed it up this way: 'We've got a very, very good working relationship with this company, up until now, touch wood, with discipline and people not carrying out their work. And we always have a chat to them and normally ... we don't have to go any further.' But it was not simply managers at Strand who welcomed globalisation and the ending of local agreements. We have already seen how employees referred to the globalisation of Strand with pleasure because of the opportunities it gave them, and many of our interviewees welcomed the changes that came with it. The BME engineer who had put up with years of ill-treatment said that it meant that 'they are having to adjust procedures about dealing with other nationalities'. A BME programme leader thought Strand would now 'pick the best people from wherever they can get them'. He also thought that there was a new openness to other ways of doing things which was more in line with international practice, whereas the only standard used to be how things were done at Longstretton (not even elsewhere in Strand's UK operation).

In effect the programme leader agreed with the senior HR director's view that local agreements were an unnecessary complication – with over 2,000 live agreements in the United Kingdom alone – and not 'fit for purpose'. In Longstretton alone, there were five different grievance procedures. All of this made the role of managers unnecessarily difficult and, unless it was simplified, the devolution of some HR functions, in line with modern HR practices, would be vey difficult and risk causing ill-treatment and/or making it unlikely that ill-treatment could be dealt with promptly. The director may have been right to think this could cause all sorts of problems which could lead to trouble at work, but the danger seemed to have been exacerbated by a lack of resolution on the part of the company before she joined. The staff convenor cited 'a lot of the agreements we struck with the company over the years, talking about flexibility and no demarcations, and everybody doing anything they're asked to do provided they're trained'. But 'the company has never kind of really driven that', so it came as a nasty surprise to some when they found Strand taking flexibility and a 'can-do attitude' seriously: 'just waiting to be told what to do is not the way the company expects people to behave anymore.' He gave the example of Strand vacillating over whether blue-collar workers needed foremen, and the extent to which they were really prepared to empower shop-floor teams to get on with things themselves.

Management roles and responsibilities

In the modified matrix style of management Strand adopted – a long time ago in blue-collar work, much more recently for white-collar employees – employees moved around from project to project with local control over what they did resting with the managers there. At the same time, their careers were in the hands of a 'resource manager' elsewhere in Strand who, amongst other things, handled their PDR and, maybe, helped them rise quickly through a fast-track procedure. In some situations, resource managers had helped employees we interviewed to escape or, at least, cope with ill-treatment from a project manager. But the matrix style is also renowned for creating risks because it contains more potential for conflicts over priorities. The technician, for example, talked about having 'four people that you're answering to really, and you're trying to keep them all happy. And they've all got possibly different agendas ... and they've all got their deadlines. The project's got their deadline and also they want theirs done now'. This placed considerable onus on the people at work on a project to behave in the way that Strand employees habitually describe as 'treating each other as adults'. In other words, the matrix style both capitalised on and put strain on the unity of sentiment and purpose that Strand employees felt.

The complexity of the matrix style of management was recognised as a real problem by the HR consultant. There could be confusion about whom the employee was reporting to, not just in terms of who had priority ('because there is always a competition for resource to get things done') but who they should go to in order to sort out particular problems (so directly relating to trouble at work). A supply chain manager told us he could not keep tabs on his team to understand who might be overworked. He could not know what their day-to-day pressures were and we should be under no illusions that there were *lots* of pressures in Strand. Managers were highly loaded and, as everywhere, senior mangers like the chief programme executive thought being given an unmanageable workload or impossible deadlines was 'part of the management challenge'. The staff convenor thought that some of this was being passed on, for example, 'managers put that in the PDR that working additional hours is a good thing', and

> there's an inconsistency with the way they're treated as managers, like additional hours is an expectation. So if they're treated that way then they kind of say 'well, if you want ... if you want to be a star like me then you've got to do the same as me'. So there's no great surprise that they transmit what's put on them.

He also thought Strand was adding to workloads irrationally and unnecessarily by giving people things that they did not need to do. There were others who agreed wholeheartedly, for example, the technician who described team leaders having to waste their days with 'chart engineering' – making up charts for reports and presentations rather than doing real work that added value, 'so there's all those frustrations and the clock's ticking'. According to the line manager, the shop-floor teams could also be diverted to 'mundane work' which did not add value, and held up work on other things, but management would not want to hear about the hold-ups and the team ended up putting in extra hours.

For some managers, part of the intensification of managers' workload – including their share of charts and mundane work – followed the distribution of some HR responsibilities to them. The line manager, for instance, complained of the workload entailed in handling the teams' training needs. He was backed up by the staff convenor who said that discharging all of these new responsibilities took time, and the attempt to provide online solutions was hampered because of the complexity of collective bargaining arrangements. When managers reached the wrong conclusions, this created more work for them and the possibility of complaints of ill-treatment. Even if they got it right, there were risks of resentment in the new system: why should employees have to tell their managers all about their health problems if they did not want to? Only the manager could now book an occupational health appointment, though the HR consultant did not think it was a requirement of the system that employees had to disclose the nature of their problems to their managers in order to do this. On the shop floor, the line manager was also displeased by the extra work this entailed. We need to bear in mind that all HR activity, if mishandled, can exacerbate, or even spark off, ill-treatment. The risk of setting fires was increased by putting non-specialists with no knowledge of the law, and shaky knowledge of company procedure, in charge of the matches.

Of course, there was help to be had online and there were also training courses but, as the line manager told us, 'with my own training, basically

I just work longer hours if I need to fit different training in'. Not that managers could always stretch themselves in this way on behalf of people in their teams. The HR consultant thought that 'sometimes people feel … that they don't get enough support from the management … And, in some instances, there's a lack of it because managers are too few and overworked, perhaps. So they don't really have the time to do the coaching that they should do'. The manager of the Greek engineering team leader subjected her to weekly bullying: she said he set her up to fail, and to overwork to try to please him, but at the same time he humiliated her. He was generally bad at giving support to the people he was responsible for: 'Because I was appointed to this job not with loads of experience; it could be because I didn't have loads of experience and he didn't have the patience to deal with me.' She said he complained about being under loads of pressure (though she wondered why he thought this a justification for passing the pressure onto others when she herself did not do this). Elsewhere, the commercial development manager complained she had had little support because her manager thought it would be 'spoon-feeding', and she was stuck with learning the job the hard way when he could have helped her to be more efficient and productive, not making lots of mistakes. ('I think he's once said one thing to me about you did that well. That's in the whole five years I've worked for him.')

Strand's informal approach to trouble at work

Let us take stock. We have seen that Strand counted on a level of commitment from new employees that most big companies could only dream about and that this was an ideal situation for reducing trouble at work. We have also seen how the normal threats to these conditions – office politics and racism, misogyny and other prejudices, badly behaved customers – occurred, and we have seen how Strand's strategies for reducing costs and increasing productivity put the basis of the collaboration and openness at risk. We have covered redundancies, changes in reward structures and work organisation (flexibility, empowerment and intensification), deskilling, changes in HR including the performance and development of employees. We would expect that Strand would take steps to minimise the risks to engagement entailed in all of these.

Some aspects of changes in work organisation were actually calculated to increase commitment. So people may not usually like change but they do sometimes welcome empowerment and other things which increase collaboration and cooperation like flat hierarchies, more autonomous team-working. The supply chain manager, for instance, said Strand had 'gone into self-contained teams as such, and you feel part of the task you're doing'. These things encouraged the more 'adult' behaviours that we know from the interviews that employees wanted, and which also served to stop sowing or nurturing the seeds of trouble at work. Sometimes this happened in a straightforward way; for example, the chief programme executive enjoyed not being 'second-guessed all the time'. The way his teams were performance managed – against cost, schedule and quality – also mapped on well to what the individual team members wanted anyway. In other cases, it happened not because adult behaviours were directly encouraged but because people had to build them up to help them follow through on their primary commitment to the product. As we know, the modified matrix put extra demands on workers. The possibility of confusion and conflict increased, and there needed to be a lot more deliberation and decision-taking locally; otherwise there was gridlock. If the employees were already deeply committed to the product, then they would align their own behaviours to make this work. They would demand of each other that they behave responsibly, as adults. But the company also made its own contribution to ameliorating the potentially damaging (to commitment) aspects of changing work organisation.

Leadership

The senior HR director explained that Strand now saw leadership as just as important for managers as technical knowledge ('it's no good to us to have somebody who is technically brilliant but actually can't lead a team of people to deliver'). She wanted to talk about what they were doing to achieve this in 2011, even when they were still grappling with the fact that as in 'any other large organisation' people got 'promoted on the basis of technical excellence' and then gradually moved up the organisation until they were no longer using that technical expertise but 'find themselves doing more of the people side of managing and leading that perhaps is not their natural skill set or something that they particularly value'. For the director, the remedy was to tell managers exactly what behaviour was valued, change how they selected people for 'critical roles' and change how they were performance managed, making it more about how they managed people than it was at present: making sure they were rewarded for certain behaviours at each level of managers and leaders. While it was a work in progress, some of this had already been in place 18 months before when we began our interviews.

The HR consultant explained that they took on graduates each year for technical/professional development but also, now, a group to be developed as 'leadership people': 'There is work done at early points on in trying to instil in people the understanding that they have to observe what's around them in terms of the teams that they work with and that they may need to intervene when they see issues going on.' He told us managers were told to watch out for any behaviour that was unacceptable and report it (and we heard from the chief programme executive that this was now happening in his programme). The HR consultant had to admit, however, that there might be more incentive for managers to report their teams were running smoothly and hope such trouble fizzled out because reporting problems might reflect badly on their own performance. All the same, the staff convenor was complimentary about the leadership programme that made it possible for the poor people skills of 'technically brilliant' managers to be addressed. He also knew that poor managers had been eased out into more suitable technical positions. However, one managing director had been particularly important in pushing for this, and there had been less progress since she left Longstretton: 'We do have some people who are, in my opinion, wholly inappropriate still managing teams and creating havoc, and not being dealt with.'

Communication

Another priority area for Strand was communication, which had three elements: the physical layout of their workplaces, face-to-face communication and electronic resources. The physical layout, as the chief programme executive explained, was all about making 'sure it's easy to communicate and get in formal meetings together'. His team had the typical Strand seating arrangement in the same enormous room: 'There's everybody from, I guess myself, down to some of the admin assistants, and we all have the same desks, the same kind of environment, and we all sit pretty much close together. In some natural groupings I guess, but we're all in that room, pretty much.' It was not only this executive who thought such groupings important, and the importance of (fine-tuning) the physical layout to help with collaboration and other aspects of what he called 'complex interaction' was made clear to us.

Most of our interviewees praised Strand for the great improvements made in face-to-face communication in the past few years; indeed occasionally they thought it might now be a bit over the top. The ex-foreman, now an 'efficiency sponsor', thought it was 'far superior' to what it used to be with weekly meetings with shop-floor staff and a promise of answers to questions by the next meeting. There might be still room for improvement but the workers could ask any question they liked, and there were also communication boards and a diary showing who would be visiting the area. The young woman fitter on his team was a little less enamoured of the weekly meetings:

> Yeah, you've got the quiet ones who just sit there and just want the comms to hurry up so they can go to lunch. And then you've got the ones who just want to yell about everything. And then there are the ones who are kind of in the middle and actually have a point to make but don't get listened to because there are people yelling over the top of them.

The project accountant had the same weekly meetings plus regular, individual-tailored briefings for a team of about 30: 'on what's going on in the business. And on top of that, we have those ad hoc briefings if there's anything happened. Yeah. So for employees, we all know what's going on in the company.'

For Strand, electronic communication meant much more than sending newsletters by email. The HR consultant said everyone had an account on the intranet, but despite some investment in it lately, not all works employees had PCs they could easily access to get on it. There were PCs in resource areas they could get access to, but this was not very convenient. This was important because a lot of the resources the company wanted to make available to employees – for example because of the model of distributed HR responsibility – were accessed through the intranet. Individual employees could use it to find out about

> company policies on leave, on family friendly issues, on all sorts of things. It includes such things as harassment and whatever, and it provides information for the employee about what our policy is, where they should go to if they want to follow up something, access to any, if they need any, particular forms to go with something, then links to things like that.

He thought this was empowering because employees could find out themselves without having to contact HR or their manager.

Personal development

While Strand had only begun to pay close attention to leadership and communication relatively recently, one of the long-standing characteristic features of employment there was that considerable attention was given to staff development and multi-skilling. As mentioned earlier, development usually involved people moving round the company, so it allowed them to escape from troubled situations but, more importantly, it reinforced their commitment to, and belief in, Strand. Of particular importance here was the way that the resource managers were able to make the employees they were responsible for feel that their development plan really was personal. The feeling of being treated as an individual was reinforced by the assessment tool Strand used to score employees' development and identify their needs. The kind of people Strand employed thrived on this. Take the supply chain manager who was

> trying to grow. When I take a role, I want to try and grow and move as far as I can. So it's not so much just taking a role and saying oh right, I'd be good in that position. I try and think about where does it want to go? Where does that organisation want to go which I'm working for … have I got the right skills to start off with? And that's the challenge from thereon basically to establish those skills and actually try and enhance what I've got currently, so I can move on to something else.

In a PDR it could be the employee who pushed for this – 'they're open to suggestion and just put your hand up and discuss where you want to go next – or it could be the manager asking if you have thought of trying something different.' Either way, Strand was regularly making sure individuals were 'on the right path or ensuring how they could enhance the individual in that respect'.

The supply chain manager said Strand gave him 'all the resources and facilities' he needed to get the skills and an open door to apply for new posts – so far, he had always got what he wanted. He had also taken Open University management courses and, like many others at Strand, his horizons were not limited to Longstretton, and he really wanted to pick up the 'different cultural awarenesses' so that he could work abroad and maybe even leave the company. The Greek engineering team leader had the same idea, but first she was taking a break to complete an MBA at one of the United Kingdom's very best management schools. But personal development was not something that was only available to, or only prized by, Strand employees with Higher National Diplomas (HNDs) (like the supply chain managers) or degrees (like the engineering team leader who already had a master's in engineering). The technician we have mentioned several times before joined Strand as an apprentice more than 20 years ago, and he was still driven by the need to develop himself, do interesting work, and take on new challenges. He moved away from too much 'chart engineering' (see above) a year ago; for example, he did not have

> an issue staying at Strand, it's a good company. But I want to be happier for longer. And I could see the job role deteriorating to a technical dogsbody. So for that reason, I applied for another job, which is the one I'm in now, which is manufacturing engineering, which I am over the moon that I took, because it's great.

This was normal. As the engineering team leader told us, 'I get quite bored easily and I move jobs quickly, and the company has allowed me to do so. I think they look at the type of people that work in the company and, depending on their needs, they allocate people quite wisely, I think.' The individual attention paid to personal development in Strand helped to keep the Longstretton workplace relatively untroubled.

Management of illnesses and disabilities

Another important factor in Strand's relative success in minimising ill-treatment was their sickness policy and associated good managerial practices. Given the significance of sickness policy in the BWBS and some of the other case study chapters, this is no surprise but, at first glance, there was little to choose between what Strand did and what the other employers we studied did. In fact, the commercial development manager we talked to thought Strand had, as in many things, a

> traditional attitude, you have to keep the workers in their place kind of thing. And sickness … is a big deal … I learned recently they have some kind of measure, where they measure how often you're off sick and what days you're off sick, and they give you a result at the end of it. I don't know what mine is. Apparently, it's best to have three days off than it is just to have one day off.

She was referring to the Bradford Score (see p. 209) but we should add that she told us she used sick leave to cover for her children as she was a single parent and could not find alternative childcare. Certainly Strand used a similar framework for its sickness policy to more troubled employers, but the difference lay in how they operationalised their policy within this framework.

We heard a case study of how a manager worked with this policy from the line manager who described the way in which he, with the help of the man's colleagues, carefully and sensitively managed the absence of an employee with clinical depression in a manner which Walker and Fincham (2011) consider to be all too rare. The key to this was low-key but regular communication throughout the many months the man was absent. None of this was seen as invasive because the manager had a 'good rapport with my guys I guess and that helps', but the policy was also well-understood and widely seen as supportive by staff and certainly not as coercive. Nevertheless, he was well aware of the potential problems or pitfalls: 'It is quite a delicate situation, sort of just teeter around it and just have a chat with him to see how he is and how he is getting on, just to touch base really.'

Several employees mentioned the possibility of stigmatisation of Strand employees with impairments. With the potential for the stigmatisation of mental illness, there was always the possibility of non-disclosure and it was fortunate that this employee had told everyone he was depressive, including the manager. That meant 'everyone kind of helped along with the situation really ... and his colleagues kept in touch with him as well and made sure he was alright and just ... because they're friends really'. He actually found it helpful to his recovery to keep in touch and come in occasionally. Not that everyone could be so open; another member of the manager's team had a serious physical health problem and told nobody, not even when he went off for a major operation: 'no one knew where he was basically. And I didn't have his mobile or home phone number because he didn't want anyone to have that either.'

Good practice in the management of sickness absence meant paying careful attention to the return-to-work process. The employee with depression was phased in with part-time working and regular monitoring of how he was feeling. The line manager understood he had to 'tread carefully' and forcing him into full-time hours would have meant 'he's going to snap again and it's not going to be good for him or the company'. We wondered how he had the space to do this and whether there was any pressure on the manager to meet targets and get the work done. How could he afford this leisurely return to work? He agreed about the pressure – describing it in careful detail. Because he and his team worked on several projects at once, they had pressure from multiple sources. The people who were responsible for delivering those projects were all quite capable of pointing out that there was a man missing from the team working on their projects. The line manager insisted, however, that this might mean juggling, and sending work to some other sections/sites and working weekends, but it would not mean pushing someone to come back to work before occupational health said they were ready.

The white-collar convenor agreed. He thought Strand would 'bend over backwards to try and rehabilitate' workers with serious illnesses. This could include part-time working, changing duties or place of work, 'all kinds of things, provided they can kind of see an end to it'. Strand did not mind their employees managing their illness or condition at work, but they had to see a potential end to a sickness absence or they would move to a dismissal as incapable of the job or ill-health retirement (this was confirmed by the HR consultant). The convenor explained how this entailed difficult judgements; for example, there were some mental health problems that would eventually respond to medication and others that would not. He also told us how Strand HR countermanded a manager who wanted to sack someone diagnosed with bipolar disorder who did have effective medication (and the convenor knew very well that this would have been a DDA case if Strand had sacked this employee).

How did the convenor think Strand fared in respect of the DDA more generally? He had had a few potential DDA grievances that had all been very complicated. He said that once you got into a case it always seemed extremely difficult to see how the DDA could be applied to the benefit of the worker. He implied that this difficulty lay in the nature of the legislation rather than Strand's behaviour, and he told us, 'my genuine impression is that they will try to avoid breaching the law to the point where they're going to get claims against them' and they would make reasonable adjustments. Even though he gave Strand grudging praise in this respect, he thought disability was the poor relation in the equality and diversity field, perhaps because the idea of different treatment was so challenging. In effect, he argued for a move towards the adoption of the social model of disability. The blue-collar convenor was more critical of Strand. He said they did not have many employees with disabilities, certainly on the works side, and those who had became disadvantaged after they joined the company were 'penalised through ... people not understanding their disabilities'. He had one such case at the moment where a young employee who was covered by the DDA had been made redundant several times and was being refused a transfer to a job 'she's quite capable of doing', indeed had 12 years experience of doing it. She was taken off training while having treatment for cancer ... obviously, she's being disadvantaged because of her disability'.

The HR consultant agreed, 'DDA issues will make a case more complex', and it was up to the specialists designated to talk to employees who might be in this position to tease out such issues and, if need be, make the referral to occupational health. He thought they could cope even with a previously undisclosed DDA issue: 'I believe that we do very well in ensuring that we seek to make sure that we understand any conditions, make appropriate adjustments for those conditions, and certainly wherever possible, make sure that they can continue to be employed.' His examples including paying for staff at all levels to spend time on addiction programmes and for private consultations where employees were at the bottom of an NHS waiting list.

The consultant also thought Strand had been very proactive in making sure employees in general understood the implications of the DDA, including applications to the mental health problems the line manager had told us about ('if you get 25/30 people in a room, chances are that at least one of you is covered by the DDA, but you may not know it'). We could speculate whether such intervention was part of the reason the man's colleagues behaved so well in the case described above. The consultant also pointed to the expert advice available from the management HR helpline if there was uncertainty over whether something qualified as a DDA case or a case of harassment. In addition, there were promotions from the occupational health department about topics such as workplace stress, and the potential mental illnesses related to it, which should sensitise managers to these possibilities. Managers were also heavily dependent on occupational health for guidance (made freely available to the employee concerned) on what was appropriate action in individual cases. They had some success in getting people with mental health problems back to work in this way.

This, naturally enough, raises the question of Strand's treatment of work-induced stress. Most employees we talked to acknowledged that the company paid considerable attention to the topic. According to the supply chain manager we talked to, Strand did 'quite a bit of work there, from that point of view. They regularly communicate and put on courses where people can feel that they can learn about the stress levels and understand what to do about things'. He also reported life-coaching sessions (which were subsequently discontinued) in which employees could be helped to manage pressure across home and work. As this suggests, work-life balance was a potential source of stress that the employer could relieve with flexibility.

Flexibility for commitments outside work

We have already noted that a commercial development manager we interviewed used her own sick leave to provide cover if her child was sick:

> They expect you to take a day's holiday because you're not entitled ... you don't have to do legally, but they expect it. And the other thing is that my boss, again, says, 'Well my kids are never sick, we send them to school anyway, no matter', that kind of thing. And I just think well, 'what do you expect me to do when she's got a temperature, you expect me to send her to school?' I wouldn't feel right as a parent.

This manager's attitude might well be experienced as ill-treatment but what was the company policy? Our interviewee thought that they were not flexible and she paid the price for it when she racked up her sick leave and lost most of her holiday entitlement, but she did think other managers might be more flexible. Her resource manager had asked her to 'speak to me about it and we'll try and work something out where you can make up the hours and so on'. Indeed, this was what she did when her children visited their father ('So, I have a week of freedom that I can spend at work. Yippee!'), but this was not always possible because of the structure of work tasks in a 'very defined working week'. She also raised the question of working from home while caring for her children – easy if she had a laptop but Strand was not that 'advanced'. They 'talk about it a lot and certain people have laptops. And they tend to be managers or new graduates who are very valued in the company. But other people don't. And there doesn't seem to be any rhyme or reason'.

Where in the workplace an employee was situated, and the way the workflow was structured there, might have determined whether more flexibility was available short of working at home. The chief programme executive told us, 'I operate a fairly flexible kind of … It's not strictly flexitime but a flexible kind of working thing, so I don't, we focus more on deliverables than being at work, sort of thing.' This suggested that local senior managers like him had quite a bit of freedom in this respect, but lower down the hierarchy the ex-foreman simply did what the code he found in the online HR advice told him. If he was allowed to give them time off, 'whether it be for doctors' appointments, whether it be for dental or funerals', he would (though he was surprised to learn that one of his workers was allowed the day off to get married if it was for a *second time*). If the request came under an agreement where he could make up the time, the online code would tell him that too.

The HR consultant explained the policy framework behind this. Long-standing detailed agreements on how many hours blue-collar workers could take off, paid or unpaid, for every conceivable reason, had been overlaid by the 'new working arrangements'. Under these 'the focus went from attendance to delivery', although everyone had to put in their 37 hours. This meant that there was more informality and fewer people like the ex-foreman looking up HR online to find out the code for every eventuality. Indeed, blue-collar workers, like the ones he looked after, worked shorter hours than they did when the old agreements were struck. Since they now worked a nine-day fortnight they were 'encouraged' to take their time off on the tenth day.

None of this was particularly generous and, in the judgement of the white-collar convenor, Strand kept to the 'absolute bare minimum' required by law, for example, on paternity leave, because they were 'quite conservative' and not looking to take the lead. The HR consultant flatly disagreed: he said that Strand had better pay for 'things like maternity leave and all those sorts of things' than the statutory requirement. They allowed people to 'vary their working time because of family issues before even the legislation came in for the right to ask for part-time ... And certainly, we've got an ever-increasing number of people who are working part-time or varied hours for things relating to either personal issues, family issues, caring issues'. This did cause problems sometimes,

> [But he was] not aware of many occasions, almost if any, where we have not been able to provide some flexibility for somebody because of an issue. I mean, the expectation of us as a large employer is, if we have to find a job share to cover two halves to make one, that we ought to be able to do it. And sometimes it's difficult but, in general, we seek to be able to cover that.

The white-collar convenor thought Strand would certainly find it hard to argue in an employment tribunal that such a large company could not afford to cover a few people working part-time. The HR consultant also explained that Strand operated part-time or full-time career breaks.

We asked if managers might reply to such requests by saying 'if you take that kind of contract, you'll never get on in Strand'. The consultant said he didn't think so and, if such a thing was reported, 'we'd take an extremely dim view of it.' However, he admitted that the only way they would hear about this would be if an employee told HR his or her manager had turned down a request, or that they felt the employee's career had been adversely affected by making such a choice. The evidence was, however, that this had not happened because 'we have people who are part-time in some of our most senior positions'. There was 'potentially' some resentment about this from people who did not have dependents. After all, there was even resentment, passed on by the unions, about people taking smoking breaks. The white-collar convenor disagreed about where the balance of this resentment was; for example, in relation to family friendly policies, 'there is a thread of resentment in the company that they don't like that very much. ... less from other employees, mostly from the management.'

The importance of fairness and rationality

Sensible practices on sickness absence and flexible hours may have helped to ameliorate some of the effects of the riskier initiatives Strand was taking. We would argue that it was important that employees saw these practices as fair and rational, and the same applied to all the other policies that might affect employees, including selection for redundancy. The young project accountant was adamant that basing selection for redundancy on PDR was needed to keep her faith in the company: 'It's purely based on performance, not based on anything else. And I think that's very fair.' One of the benefits of fairness and rationality in the policies that employees *did* know about was that those same employees tended to assume that Strand was being fair and rational in the policies they knew little about. The supply chain manager, for example, expressed his faith in the company's policy on bullying and harassment in just these terms. He was very vague about what the procedure might actually be, but he trusted Strand to behave rationally and fairly because of the business imperatives of such a policy.

It was Strand doctrine that trade unions were crucial to keeping the appearance of reasonableness, rationality and fairness in place. For example, in planning redundancies, the senior HR director said they had 'fairly intensive discussions at early levels with a whole range of our employee representatives, partly because we're very highly unionised, so worldwide we're sort of at about the 70 per cent mark, which is pretty high'. The director said their communication structures with the union were 'gold-plated' rather than the 'bronze standard' required by legislation, and 'we tend to do a huge amount of communication around changing business issues, effect on workplace, trying not to get this element of surprise.' This was not to say that there could not be some difficulties in this relationship. In 2009, 18 months before we interviewed the director, the trade union convenor for hourly paid workers at Longstretton told us that he thought Strand was changing fundamentally, becoming more 'ruthless', and no longer bothered to consider alternatives to redundancy like retraining. The convenor had left Longstretton at the time we talked to the director, and she was undoubtedly relieved he had because relations with the shop floor 'can be a bit of a bumpier road. It will depend much more upon relationships that you have with particular power bases in the various parts of the shop floor'.

Strand's formal approach to employee and public relations

Alongside its relations with the trade unions, Strand operated successive initiatives which were designed to reinforce faith in the company and particularly in Strand's commitment to fair, rational and ethical behaviour. We are going to look at three of these programmes. The first was an integrated Strand People Framework which rolled together and updated the previous policies on such things as equality and diversity, dignity at work, and bullying and harassment. The framework was made available in one glossy booklet and on the intranet. There is no doubt that the employees we talked to were aware of both the framework and its predecessor policies. Although she did not think it made much difference to the behaviour of her colleagues, the logistics manager said, 'the one thing that Strand does really well, I think, is making sure that people who are non-British or of different skin colour or has got a disability of any sort, they bend over backwards to make sure you're okay.' Several of our interviewees told us they firmly believed Strand treated its employees fairly. Eighteen months later, the senior HR director was very happy that the latest engagement survey had some good news about fair treatment, for example, harassment of protected groups. This was 'an area universally that we actually see we get very positive results on' even amongst blue-collar employees.

We asked the HR consultant about the equality and diversity policies, and he, like many employees, found it difficult to 'remember all the bits and pieces'. All the same, he thought Strand had made big efforts in this area lately: 'There has been far more emphasis on the need to understand and ensure that we eliminate wherever we can issues around discrimination of any form.' Admittedly though, this was against a background of heavy male domination of the industry. It was very difficult to get women to think about doing engineering jobs so the machismo and banter remained, 'which we have to recognise and seek to help stamp out wherever we can'.

He thought it was a tough job breaking down sexism and misogyny and the white-collar convenor agreed – these were bigger issues than racism in the company – but he also agreed on 'creating a culture where people should expect to be respected, which I think on balance I'd have to say the company does try to do'. He also thought that the company had done its equality and diversity training very well. How did it look to those on the receiving end? The employees we talked to mostly said they would feel more confident about acting on things now. For example, the BME programme leader we interviewed would act on the abusive anonymous letters he received at his home address (but from work colleagues) some years ago. When it happened, he thought 'am I really totally safe here if I raise this any further?' A BME commercial development executive would act on the discrimination he repeatedly faced when he applied for promotion. He now thought the system to be much better and he would be prepared to 'take them to the cleaners'. Like others, he put much faith in the outside, confidential helpline that Strand had made available to its employees.

A woman project officer said that she had not made a complaint about bullying by her manager because she did not think the people whom she knew had witnessed the bullying would come forward, and she did not even want to approach them because she thought they might be ill-treated because they had spoken to her. Moreover, she said, 'some managers are very cliquey so if you'd have gone to the next level it would have been brushed under the carpet.' She also feared being 'blacklisted' and being singled out for redundancy herself, but these days, she would act because she knew there were support groups and she believed Strand was 'serious in supporting you'. She was particularly reassured by the 'external organisation that actually is brought in to deal with bullying', but she had only heard of this innovation by accident and, in cases such as hers, confidence was combined with vagueness about the details, a vagueness the HR consultant shared.

Some of the principles of the Strand People Framework were cross-referenced in Strand's Ethical Judgement Policy, an initiative which may have been kick-started by Strand's growing involvement in the United States where corporations were covered by the Foreign Corrupt Practices Act (1977) about bribing foreign officials. There had also been some unrelated, public relations debacles in the industry. It was unsurprising, then, that the senior HR director explained the point of the Ethical Judgement Policy was for customers to see Strand took its 'responsibilities seriously, not just in terms of the products we deliver, the communities in which we operate but also around how we conduct ourselves in doing that is quite important. So ethical judgement in that context was a very easy decision'.

We were interviewing at the time the policy was rolled out, and we found that the notion of ethical behaviour resonated strongly with some of the employees we talked to, employees like the commercial development executive who had told us that, no matter what power allowed people to get away with, 'morality is morality'. Like fairness and rationality, the perception that it behaves in an ethical manner strengthened the faith of Strand's employees in policies they actually knew very little about. Like the specialist illustrator, for example, they trusted Strand to be moral: 'They try to do the right thing, ethically definitely they do, which is why they have agreed to this, I am sure' – 'this' was the interview that we were conducting with her.

The chief programme executive certainly saw the connection with people's belief in Strand when he was hosting a few sessions on ethical judgement:

> And clearly ethics is quite a broad subject; it was actually just at the time when *The Telegraph* was rolling out their stuff [a series of scoops which sparked off the MPs' expenses scandal] – perfect introduction! And part of the ethics training is ethics in the workplace as well. So it kind of touches and emphasises a little bit on the People's Framework there.

For the supply chain manager, the policy was to do with 'mission statements such as the ethical and to be trustworthy and so on – respect. So I can imagine it stems from those sorts of beliefs or behaviours as well. I couldn't clearly state exactly in words what it is'. The project officer we interviewed was quite clear it was about 'not bringing the company into disrepute. So, for instance, talking to the ... newspaper or something about something you're involved in at Strand'.

The last of the three strategic interventions that we shall discuss was, according to the senior HR director, intended to educate employees in what mattered to Strand. As she put it, this involved picking 'stories' that chimed with employees' principles and helped to deepen their engagement. As part of her latest Vital Signs initiative, employees might be given real stories about people in life-threatening situations in which Strand employees' contribution may have saved lives. Vital Signs was explicitly intended to reinforce 'the reason for being in SGS and the reason for getting up in the morning and coming in and doing the work that you're doing' with which we started this chapter. For the director this was quite consciously about connecting with 'deeply held values and beliefs'. To achieve this, groups of employees received an interactive presentation 'with a combination of text, picture, intervention ... video, question and answer'.

Strand now did something like this every year. The director said, 'the theme might be the same but it's refreshed. And it's refreshed every year in terms of what is topical, what reinforces, what comes back to that sort of ... that core element that makes individuals very proud to work for Strand.' Her emphasis on the individual was telling and quite conscious, 'and it does sound trite, but it is finding appropriate ways to make every individual who works for you understand that what they do is important', and for the director, this made traditional forms of employee communication useless:

> The things that tend to work better in our environment is making it more *personal*, so how do we take the context of what is a very complex business, make it simple, make it relevant for an *individual* and *individuals* at very different levels of understanding of business, interest in the business and awareness of what goes on? How do we get them to a *common* understanding of what Strand is so that when we start to give very specific messages on things that are important to us they have a context?

Strand implemented these annual initiatives by telling managers it was their job to 'start to bring the jigsaw pieces together so that individuals, who would possibly only see one piece, can now see how that connects with a range of others to provide a picture and a story and it becomes meaningful'. They were given training and support to accomplish this, though pains were taken to try to ensure managers did not deliver a standardised experience. They must make it 'compelling' and 'direct, jargon-free', and they had to personalise the package for their teams. We saw some evidence of the way this could be done in the chief programme executive's teams 18 months earlier, and we would agree that for him, at least, it was 'very easy to create that compelling vision of what we all need to do'. The director also expected managers to 'encourage interaction, encourage questioning. So as a business we are reasonably comfortable, compared to the norm, with people challenging and asking questions, and we put a lot of time and effort into constructing avenues for employees to do that'.

Having said all of this, several employees told us that what the company did to reinforce employee commitment was nothing special. The commercial development officer thought Strand had started to make progress, but they needed to do more to communicate 'a bit more of a company kind of feeling ... giving us a bigger feeling of well actually we're part of this amazing organisation'. She and others saw Strand's stance towards its employees as traditional, even a bit backward, not cutting edge, but as having made some real improvements. The project officer said, 'over the years the company has got better, a lot better.' The white-collar convenor could find examples where 'the behaviours aren't right ... [but] probably the company gets it more right than wrong'. The commercial development officer agreed: Strand was 'progressing' though remaining more backward than her previous employer, 'It's a company that you have a lot of respect for, in terms of what they produce. And technically, I think they're very good but I do think in terms of employee relations, they're still quite behind when they should be.'

This is also a good point to recall the importance of adult-to-adult relationships to our interviewees, and some of them still considered that Strand needed to make progress here, particularly in the way young people were treated by managers and colleagues. The technician we have quoted extensively in this chapter explained the negative and uncooperative habits of behaviour this could breed, and he was happy that nowadays 'everybody's mature and reasonable, like you would have liked it always to be'. Others were not sure. The commercial development officer certainly thought Strand fell short of the mark in the way it treated its staff. Strand needed to show more respect to employees and

> treat them like adults and as people who are there, earning a living, running a household, grown-ups ... it feels a bit like ... I have to say a little bit like a teacher/child relationship sometimes, not actually you're a respected adult doing a job.

Strand's formal approach to trouble at work

Both trade union convenors thought Strand did not hesitate to deal with bullying and harassment unless the perpetrator was a manager. In fact the works convenor would have liked a bit less haste, and his preferred option was for managers to leave problems of bullying by colleagues to the union which would sort out the problem, probably by separating the two parties, without anyone losing their job. He had also taken 'statements and put them in envelopes, signed them with a date on. I said if it happens again, I'm going to give this to the company. And in the main, it ain't happened again, it's isolated incidents'. This worked well where, as they often were, people were reluctant to pursue the matter – in fact he thought 90 per cent of cases fizzled out.

We know, however, that ill-treatment by managers is the major element of trouble at work, and both convenors were dismissive of Strand's performance in this respect. The works convenor described how he persuaded a 'young lady' to take a complaint about a manager to a harassment counsellor in the new system Strand had introduced. As a result, she was called to a meeting with the manager in the same room, not a confrontation she wanted at all. He gave another example where, although a racial harassment case against him was successful some years ago, an employee was eventually reinstated as a supervisor. The convenor had no faith in the new policy: 'I think there's a lot of bullying goes on with management here that goes unnoticed, that goes undetected. I've seen grown men cry in here … worried about their job.' The white-collar convenor thought that most problems like these did not come to light because 'people don't rush to complain. You know, you don't come to work to create waves, do you? So if you have a bit of an arsehole as a manager, you know, you put up with it generally'.

We have mentioned before that Strand employees who would not have complained about bullying or harassment (or discrimination) in the past were sure that if the same thing happened again now they would act. As the white-collar convenor suggested, however, it was by no means certain they were in the majority. The commercial development officer told us she 'wouldn't go to personnel with a problem about my boss, unless it was something really major. Because ultimately, they're working for the company, they're not working for me. I'd be more likely to leave.' Others said things like 'there are certain things that you don't do in The Company … I think that your card gets marked. Maybe I shouldn't be saying this.' And they thought that complaints must lead to slow progress through normal channels or the Strand fast-track system.

Like the works convenor, the white-collar convenor believed Strand often acted in haste instead of 'trying to really burrow down and find out what's going on and dealing with the issue'. Investigations were conducted by a case management team (usually an independent manager and the case manager within HR):

> But it won't go beyond the statements they give, and they won't ever go out, look out and find out the truth behind it, other than to go back to the management team and say 'Is all this true?' 'No, it's not true'. 'Case dismissed' like.

However, neither convenor discussed the possibility of addressing a manager's ill-treatment through their PDR and development plan. The PDR scoring criteria may have made this a possibility but that seemed to be of scant comfort to those, like the Greek engineering team leader, who were told this would be the way bullying by her manager would be addressed. At the suggestion of her resource manager, she wanted something more tangible on the manager's record, but HR had said this was not possible unless she made a formal complaint. She felt it needed to be recorded to show that there was a pattern if it happened to someone else in future, and she made the link to ethical judgement and social responsibility: did they not require this safeguarding? Indeed, in this respect she thought she might have failed to meet her own moral responsibility by not following through the complaint herself.

The white-collar convenor was no keener on seeing a bullying manager sacked than the works convenor was to see his members sacked for bullying. He recalled a case in which harassment and bullying by a manager had happened in front of two witnesses. The subsequent investigation decided there had been inappropriate management behaviours, but nevertheless there was no grievance.

The rest of the team were so incensed they put in a collective grievance against this same manager, and some also alleged fraudulent behaviour. The company only acted on the latter and simply sacked the manager. The convenor would much rather they had kept him on and got to the bottom of the bullying. The team had not wanted him dismissed, 'they wanted him to behave in a different way. And because of the complete inability of the management team to really get to grips with it, it ended up with this guy being sacked.'

In another case he had handled, there were counter-allegations of harassment between employees but quite clear indications that the much more senior one of the two was more culpable. No action was taken against the more senior person but, if it had been the other way round, the convenor believed the junior person accused of improper behaviours would have been dismissed or disciplined simply on the evidence of a manager's complaint: 'The bullying and harassment policy on paper looks reasonable in terms of best practice. In practice, I don't think it's applied uniformly or fairly.'

What other improvements were suggested? The one thing we heard most often was that Strand did not follow through on the changes it wanted to make, including the initiatives that the senior HR director considered so vital. As we have seen, people could be extremely vague about the detail of what had been rolled out, and this applied to both bullying and harassment and the very recent Ethical Judgement initiative. The logistics manager thought that employees could talk to their trade union representative about bullying and harassment, and perhaps there was a confidential way of reporting it to headquarters. She also said, 'we do ethics and diversity training.' The specialist illustrator was clearer about bullying and harassment because we 'had a booklet recently', but the Ethical Judgement initiative had fallen on stony ground:

> We had another thing which was about ethnic recognition or something like that, I can't remember what the title of it was called, but it was everybody had to do it, it was a compulsory course ... Exactly that is what it was about really, is about the company image, essentially at the end of the day but they called it ethnic, ethical, I can't remember but it was ethical something or other because we were all coming back saying oh we have been ethically cleansed. Yes it was treated as a little bit of a joke by the staff I have to say.

She wasn't the only one who told us that nobody in their group took these roll-outs seriously. They frequently described them as 'tickbox activities' and reported colleagues' resistance to them. The commercial development officer told us about the homophobic comments made by managers on diversity training, 'what a waste of time it is and all this kind of stuff. So, I don't think it's well appreciated by the managers, is my impression. They do it because they have to do it. I don't think any of them really believe in it.'

Our technician interviewee talked about such 'negative attitudes to company initiatives' that they might even make things worse, for example, giving the shop floor ammunition to fire at management. He also noted the way the company neglected to explain the benefit of its initiatives once it had bedded in. Instead it was just one initiative after the other with no information on impact, and that meant people became disillusioned: '60 to 70 per cent of the people walk in there only so they can have a couple of hours off. And some people get around not going at all.' The white-collar convenor also drew attention to process compliance (making sure Strand always follows proper procedures, in other words) as 'one of those things that the company kind of majors on for a bit, and then it all seems to like drift out of consciousness a bit'.

The workforce's concern about all of these things was that Strand did not really care if anything changed or not, and they were putting out whatever initiative it was simply in order to 'tick a box'. As the project officer said,

> It's like, what's the latest, I don't know, environmental issues. The company now has issued everyone with a leaflet and so HR were involved in giving out the leaflets because it's a tick in the box. It's a corporate policy that they've got to be seen to have discussed and communicated to the rest of the function ... last week we had ethics training.

In other words, the appearance of doing something was all that was required. Who was the box being ticked *for*? Our interviewees weren't sure about this. Perhaps it was the government (or some other regulator), Strand's customers, public opinion, Strand's competitors, corporate or social fashion. The point was that, even if these were valid reasons, there had to be a business reason for doing it, as the BME engineer said, 'they have diversity policy and things like that, but the main thing behind all this improvement is that the company's realisation of wanting to realise that if the employees feel better then their performance is better and it is better for the company.' The employees we talked to wanted Strand to go the extra mile and find out whether there was evidence for that business case after a roll-out.

The white-collar convenor was one of those who thought it was corporate fashion which Strand was always trying to catch up with. When they did finally catch up with something, other companies had already moved on to the next thing. This meant that before Strand could 'really embed' its latest development, 'the next sort of wave of management nonsense comes along and they kind of leave all that and do something else'. He also thought that another reason for not embedding might be that different initiatives came from different senior managers, and the successive waves reflected the rise and fall of individuals' fortunes in political struggles. You would not then expect to see follow-through as there would be no widespread support at the top: 'Oh, you know, just let them fail and then we'll go back to what I want to do.' We need to bear in mind he was talking about changes which involved formal union agreements in which everyone was fired up to make a big change 'with a huge fanfare and great charts on the walls, and graphics, and seven 'Rs', and workshops'. The fanfare stopped and there was nothing else: 'You start the journey and then stop, you know, at the first services you stop and then never get moving again.'

Conclusions

In Chapter 9 we consider whether Strand's (formal and informal) approach to ill-treatment worked by preserving their employees' faith in the employer's commitment to them as individuals and to general principles of fairness and rationality. When we consider this qualitative support for the quantitative results reported in Part Two, particularly on the FARE score, we shall bear in mind that Strand was able to rely on a reservoir of employee belief, which was shrinking at Banco and may have dried up at Westshire. Strand could still test its employees – by making them fear for their jobs, for example – without damaging that belief. This even applied to those few members of minorities that Strand employed and who appeared to suffer a disproportionate share of ill-treatment. In Part Two, we suggested that minority employees may actually try to avoid workplaces which they suspect might be troubled. If effective, this tactic might lead to some minorities, for example, employees of Asian origin, being under-represented amongst workers who were ill-treated because they were under-represented in troubled workplaces. This chapter helps us to make it clear that Asian workers may still suffer more ill-treatment than white employees in the same workplace no matter whether they work in troubled or less troubled workplaces. Almost all the BME interviewees we talked to at Strand were of Asian origin. They may have suffered much more ill-treatment if they had gone to work in a troubled workplace, but they still had to put up with far worse than most Strand employees. It is worth adding that women (and perhaps also LGB) employees seemed to be in a similar position. The common thread to the ill-treatment received by minorities at Strand also recalls another of the results of our analysis of the BWBS. Members of all minorities reported that they had been told they were no good at their jobs and should not have been hired in the first place. While minority members reported some improvements in their time at Strand, it should be noted that this kind of ill-treatment was not necessarily addressed by Strand's formal or informal tactics for minimising trouble at work. We shall return to this point in Chapter 9.

PART FOUR

9

The Troubled Workplace

Although the literature we discussed in Chapter 1 was largely concerned with workplace bullying, rather than the broader category of trouble at work, many of the topics covered in that literature have reappeared in our analyses, although we have not always presented them in the same terms as the bullying researchers. For example, most of the ill-treatment we found was of employees by their managers, but we found it more helpful to interpret this finding in terms of conflicts over authority and control rather than power distance. Moreover, we found that it was generally not the weakest and most vulnerable workers who reported the most ill-treatment. Other subjects discussed in Chapter 1 which received extensive coverage in our analyses included autonomy, communication in organisations, conflict escalation, employee participation and representation, high-commitment HR management, job insecurity, industries and sectors, leadership, management styles, minorities, occupations, organisational change (including chaotic workplaces), role conflict and role ambiguity, routine organisational processes and activities, workload and work intensification, workplace culture and workplace diversity. In this chapter, we shall summarise our findings on all of these themes, however, even though there is some overlap between bullying and trouble at work (see pp. 25–6); we do not think it would be legitimate to suggest that our findings confirm or challenge those of the bullying literature. In fact, we shall only refer back to those parts of the literature that we think have paved the way for a more sociological approach.

We have not looked to psychological factors to explain why any of these subjects are relevant to, indeed can help us to explain, trouble at work. Instead, we have looked to the characteristics of the workplace itself. Our research has revealed the two workplace characteristics which are most strongly associated with trouble at work: conflict with employers over workplace norms and the ill-treatment of those who provide public services by members of the public. Where one or both of these vectors for trouble at work is present, there will be an increased chance of a troubled workplace which has a concentration of ill-treatment. Employees who work in a troubled workplace are more at risk of ill-treatment than other employees, and the members of the troubled minority are largely drawn from their ranks.

In the following section, we illustrate how different the sociological approach is from the individualised medical and psychological approaches by exploring the different views taken in each approach about the harm caused by trouble at work. It is most commonly assumed in the literatures on bullying and stress that ill-treatment is a problem for everyone concerned, including the employer, and not just those who suffer directly from bullying and stress. The sociological approach makes no such assumption and we discuss the extent to which our research has suggested that some employers may not only encourage trouble at work but, as suggested by Beale and Hoel (2011), actually benefit from it. Before we do this, however, we must summarise what we know about the impact on employees of trouble at work.

Whose trouble is it?

By saying trouble at work has more sociological coherence than either workplace bullying or work-related stress, we are not denying that ill-treatment has very serious effects on people's health, finances, relations with family and friends, relations with their employer and their feelings about their work. All of these effects were documented in the first half of this book, but it is also worth remembering that the aspects of trouble at work which we had initially thought would be most serious were not always those which employees identified as having the most impact on them. Unreasonable treatment had greater impact than denigration or disrespect and the violence from clients and others, which employees seemed to be so reluctant to consider as criminal behaviour.

Although managers were responsible for quite a bit of incivility and disrespect, they were responsible for most unreasonable treatment. It was this kind of ill-treatment that signified something had gone wrong in an employee's relations with his or her employer, and which affected his or her feelings about work, and we argue that this was why employees felt it had the greatest impact on them. In order to fully understand this finding, we need to bear in mind just how important work seemed to be – not as a means to an end (such as status or income) but as an end in itself – to the vast majority of the people we interviewed in our case studies. The meaning and significance people found in their work lives, and the emotional satisfaction it gave them, were obvious, though perhaps not unexpected, at Strand and Westshire and even Banco. It is therefore worth recalling that most Britscope employees also felt like this. Indeed, we described their expression of positive commitment to their work as a striking feature of the Britscope interviews. Two-thirds of the interviewees reported in different ways that they enjoyed their jobs. Some went so far as to say that they loved the work and felt 'proud' to work for the organisation. When we remember that this level of commitment was central to many of our interviews, we can see how people might be particularly affected by treatment which seemed to demonstrate that their work was not valued, and their employer felt no reciprocal commitment.

In fact, the key to changing how people felt about work was – as Pearson *et al.* (2001) might have predicted – the presence of a *moral* element in the employer's evaluation. Many of our interviewees told us they had been model employees – always being prepared to go the extra mile, like the Strand workers who were prepared to do something 'a bit special' or the Britscope employees who never wanted to take time off when they were ill – but found themselves no longer well regarded for reasons they could not fathom. To such employees, trouble at work felt like an existential crisis: what they used to believe was best for the organisation, and their clients or customers, and what they used to be praised for doing was no longer good enough. It was through the experience of ill-treatment – both unreasonable treatment and incivility and disrespect – that an employee learnt that his or her employer had found himself or herself at fault.

The very fact that an employer seeks to change the way an employee works is sufficient proof that the employer is no longer satisfied with the employee's work; yet this need not amount to blaming them, and thereby devaluing the work they have done, and personal sacrifices they have made in the past. It is perfectly possible for past contributions to be fully recognised even when employer and employees agree that newer, and better, ways of working are now possible. It is, however, unlikely that this will happen where employees are being ill-treated. Employees told us that ill-treatment signalled to them they were mistaken to believe their work had been valued in the past and, in their conversations with us, they revealed some of the deep-seated conflicts which underlie trouble at work. Where they had been convinced they had been model employees, the ill-treatment meted out by their employer was now signalling something completely different.

In these cases, ill-treatment was a marker for a fundamental disagreement between employer and employee about the nature of valued work (as described by Roscigno, Hodson and Lopez 2009). No matter how steadfastly the employee held to the view that they have been a good and valuable employee, they now knew that their employer thought they were deluded. It was this slur on their integrity – or dignity (Bolton 2007; Hodson 2001; Hoel and Beale 2006; Peyton 2003; Rayman 2001) – that had such a great impact on so many of the employees in our study. It is perhaps not too dramatic to say that the experience demoralised them, not simply in the conventional sense of lowering their morale but also in the sense that it showed that others were prepared to question whether they were behaving in a moral way. This is something that a clinical idea of stress (Walker and Fincham 2011), or a psychological concept of bullying, struggles to encompass but it is all of a piece with the classic sociological concern – present in the writings of both Adam Ferguson and Émile Durkheim, for example – with moral relations between people (Fevre 2001; Pearson *et al.* 2001).

The literatures on bullying and stress would not, of course, deny the effect of ill-treatment on morale. Indeed, the effects of lowered morale on productivity, attendance and labour turnover (resulting in the associated costs of hiring and training) routinely make up the prime elements in any calculation of the cost of bullying to employers (Beale and Hoel 2011: 14). As we hinted at the end of the previous section, these literatures thereby assume that ill-treatment is as much a problem for the employer as it is for the employee. If it is assumed that ill-treatment results from the behaviour of bullies in the workplace – who are as, or more, likely to be co-workers than managers – this might seem a logical conclusion to reach. Yet when our study shows the dominant role managers play in creating trouble at work, this is bound to raise the question of why managers persist in condoning, if not causing, trouble at work if it loses them money. This also reveals one of the major defects of the usual calculation of the costs of bullying to employers: not only are such calculations usually based on guesswork about costs and, especially, any productivity effects, but they almost never balance these costs with any *gains* that might accrue from ill-treatment.

In our analysis, we have not assumed that trouble for one side of the key moral relation between employees and employers necessarily spells trouble for the other. Indeed, our research has demonstrated what Beale and Hoel (2011) proposed: that employers might be quite prepared to put up with a bit of trouble to achieve their aims. Perhaps the best way to grasp this point is to discuss those situations where employers were trying to change the terms of their relationship with their employees. We are not denying that, if employees associate organisational change with trouble at work, this can sometimes cause difficulties for employers. We shall consider the possibility that some employers are put in this position by managers who either do not understand what is in the best interests of their employer or are incapable of acting on this knowledge. For now, however, we need to raise the possibility that trouble at work is a price employers are willing to pay when they view change as essential to the progress of the business. If change cannot be achieved by methods which avoid upsetting the workforce, then so be it. We also have to consider the possibility that, for some employers, it could be that upsetting the workforce is actually the object, inherent to the change they want to bring about.

From what we learnt in our research, for example, at Britscope and Banco, it is not at all far-fetched to suggest that employers may sometimes want to shake up the way that employees feel about their work and their relations with their employer, to shift them out of their comfort zone and dispel their complacency. In such instances, the usefulness to employers of the notion of an identity of interests between capital and labour is at an end and, if not wishing to demoralise their workers, employers may certainly want to make them uncertain of their position, and worth, and anxious to please. So, either because it is a necessary means to an end or because it is an end in itself, employers may consciously set out to create trouble at work. In this case, the association between change and ill-treatment is a result of the employers' actions. They are prepared to risk the demoralisation (in both senses) of their own workforce because of the fundamental disagreement they have with their employees over the nature of valued work.

In order to fully understand the normative conflicts that occur in such cases, we ought to recall that the BWBS showed that, for the most part, trouble at work was not about bad employers victimising the marginal and vulnerable. In fact, it was the more privileged employees who were more likely to complain about their employers, and particularly their managers. It is no surprise to us that, when the pretence that employers and employees have identical interests is dropped, the strongest employees are most likely to stand up for themselves. Of course, from the employers' side of the normative conflict these complaints might be heard as cries of pain from the comparatively well-off who felt they were being asked to work a bit too hard or take less time off. Or perhaps they were being given more oversight and less freedom to do what they liked.

In such normative conflicts, British employers (and a succession of sympathetic governments) can argue that trouble at work is the necessary price that must be paid to modernise unproductive work practices. Thus it was argued that Britscope's effort to bargain with its employees had been struck when the organisation was in a very different market situation and faced little if any (and often non-unionised) competition. Similarly, Banco was trying to do something about unprofitable parts of its organisation apparently operating on the wrong business model with outdated practices. Indeed, Westshire had benefited from considerable investment but was struggling to show the benefit of all this spending because, the employers argued (under political pressure), of unproductive work practices. It should not be forgotten, however, that these *are* the employers' accounts and that they were contested.

The BWBS provided evidence that organisational change is associated with ill-treatment, but it is also important to remember the type of change that was involved. The evidence was strongest in respect of employees' reports of loss of control. This factor was more strongly associated with all three types of trouble at work than almost any other factor in our analyses. It is of considerable importance to the interpretation of this finding that simply working in a job with low autonomy was not associated with any kind of trouble at work. We take this as evidence that, when they added ill-treatment to reduced autonomy, employers were trying to take relatively privileged employees down a peg or two, wrest the initiative from them, enforce the manager's right to manage and move the business on in the way they wanted to. From their viewpoint, this made obvious sense but it did, however, risk demoralising the employees who were on the receiving end.

Employees who work in a job with little autonomy will have no prima facie reason to believe they have failed to fulfil others' expectations of them, but an employee who has *lost* autonomy and, at the same time, been subject to ill-treatment is much more likely to reach this conclusion. While their managers may feel that they are simply reasserting their right to manage in order to redress a problem, from the employees' point of view it seems that their input, apparently so valued in the past, is no longer needed and, indeed, might be part of the problem managers are addressing. This was a feeling that the financial advisers of Banco appeared to share with those who complained of the 'target culture' replacing professional judgement at Westshire. In both cases, where once employee autonomy had been indispensable to the success of the organisation, it was now an obstacle. The turning of a potential difference of opinion into actual conflict was marked by the occurrence of ill-treatment. This ill-treatment might reside in the tactics employers used to force through the changes they wanted to make, or employees might simply see the accomplishment of these changes as constituting ill-treatment. At Banco, for example, the field force of financial advisors complained both that their loss of autonomy amounted to unreasonable treatment *and* that their managers were treating them with incivility and disrespect as a tactic to achieve the changes they wanted.

If the combination of reduced autonomy and ill-treatment was clear evidence of deep-seated conflict over the nature of workplace norms, the same applied to those cases where employees experienced a combination of ill-treatment and super-intense work. Where trouble at work was associated with working too intensely, there was a conflict over what level of work was appropriate or possible. Like less control, super-intense work was strongly associated with all three types of trouble at work, whereas the alternative measure of *increased* pace of work only predicted one type, unreasonable treatment. There is, therefore, a possibility that less conflict was entailed when work intensification occurred than in cases where employees simply felt the work they already had was too intense. It may be that, in a similar way to the Banco example in the previous paragraph, employees saw an increase in the pace of work as constituting unreasonable treatment in itself. It could also be that there was more scope for employees to agree increasing the pace was reasonable – because, presumably, they had spare capacity – than there was for them to agree that they should be working too intensely.

People's judgements about whether they have spare capacity, or are being asked to do too much, are obviously amenable to clinical assessment, for example, of levels of stress, but such judgements are also social ones (Walker and Fincham 2011). Deciding that work is too intense is not just a matter of employees diagnosing the causes of their own physical or psychological symptoms. Take the Britscope employees who said they could not manage to complete their schedules yet still considered themselves model employees, or the Westshire employees who were forced to come in at weekends and evenings to cover the work of colleagues who were sick. In both cases, employees believed the level of work they were being asked to cope with was being deliberately increased by understaffing. This belief, rather than how tired or stressed they felt, was the key to their disagreement with their employer about the level of intensity of work that was appropriate. For example, at Westshire we heard many complaints of the 'overbooking' of clients in an attempt to meet performance targets and of understaffing as leavers were not replaced because budgets were cut.

Of course, managers at Westshire or Britscope saw things differently. The combination of ill-treatment and super-intense work signified a conflict over what level of work was appropriate so we would expect that the level of work which the employees complained about would be seen as perfectly reasonable. Thus managers would believe employees were attempting to limit their effort in order to keep employment higher than it needed to be to the detriment of the company and their own job security. Therefore, understanding conflicts over work intensity requires us to do more than measure workers' stress and well-being since they have a great deal to do with what used to be known as industrial relations issues about appropriate staffing levels and, even more fundamentally, what constitutes a fair day's work (Beale and Hoel 2010, 2011; Hoel and Beale 2006; Ironside and Seifert 2003; Roscigno, Hodson and Lopez 2009; Walker and Fincham 2011).

Thus far, we have been treating not only the employer as a single actor – something we shall address when we consider whether managers ever act against their employer's interests – but also employees as a homogeneous group. From our survey, we are aware that we know very well this could be misleading. Based on results for the troubled minority, roughly one in five incidents of unreasonable treatment and incivility and disrespect (and one in 10 incidents of workplace violence) took place between co-workers. In the case studies, too, we heard of ill-treatment by employees, even in relatively untroubled workplaces. At Strand, for example, we heard a white-collar employee use the term 'viper pits' when describing particular groups of blue-collar workers, and we heard a fitter describe the places where managers and engineers worked on the shop floor as 'pig pens'. We would argue, however, that managers and employers were directly implicated in much of the inter-employee conflict revealed by the survey and the case studies. For example, at Britscope we heard several complaints from employees about managerial reluctance to tackle the problem of fellow workers who were thought to be not pulling their weight. This was perceived by Strand managers to be the most common complaint made by employees, for example, as measured in employee engagement surveys. Evidence of employee concern, and indeed anger, over this perceived unfairness featured in several of our interviews.

It seems conflict between employees at Strand was actually exacerbated because it took the task of making change without initiating conflict very seriously, and some employees saw this as unduly lenient to others. All the same, we would not expect the association between ill-treatment and reduced autonomy or super-intense work to be anything like as strong there as it was in other companies, for example, Britscope. In general, Strand appears to have been extremely reluctant to consider the ill-treatment of its employees to be a price worth paying in order to get its employees to match global standards of productivity and innovation. In the chapter on Strand, we described ways in which the relations between employers and employees might be so constituted, and so managed, that it was possible for employees to accept that a fundamental change to the way they worked was both fair and reasonable. It is possible that the employers who, unlike Strand, see trouble as a necessary but unwelcome side effect of change simply lack the capacity or competence to be able avoid it. It is also possible, as we have hinted already, that any capacity problem points to deficiencies in managers (see p. 139). We should, however, bear in mind that Strand employees earned considerably more than the majority of Briscope and Banco employees and possessed high-level skills that were valuable to their employer.

Reduced autonomy and super-intense work were not the only characteristics which were associated with ill-treatment in the BWBS. The association between all three categories of ill-treatment and all of the FARE questions was just as strong, if not more so, and this led us to similar conclusions. If people were more likely to report ill-treatment if they had not been treated as individuals, had to compromise their principles, or found the needs of their organisation always came first, this suggested there were deep-seated conflicts between employees and employers about workplace norms. If they reported that they compromised their principles but did not report ill-treatment, we must assume there was no deep-seated conflict and, perhaps, employees had low expectations of respect and fairness in the workplace.

It is important to give some examples from the case studies of the kind of conflict that can occur in respect of each of the FARE questions. There were many examples in our case studies of employees complaining of ill-treatment in relation to not being treated as individuals. For example, we were told of employers failing to recognise the special nature of a model employee's contribution and the individual needs of employees. The needs of individual employees which were not recognised by employers might be the training they needed to help them do their jobs better or needs associated with their health problems or impairments. Time after time we were told – for example, by Britscope employees – that employees with health problems were not being treated as individuals. Other examples of ill-treatment associated with not treating people as individuals concerned employers' attitudes towards their clients or customers. For example, Banco employees complained of the way they were no longer allowed to tailor their service to customers to fit their individual needs.

This example from Banco illustrates the difficulty of finding examples which apply to only one of the FARE questions, since treating customers in this way may well require an employee to compromise their principles. This is what Banco employees thought was happening when they were made to comply with the new high-pressure sales practices introduced by the company. Banco had created the conflict by telling its employees to change their relationship with their customers in a way some of them found morally objectionable. Westshire employees also reported conflict over moral principles to be a correlate of trouble at work. Many of them assured us that they were morally principled and strongly determined to defend those principles even when this led to conflict with their employer – for example, when they felt that managerial targets were placed ahead of the needs of patients or clinical priorities – and trouble at work.

Either of these cases could be used to illustrate examples of ill-treatment where employees felt the needs of their organisation always came before the needs of people, whether they be Banco customers or Westshire patients. In Westshire, for example, employees felt that managers categorised patients as a single homogenous group. Thus in Chapter 7 we gave the example of one employee who dealt with children with learning disorders, who complained that the organisation failed to take into account the varying needs of a child with autism and one suffering less severe learning difficulties. Such differences would interfere with the standardised measuring requirements of the target culture. The political impetus behind this culture may have made it easier for managers to excuse themselves from responsibility for such failures.

As in the discussion of conflict over reduced autonomy and super-intense work, we must acknowledge that the existence of conflict over the issues covered by the FARE questions means that employers will have a very different view of things to the employees who are concerned about these issues. For example, Britscope managers would argue that their sickness absence procedure was fair because it applied to all its employees in the same way, and the logic behind the three-stage warning procedure was soundly based on good practice and academic research (which led to the ubiquitous Bradford score for evaluating employee absences). Banco managers would insist that the changes they introduced were not to the detriment of their customers and had a strong business rationale. Without them they could not continue to provide the services and products their customers wanted. Westshire managers would say they were finding ways to deliver an effective public service without wasting money.

However, the example of the way Strand treated its employees or, at least, its white-collar employees, reminds us that employers can pursue their objectives without courting conflict. Perhaps this depends, however, on the kinds of objectives they have in mind and short-term goals like reducing costs which may conflict with treating people as individuals, not compromising their principles, or making sure the needs of the organisation do not always come first. Strand was a very successful company operating in a sector where taking a medium- to long-term view was the norm. This is a good point to recall some of the work that Strand had done, with an eye to the medium to long term, to persuade its employees that they were treated as individuals, that their principles were safe at Strand and that the needs of the organisation did not always come first. While we do this, we can see that Strand was far better placed, and far better resourced, than most organisations to be able to deliver this work.

We have already reminded readers of Strand's policy on personal development which our respondents believed was fully responsive to individual needs. We remember from Chapter 8 that Strand's policy of moving employees around the company meant people could leave troubled situations but also reinforced their belief in the FARE principles; for example, they were made to feel that their development plan really was personal. We described Strand's initiatives designed to reinforce commitment to principled behaviour, and we noted that many employees volunteered that they believed Strand operated in just this way. In particular, we commented on the success of the Ethical Judgement Policy in reinforcing Strand's ethical approach to its employees even though it was designed to address other concerns, specifically Strand's approach to doing business with foreign governments. We concluded that when Strand employees believed the company behaved in a fair, rational and ethical manner they assumed that this also applied to everything they did, including things our respondents knew very little about. This had once, perhaps, also been the case in all of our cases studies, but the employees of Britscope and Westshire had largely lost their faith in their employers. At Banco, the formal commitment to ethical behaviour was as strong as ever, but some staff now believed it to be empty rhetoric.

Of course, the initiatives that Strand took to reinforce their employees' belief that the organisation's moral principles coincided with their own were also an occasion for emphasising the way in which employees were treated as individuals. We heard that, as part of the process of connecting with 'deeply held values and beliefs', Strand had to find 'ways to make every individual … understand that what they do is important'. This meant communication had to be '*personal* … relevant for an *individual*', and it was very important to Strand that this appeared to be a two-way street with managers encouraging employees to raise difficult and challenging questions. A prime example of the evidence Strand employees could point to in order to show their employer did not always put the organisation before people was the implementation of their sick leave policy. For example, in the case of the employee with clinical depression, described in some detail in Chapter 8, the health of the employee was the company's priority throughout (cf. Walker and Fincham 2011). Whatever formal policies might say, the way that sickness absence was handled in practice tended to suggest Strand had a genuine concern for its employees.

Sick leave, return to work and adjustments to work, and the workplace, were all made in order to accommodate the individual needs of employees.

These are the conditions an employer needs and, indeed nurtures, in order to avoid the generation of conflicts with its employees. For example, the presumption that most white-collar employees at Strand would make about any changes the company initiated would be that they would give no genuine cause for concern. This all sounds like a lot of work for a company to have to engage in to keep its employees onside, but we must not forget that Strand employees were ready to generalise their belief in Strand's good behaviour well beyond those occasions when they had access to some evidence to justify their faith. The conflicts that can lead to trouble at work occur because organisations fail to measure up to the commitment to rationality, fairness and respect that their employees expect, but employees are generally well disposed to believe that their expectations are being met. This is perhaps because they assume that the default settings of bureaucracies and markets – especially in 'modernity's shop window' – are always set on rationality and fairness and respect. Employees believe that emotions are irrational and dangerous and that it is reason that guarantees civility and respect. It is not religious convictions, or secular love for fellow man, that the Strand employees thank for the sympathy and forbearance and forgiveness they show each other. As they all told us, this was simply 'treating each other as adults' in the way which would be expected in a rational organisation.

We have discussed what employers can do to keep employees onside, so minimising conflicts and indirectly keeping trouble at work low, but we have not fully dealt with the question of what employers can do to avoid trouble at work. The remaining issues concern what companies can do more directly to minimise troubles at work through company policies on dignity at work and sickness absence, improving the quality of management and leadership, and managing relations with employees and the employees' relations with each other. Before this, we conclude this section by discussing those explanations of trouble at work which point outside the workplace to wider social problems. In a moment, we shall summarise what we know about the treatment of employees within the various equality strands, but first we turn our attention to the ill-treatment of employees in the public sector and violence in the workplace both within the public sector and more generally.

We mentioned, at the beginning of the chapter, that the second main sociological factor behind trouble at work concerned the risks of ill-treatment from the public when providing a public service. In Chapter 3, we learnt that public sector workers were more likely to experience incivility and disrespect, and in Chapter 4 we learnt that they were also more likely to experience violence. In both cases, we were satisfied this was largely a matter of ill-treatment from people who were not managers or fellow employees. Rather, ill-treatment originated with the clients of public service organisations and other members of the public employees of these organisations come into contact with. Because of this ill-treatment from the public, these public sector workplaces were on a par with workplaces that were troubled for the other reasons we have already discussed: the conflicts over workplace norms occasioned over reduced autonomy, super-intense work or questions of fairness and respect. There was no evidence that any of these normative conflicts were more likely in the public sector, but the behaviour of clients and others filled the gap.

For the BWBS sample as a whole, working in the public sector made an employee much more likely to experience a variety of different types of incivility and disrespect. Within the troubled minority, being in the public sector increased the risk of being humiliated or ridiculed in connection with work. This is consistent with the idea that the troubled minority were almost all working within troubled workplaces. Employees in troubled workplaces outside the public sector also experienced incivility and disrespect and, for the most part, they experienced it to the same degree as workers in the public sector. The exception was humiliation which, we have just noted, remained much more likely in the public sector. To put it another way, a public sector workplace ended up in the category of troubled workplace because the incivility and disrespect from the public made up for the lack of incivility and disrespect from colleagues and managers. That being said, the humiliation and ridicule dished out to public service employees had no counterpart in the private or third sectors. Some service users, it seems, think that humiliation and ridicule is an appropriate response to the services they receive.

Before we go on to discuss violence in troubled workplaces, and particularly within the public sector, we need to remind readers of the way in which we are interpreting the differences between results for the troubled minority and the sample as a whole. By far the most important factors in determining whether an individual employee will be ill-treated are those which make for troubled workplaces. The impact of these factors is so great that the fine detail of further differences between troubled workplaces is largely invisible in any analysis for the sample as a whole. Once we shift to the analysis of the troubled minority – most of whom work in troubled workplaces – this fine detail becomes visible because the factors which mark out troubled workplaces are no longer dominating the picture.

Thus, in Chapter 2, we explained that it was likely that ill-treatment of the troubled minority would have different correlates for ill-treatment than the wider sample. Because members of the troubled minority were more likely to work in a troubled workplace to begin with, the factors that distinguished troubled workplaces would not show up strongly, or at all, in an analysis of the ill-treatment they experienced. Multivariate analysis of the troubled minority did not reveal the factors distinguishing a troubled from an untroubled workplace but rather what factors dictated who had the worst experience inside troubled workplaces. To make this clearer, we gave the hypothetical example of a particular group of workers which experienced less ill-treatment because they avoided working in troubled workplaces. They might do this because they knew that in those workplaces they would certainly experience much more ill-treatment than anyone else. The result of such a pattern would be that this group suffered less ill-treatment overall but more ill-treatment when they were unfortunate enough to appear within the troubled minority.

We know now that women in the BWBS fitted this hypothetical pattern to the extent that women were more likely than men to suffer some forms of ill-treatment in troubled workplaces (see p. 77). We also know that this effect was not visible in the sample as a whole because it was masked by the factors which distinguish troubled workplaces. Women were no more likely to work in troubled workplaces than men, and having the misfortune to work in a troubled workplace was a much more important factor in determining an employee's chances of ill-treatment than anything else, including gender. This factor was so big that it could swamp a gender effect even if it was common to all workplaces. Although we shall not labour this point each time we discuss the troubled minority and troubled workplaces, readers should at least bear in mind the possibility that the detailed patterns we found within them (particularly for disability, gender, sexual orientation and ethnicity) could also apply to all workplaces. In the terms of the hypothetical example we used in Chapter 2, any one of these groups might try to avoid troubled workplaces because they expect to be particularly badly treated there. They might also suffer more ill-treatment than others in untroubled workplaces, but this effect would be masked by the effect of their avoidance of the worst workplaces.

All of the analysis of violence we have presented has, of necessity, referred to the troubled minority, so we would not expect multivariate analysis of the correlates of violence and/or injury to be able to show us those factors which distinguished those who were employed in troubled workplaces from the rest. Since the bulk of violence took place in troubled workplaces which had concentrations of all types of ill-treatment, we would expect that violence, just like unreasonable treatment and incivility and disrespect, would be greater where there was conflict over workplace norms or ill-treatment from the public. In fact, multivariate analysis showed that, even within troubled workplaces, injury from violence was more common where people were not treated as individuals. This suggests that, to some extent, conflict over these norms even served to distinguish troubled workplaces where workers experienced violence from troubled workplaces where they did not. There were greater effects from other factors, but it does seem that employers could probably do more to ameliorate workplace conditions that contribute to violence and injury from clients and other members of the public. Similarly, the association between injury and not treating people as individuals may have something to do with employees' dissatisfaction with employers' responses to injuries inflicted at work.

Within the group of troubled workplaces, violence and injury were far more likely to occur in the public sector and in workplaces with higher proportions of BME and women workers. So it was not just public service that exposed employees to violence and injury, but employment in public service workplaces which tended to employ higher proportions of BME workers and women – as might be the case in health and social care, for instance (compare to Hodson *et al.* 2006 on workplace diversity in Chapter 1). The public sector had more of the troubled workplaces where employees were exposed to violence, but this experience was not common to all the workplaces in the public sector. This makes perfect sense because we know that clients and other members of the general public were responsible for the great majority of violence and injury, and we also know that employees in some public sector workplaces have more face-to-face contact with clients and other members of the public. We also know some public sector organisations, particularly those tasked with the delivery of public services, have more potential for both conflict with clients, and others, and contact with potentially violent people.

We suggested above that employees tend to assume that the default settings of bureaucracies and markets are set on rationality and fairness and respect. Employees tend to believe that emotions are irrational and dangerous and see reason as the guarantor of civility and respect (Bauman 1991, 1993). The reasoned, restrained and temperate reaction of organisations to the incivility and disrespect, and violence and injury, meted out to some public servants is only what most of us would expect. Indeed, it is the expectation of the public servants themselves, who tend to take it in their stride as part of the job, perhaps not even recognising criminal behaviour. But just because public servants are prepared to put up with this ill-treatment, should the rest of us be? Managers were more likely to report violence and injury, but so were the associate professionals and personal service workers in health and social work, public administration and defence, and in education, some of whom were comparatively poorly paid employees. Should we really be prepared to accept that this ill-treatment is an unavoidable feature of some not very well-paid jobs in the public sector?

When we said that employers might sometimes set out to create trouble at work we were thinking, typically, of the tactics used by aggressive managers who were determined to ignore resistance from what they felt were intransigent employees. But here we have another employer, the state (or, to put it another way, all of us), creating trouble at work for its employees by exposing them to incivility and disrespect, and violence and injury. We would not deny that ill-treatment, or the threat of ill-treatment, can have an adverse effect on the quality of public services. For example, a succession of enquiries into the deaths of children who were known to social services has suggested that the public servants who might have helped to prevent these deaths were themselves intimidated by the adults responsible (for social workers' experiences of violence, see Denney 2010; Harris and Leather 2011). Nevertheless, as we argued in relation to conflicts over norms, we would question whether a sophisticated calculation of the *net* costs to the taxpayer of the exposure of public servants to ill-treatment would suggest that this also represents trouble for the employer. Paying the hospital bills and compensation claims of injured employees and recruiting and training of replacements for those who leave their jobs to escape ill-treatment are relatively cheap compared to the cost of organising public service in such a way that the ill-treatment of public servants is reduced. Consider, for example, the expense of market solutions to issues of safety and security in education and social care. We may not be exposing public servants to trouble at work for commercial gain, but it is certainly done with an eye on the cost to the taxpayer. It might be salutary to be able to compare this cost to the (presumably paltry) cost of the dubiously effective zero-tolerance approach towards violence against public servants.

We conclude this section on who suffers from trouble at work with some discussion of the various groups of employees covered by equalities legislation. We begin with the employees with disabilities and health problems who we know were more likely to experience both unreasonable treatment and incivility and disrespect. In common with other equality strands, the presence of a disabled employee was a predictor of troubled workplaces. It might be possible that this tells us something about the kinds of organisations which employ people with disabilities or health problems, but, in common with Walker and Fincham (2011) we think the presence of employees with disabilities and health problems can lead to conflicts over workplace norms in the same way as the conflicts between employers and employees described earlier. Conflicts with employees with disabilities over the type work they are given and their performance, their rewards and entitlements, and their attendance and hours of work are all closely related to the conflicts over norms for autonomy, work intensity, fairness and respect. We might even say that these are sometimes the same issues simply recast with special reference to people with disabilities.

From an analysis of thousands of company employee engagement surveys, Schur *et al.* (2009) found that employees with disabilities did not feel more marginalised or disadvantaged in companies that all employees thought were more fair and responsive. They thought this confirmed an earlier theory which identified the fair and responsive treatment of all employees as the key to the treatment of workers with disabilities because, at least in part, employees without disabilities would not see adjustments made for workers with disabilities as special treatment. This would be another plausible reason why the presence of workers with disabilities would be a key predictor of troubled workplaces.

This analysis is particularly applicable, we believe, to employees with other health conditions. Where they were denied entitlements, or their employers were not following proper procedures, these were unambiguous signs of conflict over norms. When it came to the analysis of the ill-treatment of employees with psychological conditions and learning disabilities, there was more suggestion of health effects. In the Britscope and Banco case studies, for example, we came across several employees whose psychological health had deteriorated because of ill-treatment. As ever, we would simply add that, often, prior psychological problems were exacerbated by ill-treatment. In this, then, some ill-treatment may be caused by the response of others in the workplace, including the employer, to disability and ill-health (Walker and Fincham 2011).

In Britscope, for instance, it seemed that employees with disabilities or health problems had endured discrimination and harassment, and we think this may also be a part of the explanation of those cases where employees with psychological problems or learning difficulties suffered incivility and disrespect. We need to bear in mind, however, that those on the receiving end were rarely aware they were being targeted because of their condition or disability. Like the rest of us, they thought the workplace was fundamentally inimical to this kind of treatment. If discrimination was an important effect, we might expect some evidence that employees with disabilities suffer greater denigration even within troubled workplaces, and we did, indeed, find they were much more likely than other employees in troubled workplaces to have to put up with people – perhaps managers, but also fellow employees – suggesting they should leave. Being told they should quit was an experience employees with disabilities shared with both LGB and BME employees. Finally, employees with psychological conditions or learning disabilities were more likely to report violence (which all took place within the troubled minority and, therefore, mostly in troubled workplaces), although a considerable part of this association might be explained by health effects.

Age was another of the equalities issues which contributed in some way to the existence of troubled workplaces. Younger workers were a little bit more likely to experience most forms of unreasonable treatment and incivility and disrespect. Though the effect was small, it was an impressively consistent result, and it seems that the presence of young workers was a contributory factor to the existence of troubled workplaces because their employment was in some way linked to conflict over workplace norms. We know from the case studies that some young workers felt they were being treated in different ways from older ones and that they believed older workers would not, in any event, stand for such ill-treatment. From the managers' point of view, and perhaps the point of view of older colleagues, differential treatment may have been seen as well-justified by younger workers' inexperience, or lack of seniority, but this simply underlines that there was a cause of conflict here. Within the troubled minority, this pattern disappeared or was actually reversed. In other words, the ill-treatment of younger workers may well be a sign of conflict over norms, but in a workplace with this kind of conflict, young workers were no more likely to be ill-treated than others, perhaps less so.

The presence of LGB employees, like the presence of younger workers and workers with disabilities or health problems, contributed to the conditions which gave rise to troubled workplaces. As with employees with psychological or emotional problems, it was incivility and disrespect, rather than unreasonable treatment, that was the main issue. As we might expect, it would seem that the problem is not so much that the presence of LGB employees raises the possibility of conflict with employers about workplace norms. The cause of the problem looks to be much more likely to be discrimination and harassment, possibly from fellow employees, and customers or clients, as well as managers. Although we did not come across much evidence of this in our case studies, we can recall the Westshire employee who was told that she should not work with children because she was a lesbian and general remarks about homophobia amongst the overwhelmingly male workforce at Strand.

If discrimination and harassment was an important part of the story of the ill-treatment of LGB employees, we would expect this to be confirmed by the analysis of the troubled minority. As with the employees with disabilities, LGB employees were much more likely than straight workers in troubled workplaces to be told they should leave. The size of this effect was amongst the very biggest we found in any of our analyses, but it is perhaps not the most shocking evidence of discrimination and harassment. Of course, violence only applies to the troubled minority and so, even within a troubled workplace, one was far more likely to be singled out for violence if one was LGB rather than straight. As in the case of disabled employees, LGB employees rarely seem to have been aware of this discrimination and harassment. They were simply aware they were ill-treated. They did not necessarily know they were more likely to be ill-treated than straight employees and did not usually indicate they thought they had been singled out for ill-treatment because of their sexual orientation. As ever, we believe the expectation of rational and fair treatment is strong, and it takes something quite dramatic to happen before people question their default assumptions.

We were initially surprised when the BWBS showed that the presence of Asian employees was associated with *less* troubled workplaces. We noted in Part Two that many of the Asian employees in our sample were highly educated, and we suggested that the type of jobs they did might be located in less troubled workplaces. We now have the makings of a theory that Asians, and particularly highly educated Asians, tried to avoid working in troubled workplaces if they could. When we looked at the analysis of the results for the troubled minority, we found the same pattern as for the members of other equality strands. Like workers with disabilities and LGB employees,

BME employees were more likely to be told they should leave. The effect was not as spectacular as for LGB employees, but it was worse than what disabled employees had to endure. So the presence of BME employees was not generally a predictor of troubled workplaces (with the exception of the particular workplaces in the public sector where violence is more likely), but it was a predictor of who would be targeted within a troubled workplace. Although the effects were not as great as we might have expected from some of the literature discussed in Chapter 1, this was certainly evidence that minorities are targeted for ill-treatment (Lewis and Gunn 2007; Lopez *et al.* 2009; Roscigno, Lopez and Hodson 2009).

We heard a great deal about the significance of ethnicity in our most troubled case study, Britscope, and much of what we heard could be unambiguously understood as discrimination or harassment by managers or fellow employees. In the case of the shop floor at Strand, and parts of Britscope, the presence of an entrenched older white male workforce caused particular problems for BME employees and women. At Britscope we heard complaints from other BME employees, both men and women, of the behaviour of Asian employees. Although the examples of discrimination and harassment at Strand were largely historical, the company was very well aware that it continued to have low BME employment, and those who were not white British employees continued to have concerns about exclusion by their colleagues. Similar concerns were expressed at Banco. Being one of a handful of BME or women employees in a workplace dominated by older white men might have been the dramatic experience that was required to persuade people that the ill-treatment they received amounted to discrimination or harassment, but elsewhere (perhaps in Banco or Westshire) BME employees may have been less likely to reach this conclusion. Indeed, discrimination and harassment may rarely look like discrimination or harassment to those who are responsible for it. For example, at Britscope we heard of conflict over management's alleged favouritism towards BME workers for fear of being accused of racism.

The only other protected equality characteristic that was associated with ill-treatment in our analyses was gender. In contrast to disability, sexual orientation and ethnicity, gender was not a predictor of troubled workplaces (except those public sector hotspots for violence which tended to have lots of women as well as BME workers). But when we turned to our analysis of the troubled minority, that is, when we got inside the troubled workplace, we found a picture more in keeping with the view of Hearn and Parkin (2001). Women were more likely than men in troubled workplaces to be unfairly treated, insulted and also intimidated (but also less likely to be threatened). As we have already indicated in the discussion of racism, the experience of a handful of women in a largely male environment at Strand (and in some work groups at Britscope) may have been sufficiently problematic for some of them – though not all – to conclude that their ill-treatment amounted to discrimination and harassment. For example, a black woman employee in her forties working at Britscope reported how she had experienced unwanted stroking or touching from certain male colleagues as part of a broader pattern of harassment:

> He used to say things to me and that. You know, there was one night manager, I remember him, he touched me, he did touch me … come up and started stroking me, come around and started stroking me like that. I went bright red, I did, everyone was looking yeah, thinking that us two were having an affair or something. I went bright red. Even when I first started at Britscope, there was one manger, he's not working there anymore, but he come around … and put his arm around my waist. He did that and, I didn't know because I was quite new to it all and that, and I didn't want to get sacked because I was only a temporary worker. And I was like wondering that can't be right … I have had male staff come up and stroke my bum as well, I've had casuals do that. You know come up and stroke my bum and I'll go no, don't.

Can employers do more to minimise the ill-treatment of their employees?

The conventional approach to this issue is to apply critical scrutiny to company policies and procedures which are meant to prevent or limit ill-treatment, or minimise the harm it causes. We have taken this approach ourselves at various points in the book. For example, we have commented on confusion in policies over what constitutes ill-treatment and on failures to communicate, operationalise or enforce policies (particularly where managers were responsible for ill-treatment). Our research has shown, however, that employers bear a heavy responsibility for ill-treatment, and we think that finding out what employers can do to minimise ill-treatment requires more than scrutiny of their policies on dignity at work. In the first part of this final chapter, we saw that employers could sometimes minimise conflict, and achieve their objectives, by carrying their employees with them. Now we shall look at what employers can do more directly to minimise trouble at work. From what we have learnt in earlier chapters, we know that other kinds of policies – on sickness and disability – may be more relevant here than policies on dignity at work. We shall also be looking at what employers can do to improve the quality of management and leadership, and at the way they manage their relations with their employees and the employees' relations with each other.

The most important conclusion we have reached in respect of dignity at work policies is that they do little to prevent ill-treatment beyond giving employees information on the sort of behaviour that might not be acceptable in the workplace. This information is primarily of use to those who already suspect they have been ill-treated – so confusion about the recognition of ill-treatment is a big problem – but we doubt it serves to prevent ill-treatment, given how sketchy knowledge of these policies is amongst managers and others. Even when employers, like Britscope and Strand, make a determined effort to apprise their employees of their policies, employees express doubts about how much is learnt. We heard employees describing these as tickbox exercises (and even 'sheep dipping'), which meant the employer could demonstrate good governance without enquiring too closely into what the workforce knew about dignity at work beyond the fact that their employer had good intentions. Of course, we realise this demonstration can be valuable to an employer all the same. At Strand and Banco, for example, employees' belief in the company's good intentions meant they gave them the benefit of the doubt when they did not really know whether an initiative was reasonable, fair and did not undermine respect.

Not only was the preventative value of dignity at work policies questioned, but so was their efficacy as a remedy for ill-treatment. We heard about the difficulty of taking action in cases where it was the word of one employee against another with no corroborating evidence. In the case of ill-treatment by managers, employees frequently assumed that no action would be taken because the manager charged with handling the complaint would side with their fellow manager. We heard several examples in which the remedy stipulated by the policy – for example, what amounted to a confrontation with the alleged troublemaker – seemed guaranteed to discourage people from acting. More generally, people did not believe that the outcomes that could be achieved by activating the policy could justify the costs to them personally of engaging in the formal process. Probably the most common reason we were given by employees for not using their employer's dignity at work policy was that they did not want to jeopardise their chances, especially when jobs might be on the line. We were told, for example, that in these circumstances, employees' card would be marked, or even that they would be blacklisted, if they complained. No matter whether their fears were groundless or not, several employees even struggled to talk about this subject because they feared our conversation was not as confidential as we told them it was.

The use of external agencies as the first port of call for complaints, which can be anonymous, was welcomed by some employees, though not necessarily those who had actually used the services of an EAP (employee assistance programme) call centre. Yet it is salutary that some employees who were genuinely apprehensive about discussing their employer's attitude towards people who used the dignity at work policy talked to independent researchers like us. Would this apprehension have been so acute if these employees thought their employer was simply acting as a neutral umpire, acting fairly and reasonably to resolve cases of unpleasantness between employees? We think that the apprehension, and indeed the fear, about using dignity at work policies suggests employees did not see their employer as impartial. At the very least, there was a perception that the employer would perceive a complaint about ill-treatment as a challenge to managerial authority. This is most obviously the case, of course, when managers are the ones responsible for the ill-treatment but, even when this is not, employees may feel, as they told us, that they do not want to stick their heads above the parapet.

These are good reasons for concluding that, as we suggested at the beginning of this chapter, dignity at work policies are not effective because they do not address the root causes of ill-treatment. Such policies are designed to deal with problems like bullying and harassment, which are conceived as pathological workplace behaviour or unhelpful responses to workplace stresses. They are not designed to deal with ill-treatment that happens for what some people see as very good reasons. When we learnt, for example, about all the causes for conflict in Britscope and how these led, in turn, to ill-treatment, we concluded that addressing ill-treatment directly, and conceiving of it simply as bullying or harassment, was beside the point. This helped us to understand why most Britscope employees found the employer's remedies for ill-treatment unsatisfactory when they actually tried to use them. In this and other workplaces, employers (and unions) bought into a limited conceptualisation of the problem and their misunderstanding of its causes led to ineffectual prescriptions. Employers like Britscope resolutely focused on inter-employee problems to the exclusion of ill-treatment by managers. Managers mainly, and sometimes only, featured in their policies as solutions to problems. It is no accident that employees did not think dignity at work policies worked where the troublemakers were managers and, indeed, feared what would happen if they tried to use the policies.

Other kinds of policies than those on dignity at work may matter rather more for the control of ill-treatment in the workplace. The Britscope policy that had the biggest impact on their employees was actually their sickness and absence policy (see the work of Cunningham, Dibben and James; Foster; and Walker and Fincham cited in Chapter 1). Much ill-treatment arose from conflict over what was seen as reasonable practice, particularly management practice, for example, in issuing warnings to employees, in line with this policy. Britscope staff thought living in fear of warnings was 'totally wrong'. These conflicts were often heightened by the fact that the ill-health and impairments employees were suffering had been caused by their employment with Britscope. At the heart of the conflicts over reasonable practice on sickness and absence was the employer's expectation of uniform treatment of employees according to standardised expectations of, for example, performance or attendance. Very often, employees felt that variations in this uniformity resulted not from acknowledging the needs of individual employees but according to the whims of individual managers (who would make inconsistent judgements about what counted as unauthorised absences, for example). There was also considerable variation, and widespread ignorance, amongst managers about the requirements of the legislation on disability discrimination, and particularly the adjustments to the workplace, or the work itself, that could be required of employers (confirming, particularly, Foster 2007; Walker and Fincham 2011).

Similar comments were made about Banco, for example about variations between managers in what they counted as reasonable adjustments. One employee with considerable experience of trying to use the Banco policy on 'extended' or 'disability-related' absence had concluded that line managers were ill-equipped to operate the policy, and yet the division of responsibility for it between managers and HR was very unclear. Banco's formal policy implied a certain degree of sympathy with disabled employees, stating that the organisation must accept the 'unavoidability' that such employees may suffer a higher rate of sickness absence, and listing examples of reasonable adjustments which should be considered to help facilitate better attendance (such as specialist equipment and training, job redesign, flexible hours, adjusted performance measures, remote working). Indeed Banco's policy closely resembles the policy operated by Strand, about which we heard quite positive accounts in Chapter 8 (though fear of being singled out for redundancy because of a poor sickness record or disability was mentioned at both Britscope and Strand).

This, along with the variations in practices between managers in the same organisation, only serves to underline the points made in the literature about how important the operationalisation of these policies is. Being able to rely on good advice from occupational health professionals is a crucial element in this process (see Fevre et al. 2008). Proper operationalisation of a sickness and absence policy that is both reasonable and meets the FARE criteria is an obvious and effective way for employers to reduce trouble in the workplace, but there may be reasons why an employer would not go down this route (Walker and Fincham 2011). It is very likely in the case of Britscope that the employer thought that conflict over sickness absence was unavoidable and perhaps even desirable. As we noted in Chapter 5, there was a clear perception amongst employees that the tough enforcement of the company sickness policy was a result of edicts from the most senior management in the company. In this, the company seemed to share the standpoint of the UK government of the time, which had determined that stricter regimes were needed to police the access of citizens who were disabled or long-term sick to welfare benefits. This government's plans to introduce welfare tests for cancer patients during chemotherapy (see *The Guardian*, 6 December 2011) sounded like some of the more extreme examples of the application of Britscope's sickness polices which we heard of from its employees.

The proper communication of sickness and absence policies is obviously a vital part of their successful operationalisation. We saw earlier, in the discussion of dignity at work policies, how much of a challenge communication with employees could be. More generally, communication was felt to be a crucial area for managers in all of our case studies. In Westshire, for example, we learnt of the way reliance on (inadequately resourced) IT hindered good communication. At Strand, we heard more positive views about IT, when it was better resourced, though there was disquiet about the redistribution of some communication and reporting responsibilities to line managers. As Chapter 8 showed, communication policies like those operated by Strand depend on good leadership and competent managers to deliver them. How much does the quality of management and leadership matter for other ways of minimising ill-treatment?

Britscope and Westshire staff frequently told us their managers were poor. At Britscope, for example, we heard numerous complaints of unprofessional, under-confident, poorly informed managers who ill-treated their employees. In fact, there was a general perception that line managers lacked the skills they needed to do their jobs well, and ill-treatment was usually blamed on incompetence, which often came into stark relief when managers were put under pressure by their superiors. At Strand, we heard of staff who were extremely competent technically but considerably less competent at managing people, and of the steps the company had taken to ensure that such staff were not given managerial responsibilities in future. Even this last example assumes that management quality is a characteristic of individuals, and this is only one side of the story.

For example, we interviewed a mental health nurse at Westshire who had been promoted to a managerial post which had become available as part of large-scale reorganisation, which meant that the kind of work he had been doing for 20 years was changing quite radically. On taking up the post, he was given responsibility for establishing a new unit which would provide mental health services in the community rather than in a clinical setting. The nature of the services, and the work involved in delivering these services, was very different from that which had been delivered in hospitals. Moreover, he was never allowed to take over managing the unit as he was moved over to set up a second unit and then a third. With a budget in excess of £1.25 m to manage, and no financial training beyond half a day provided by his employer, he found his situation extremely stressful, and his health deteriorated badly when he was called to account for having overspent his budget.

Not only was this manager not provided with sufficient training by his employer, but he had no access to IT facilities except for a two-hour, hot-desking facility that he could access on a Friday afternoon. This required a 20–30 mile round trip from his normal workplace location and with no guarantee that he could access IT kit when he got there. Things went from bad to worse when he found himself facing disciplinary threats for failing to manage his budget and for not meeting Westshire policy for completing online returns for HR data. Despite his pleas for understanding about how his job was much larger than he had expected at the time of his appointment, and with a lack of access to IT equipment, he found himself being ill-treated by his line manager, a consultant mental health expert. On top of this, he felt he was losing his nursing skills and missed being part of a nursing team.

Stories like these should make us wary of glib judgements about managerial competence, but there has been a long tradition of criticism of British senior and executive management too. These are the levels at which the decisions were taken which made the life of the Westshire manager, and the lives of many others like him, so difficult. Unprofessional or short-sighted management has been a traditional target for many on the Left seeking to explain the problems of British industry, but the first half of this chapter has suggested we ought to be careful of concluding that employers only appear to condone trouble at work because they are put in a false position by managers who either do not understand what is in the best interests of their employer or are incapable of acting on this knowledge. Take the ill-treatment of financial advisors at Banco. Was the intention to modernise work practices, reduce salary costs and increase productivity or force them out of the organisation (Rafferty 2001; Walker and Fincham 2011)? In the former example, hints or signals that they should quit were a kind of collateral damage that the employer would rather have avoided. In the latter, managing advisors out of the door could make it much easier to move to telephone sales or even selling that part of the business. In this (hypothetical) case, trouble at work would be a means to an end, but one which an employer might not wish to acknowledge publicly.

Albeit that Westshire and other employers put their employees in impossible positions when they give them managerial responsibilities without proper training or support, the greater blame for ill-treatment might be placed on a particular style of leadership. There was a noticeable difference in the effectiveness of leadership in Westshire and Strand, for example, and the attention given to continuous improvement in the quality of leadership was evident in many of our interviews at Strand. The effectiveness of leadership is not simply a question of employing competent leaders since it also depends on the kind of relations the organisation has with its employees and the relations employees have with each other. This means, of course, that ill-treatment which sours these relations can frustrate good leadership as easily as good leadership can eliminate ill-treatment. What are the key features of the kind of relations that exist in workplaces with little ill-treatment, the white-collar workplaces at Strand and the central office functions of Banco, for example?

Trade unions were recognised for collective bargaining purposes in all of our case study organisations. Banco, for example, had a long amicable history of union involvement in all sorts of initiatives, including policies on dignity at work and sickness absence policies. Some Banco employees thought their union was too close to the company, but union cooperation had helped Banco successfully to manage redundancies before the recession. Chapter 8 described a similarly close relationship at Strand although we heard little about the union being too close to the company, particularly when it came to the representation of the blue-collar workforce. Union sources there believed they were far more effective at dealing with trouble at work than managers (the FTWS provided evidence that trade unions are similarly effective at dealing with a wide range of problems at work – Fevre *et al.* 2009). Of course, Strand employees and managers did not necessarily share these views.

Elsewhere, we noted that Britscope employees had mixed feelings about the effectiveness of the recognised union in addressing ill-treatment. At Westshire, professional staff would first and foremost see their membership of their professional body as their primary representation rather than a general trade union. Strand's white-collar employees were much less aware of the need for a trade union than their blue-collar colleagues were. In Chapter 8, we described the way in which many white-collar staff at Strand had learnt to resent what might once have been called working-class solidarity amongst the unionised blue-collar employees. The white-collar workers shared with the Strand leadership the belief that an individualised approach to employee relations was more fair and reasonable than the collective alternative. Strand leadership considered this a favourable situation because it meant that there were going to be fewer objections to the changes they wanted to make now and in the future.

The senior HR director that we interviewed explained that, especially now that it had become a truly global company, Strand senior management were also increasingly aware of the constraints they felt this solidarity imposed on their ability to keep pace with the competition through effective leadership. As the senior HR director explained, however, when the company had a history of strong cooperation with trade unions, 'going directly to the employees' (without the prior agreement of a union) risked causing just the kind of conflict over workplace norms that Strand took pains to avoid. For the director, the need to adjust to the history and even the personalities in each local situation was simply a fact of life.

This was, in part, a comment on the quality of local trade union leadership – there had been a somewhat strained relationship with the long-serving blue-collar convenor at Longstretton – but it was also about something more fundamental: cultural differences in expectations of the relations between employers and employees. The director said that in one of Strand's key locations in the Far East, for example, 'you're comparing apples and pears in terms of the industrial history, the industrial conflict in terms of trade unionism and employers ... Well for a start you don't have the complex agreements. Your employees tend to come to the workplace with a very different attitude'. These employees were 'very much more amenable' to the rhetoric of empowerment because they saw 'things from an individual perspective' even though they did have formal collective representation. This was an aspect of the employees' 'different mindset': 'I know I am generalising, but they are coming into a role with a view that it is legitimate that the company makes money and gives a return to shareholders.' This made a stark contrast with the situation in other parts of the world, including the United Kingdom but also some parts of Asia, where employees would 'recognise that you need to make money but we don't trust that the money that you make is going to be fairly distributed'. The director thought this was why employees in these countries wanted their unions to monitor the fairness of this distribution, but of course her point could be extended beyond the distribution of rewards to all the issues of fairness and respect which we know can be so crucial to the generation of trouble at work. She summed up the emphasis in their Far East location as 'much more an individualism and a trust and a "this is how life is" kind of methodology and thinking'.

This characterisation might equally apply to many of the white-collar employees back at Strand's operation in Longstretton. We have noted at several points how these employees seemed to value the team-working, and continuous team-building, they were involved in at Strand (and which seemed to be one of the necessary conditions for Strand to fulfil its ambitions for effective leadership). What we have failed to emphasise is how little this team-working had in common with not only traditional collectivism but also conventional informal social ties. Strand was once a traditional paternalistic employer with its sports clubs and hobby groups and other opportunities for its employees to cement social ties outside the workplace. The notion that privatised employees who would rather not socialise with their workmates was popularised by the Affluent Worker study (Goldthorpe *et al.* 1969). It may have been less common in the 1960s than was claimed at the time (Devine 1992), but the employees we met were largely uninterested in these opportunities, and if they did meet colleagues outside the workplace these tended to be rare events at which attendance was patchy. As at Banco, regular social contact outside work tended to be limited to employees of the same age and, sometimes, gender and ethnicity. This does not suggest that informal social relations between employees were much of an antidote to ill-treatment. Indeed many employees in our case study organisations appeared to think these relationships might be one of the causes of ill-treatment and one of the obstacles to the satisfactory remedy of ill-treatment when it did occur. Most notably, many of the employees we talked to implicated informal social relations in the reproduction of sexist, racist or ageist workplace cultures.

Returning to the main thread of this brief discussion of leadership, trade unions and individualism, we find an intriguing possibility has been revealed. It seems that leaders in the three case study organisations other than Strand may not have come to terms with the implications for their organisations of the transition from collective to individualised employment relations (which the Strand leaders wanted to see spread throughout the company). The relative ineffectiveness of these organisations in minimising trouble at work may have stemmed in part from their inability to shape *managerial* behaviour to match the individualising discourse which removes collective intermediaries and makes each employee responsible for his or her own experience of the workplace (Walker and Fincham 2011: 153). It is possible that this failure contributed to the experience of ill-treatment amongst their employees, particularly those employees who were ambitious, better paid and felt they were, or should be, valued by the company. These were the least vulnerable workers, the ones who were confident that they could prosper without the help of a trade union, and who often appeared to think that the shift from collective to individualised employment relations could not come quickly enough.

We think that there may be a great deal of potential in this argument about trouble at work arising when employers were stuck between individualised and collective models of employment relations, but there is insufficient space to develop that argument here. We can simply say that this argument contradicts the earlier discussion of trouble at work as the necessary price that must be paid to modernise unproductive work practices. For example, we discussed the idea that, when they added ill-treatment to reduced autonomy, employers were trying to wrest the initiative from relatively privileged employees, enforce the manager's right to manage and move the business on in the way they wanted to. With the addition of our idea of an imperfect adjustment to individualised employment relations, this looks like employers were using the old-fashioned tactics that might be employed when fighting a powerful trade union rather than acting as the trustworthy partner in an individualised employment relationship. It is as if these employers embraced the easy part of the new relationship, the change in the nature and aspirations of their employees, without doing the harder part of shaping their own behaviour to match the change.

To the extent that our case study research took place at the onset of a recession, we may have been encountering employers who could afford to be slow to adapt to their side of the new individualised employment bargain because falling demand, rising unemployment and general uncertainty provided very forgiving conditions for their mistakes. In more prosperous times, an employer who did not fulfil their side of the individualised bargain might suffer for it by losing its most valued employees to its competitors. At the time of writing, the UK government's plans to withdraw various employment rights, for example, rights of employees with shorter service to protection from unfair dismissal, could be seen as a way of extending further these mitigating conditions into the recovery.

Finally, there may be evidence to support this theory of employers stuck between collective and individualised models of employment relations in the results of the BWBS. We can see this evidence if we allow that the FARE questions sometimes served as measures of the success British employers were having in delivering on individualised industrial relations, particularly to more privileged employees. If the individualising discourse was to appear authentic, it required the employer to treat employees as individuals, and show that the needs of those individuals could sometimes come before the needs of the organisation, and that employees could be allowed to act on their principles. That poor FARE scores were so highly correlated with varieties of ill-treatment might therefore suggest that ill-treatment was more common where organisations were failing to deliver on the managerial side of the bargain implied by individualised employment relations.

Conclusions

'Trouble at work' is not just a convenient label which can be attached to wildly different experiences in the workplace simply because these experiences are all ones we would rather avoid. If this were all there was to it, the idea of trouble at work would have limited application, but our research provides empirical evidence that the experiences we have investigated have much more in common than this. They often coincide – in the lives of individuals and organisations – and we were able to depict this in a dramatic way in Figure 2 on p. 33, which showed the overlap between unreasonable treatment, incivility and disrespect, and violence. Not only do they often occur together, but different kinds of trouble at work often have overlapping causes and similar effects. Indeed, our research suggests that these experiences may be expressions of a single phenomenon. As in the fable of the blind men and the elephant, whenever we experience one of the forms of ill-treatment which we have discussed in this book, we encounter one aspect of a much larger, multifaceted problem which is best conceptualised as trouble at work.

The private troubles that C. Wright Mills believed sociology could help turn into public issues were those in which people felt their values were under threat. In our analyses, we have tried to show how, and why, people feel this to be the case when they experience trouble at work. Employees might feel this in respect of ill-treatment from their co-workers (Pearson et al. 2001) or customers and clients, though violence from customers and clients was often not be interpreted in this way. It was, however, more likely that they would feel their values to be under threat in their dealings with managers and employers. We found that trouble at work showed employees that their relationship with their employer had undergone fundamental re-evaluation which had a moral element. The full significance of this re-evaluation could only be grasped when we understood the expectation employees had of fair, rational and respectful treatment in the workplace. With lower expectations, and less trust in the processes that underpin recognition in the workplace, re-evaluation might not have produced such thorough demoralisation. If recognition was haphazard and capricious, employees would not care; but they did care, deeply, how they were judged by rational criteria. The discussion we have just concluded suggests that the rational criteria they expected to be judged by were highly individualised and that their employers were failing to keep pace with a change they had a great deal to do with initiating.

Sociologists are much more interested in conflicts between employees and employers over workplace norms, and incivility and violence from members of the public, than they are in psychological states. We have shown in this book that it makes more sense to conduct our analysis through the prism of trouble at work, rather than workplace bullying, because it is associated with the factors sociologists study, not least the moral relations of the workplace, and particularly the moral relations between managers and employees. The same applies to the clinical notion of workplace stress, which shares with bullying an emphasis on the characteristics of the individual. We would agree with Walker and Fincham (2011) that stress, like bullying, is a less useful way for sociology to conceptualise the problem in hand. In addition, we would argue that neither bullying nor stress are stable enough concepts to allow translation between the different categories such as different workplaces, occupations and societies that interest sociologists.

To sum up, concepts of bullying and stress are unable to capture all that we know about troubles in the workplace. They are shaped by psychological and medical conceptualisations and, since these conceptualisations have thus far tended to dominate the study of ill-treatment, more sociological questions which are important to our understanding of the causes and solutions of troubles in the workplace have received relatively little attention. We would also argue that over-reliance on concepts of bullying and stress, to the exclusion of more sociological approaches, threatens to make the actions of governments, employers, trade unions and other parties who are interested in reducing ill-treatment less effective than they might otherwise be. For example, well-meaning policies on workplace dignity, and therapeutic remedies for stress and the effects of bullying, have been widely adopted. In this chapter, we have suggested that there is little evidence that they make for less troubled workplaces because they do not address the root causes of trouble at work.

While the individualised nature of the concepts of bullying and stress make them less useful to sociologists than psychologists and clinicians, individualism itself may yet emerge as a highly significant factor in our theories of trouble at work. At the end of this chapter, we introduced the idea that trouble at work has appeared as an ailment of modernity because it is the fallout that employers and employees must cope with when the transition is made from collective to individualised models of employment relations. In collective times, conflicts over workplace norms did not get framed as unreasonable treatment but as issues for collective bargaining. Any incivility and disrespect that arose could also be dealt with by collective response (as still happens at Strand), but companies that go down the individualised route – and all four of our case studies, like the vast majority of British employers, had begun this journey – dispense with the possibility of collective solutions. Trouble at work is not only an expression of industrial relations problems (as in the theories of Ironside and Seifert, and Beale and Hoel, about the predisposition of capitalist employment relations to stimulate bullying), but is also an outcome of the transformation of industrial relations with uncertain, and often unhappy, consequences for all concerned.

Notes

Chapter 1 A bad day at the office

1 We are very grateful to Emma Calvert who introduced us to this method of utilising the qualitative data gathered as part of a large social survey (see O'Connell *et al*. 2007).

2 The roots of concepts of workplace bullying lie in a definition originally used to measure the construct in school children's behaviour (Olweus 1991, cited in Nielsen *et al*. 2010). In Chapter 8, we show how employees in one of our case study organisations used an implicit contrast with the behaviour of the playground ('we treat each other as adults') to explain how trouble at work was minimised.

3 It is frequently found that dissatisfaction levels among unionised workers are higher than among their non-unionised counterparts (Bender and Sloane 1998). Higher reports of bullying amongst union members might reflect their higher expectations, their greater awareness of bullying as a public issue, and/or the fact the employees who face problems at work may be more likely to join trade unions in order to get help to address them.

Part two

1 For example, see Notelaers *et al*. 2006. Such studies have found that there is poor overlap between the groups of 'bullied' workers when measured on each different approach. In particular, less than half of the respondents who are counted as victims of bullying by researchers analysing responses to the NAQ report themselves as bullied (Lutgen-Sandvik *et al*. 2007; Notelaers *et al*. 2006; Salin 2001).

2 Respondents for the survey were identified by screening participants in Taylor Nelson Sofres's (TNS) face-to-face Omnibus survey. A representative sample of around 2,000 adults per week in Britain (England, Wales and Scotland) was interviewed by Omnibus. It was carried out using a quota sample, with sample points (and addresses within these sample points) selected by a random location methodology. TNS fieldworkers used the CAPI (Computer Assisted Personal Interviewing) method to administer the survey in respondents' households.

3 The empirical story behind our decision is a little complicated as it relates to the 21 items having both 'original' versions and also 'confirmed' versions (the latter representing an additional opportunity for respondents to confirm whether their previous answers were indeed correct and consequently are more accurate). Therefore there were two factor analyses and the differences between them, along with the differences between the factor loadings *within* each factor analysis, suggested certain items could belong to more than one factor. Our decisions were made taking into account our understanding of extant research, our own empirical findings, and results from a factor analysis of Fair Treatment at Work Survey (FTWS) data.

Chapter 2 Fairness and rationality at work

1 Are these rogue results? We asked three of these questions in the FTWS (undertaken a year later and with random sampling instead of quota sampling): 12 per cent of employees/recent employees had been pressurised to work below their level of competence and 13 per cent complained of unmanageable workloads. This gives us confidence in the reliability of our findings. The greater variation between the two survey measurements of employers' use of improper procedures (23 per cent in the BWBS versus 17 per cent in the FTWS) probably results from the differing content of the questionnaires used in each survey. The BWBS had no questions on knowledge or awareness of employment rights or on any other problems than ill-treatment. The FTWS had many more alternative questions where respondents might record their dissatisfaction with their employers' procedures. For example, 8 per cent agreed with 'your employer not following a set procedure when dealing with a grievance of other work-related problem you had' (Chart 6.1 in Fevre *et al.* 2009). It is possible that perceived overlap may have reduced responses to the question on ill-treatment. In any event, what we find in both of these nationally representative samples with face-to-face interviewing is much lower incidence rates for these types of problems at work than are often quoted. For example, Hoel and Cooper (2000) reported in their study that nearly a third of employees reported 'pressure from someone else to do work below your level of competence' now and then or more frequently within the past six months. The comparison figure from the BWBS was 13 per cent (and 11 per cent from the 2008 FTWS).

2 The stress and bullying literature seems to assume job satisfaction or disengagement is caused by ill-treatment. We are sure this is not the whole story, just as we are sure that the bullying literature does not tell the whole story of the relationship between witnessing ill-treatment and suffering ill-health when it assumes that this is just a matter of effects on health.

3 Similar patterns were recorded in the FTWS.

4 See pp. 30–1 in the introduction to Section Two – these were the respondents who reported three or more types of ill-treatment and tended to have more intense exposure. For example, a third (87) of the 265 respondents who were asked questions about unmanageable workload said this happened monthly or more frequently. It can be recalled that we made our own judgements about what form of ill-treatment was most important, and so we tended to collect more evidence on violence and other forms of ill-treatment where the numbers involved were relatively small. Thus, there were less data about how unreasonable treatment affected the troubled minority compared with the sample as a whole. For example, we asked 265 respondents follow-up questions about unmanageable workload, but we also asked 689 respondents about incidents where people had shouted at them or lost their temper.

5 In the 27 EU countries there are roughly twice as many male as female managers (*Eurostat News Release* 32/2008 – 6 March 2008).

6 There may well be psychological explanations for the failure of individuals to recognise their own shortcomings, but the point remains that people expect reasonable treatment in the workplace even if they expect it nowhere else.

7 Note that when employees' views and opinions were ignored, this was *not* linked to being excluded from a group or clique at work.

8 As Figure 7 suggests, there was little suggestion that troubled workplaces were more likely to be found in the public sector. Indeed, employees in education were less likely to experience, and witness, unreasonable treatment. Bivariate analysis for witnessing unreasonable treatment suggested that public sector workers of any kind were more likely to report it but only in two of the eight types of unreasonable treatment.

Chapter 4 Violence and injury at work

1 For example, only 0.9 per cent of working adults reported experience of physical violence during the past year in the 2002–3 British Crime Survey (Upson 2004).

2 For example, the FTWS found that 4 per cent experienced physical assault (Fevre *et al.* 2009), and our finding is also broadly comparable to the estimate of the 2005 European Working Conditions Survey (EWCS) that 3.6 per cent of the working population in the United Kingdom were subject to physical assault from people at work (presumably colleagues), and a further 7.3 per cent had experienced physical violence at work perpetrated by non-colleagues.

3 The cognitive testing interviews that were undertaken as part of the survey development work suggested that the question about physical violence was interpreted in a straightforward way as intentional interpersonal assaults, rather than structural violence (Jones *et al.* 2011).

4 There are many ways we could group the four categories of perpetrators; however, this is the only one that is accurate in so far as it reflects the actual differences between clients or customers and the other three types. It is important to not imbue these terms with assumptions about levels of intimacy, frequency of contact or power differentials between the type of perpetrator and respondent. For example, it is reasonable to suppose that some clients/customers would be very familiar to respondents, even inescapable in terms of contact if, for example, they lived in the care home where the respondent worked. However, some clients might feature prominently in the lives of respondents, and wield enormous power over them in their working lives, if, for example, they were long-term clients and the respondent was relatively new to the organisation. These examples only serve to illustrate how much we still do not know about the nature of the relationship between the respondent and perpetrator, despite our best efforts to collect data in this regard (and within the financial constraints of our project).

5 To avoid complication, we here include violence perpetrated by 'employers' under the broader category of 'employee' violence, in order to demonstrate the key distinction between violence carried out by people working in the same organisation (whether employees or the employer) and that carried out by those who do not work in the organisation.

6 Based on analysis where the perpetrator was a client in any of the three incidents.

Bibliography

Abberley, P. (1987), 'The concept of oppression and the development of a social theory of disability', *Disability and Society*, 2(1), 5–19.

Acas (Advisory, Conciliation and Arbitration Service) (2006), 'Workplace bullying and harassment: Building a culture of respect', Acas Policy Discussion Paper, no. 4, London: ACAS.

Acas (2007), *Research Summaries: Sexual Orientation and Religion or Belief Discrimination in the Workplace/The Experiences of Sexual Orientation and Religion or Belief Discrimination Employment Tribunal Claimants*, London: Advisory, Conciliation and Arbitration Service.

Agervold, M. (2007), 'Bullying at work: A discussion of definitions and prevalence, based on an empirical study', *Scandinavian Journal of Psychology*, 48, 161–72.

Agervold, M. and Mikkelsen, E.G. (2004), 'Relationships between bullying, psychosocial work environment and individual stress reactions', *Work and Stress*, 18(4): 336–51.

Appelberg, K., Romanov, K., Honkasalo, M.-L. and Koskenvuo, M. (1991), 'Interpersonal conflicts at work and psychosocial characteristics of employees', *Social Science & Medicine*, 32(9), 1051–6.

Aquino, K. and Thau, S. (2009), 'Workplace victimization: Aggression from the target's perspective', *Annual Review of Psychology*, 60, 717–41.

Ashforth, B. (1994), 'Petty tyranny in organizations', *Human Relations*, 47(7), 755–78.

Baillien, E. and De Witte, H. (2009), 'Why is organizational change related to workplace bullying? Role conflict and job insecurity as mediators', *Economic and Industrial Democracy*, 30, 348–71.

Baillien, E., Neyens, I., De Witte, H. and De Cuyper, N. (2009), 'A qualitative study on the development of workplace bullying: Towards a three way model', *Journal of Community and Applied Psychology*, 19, 1–16.

Baillien, E., Rodriguez-Muñoz, A., Van Den Broeck, A. and De Witte, H. (2011), 'Do demands and resources affect target's and perpetrators' reports of workplace bullying? A two-wave cross-lagged study', *Work & Stress*, 25(2), 128–46.

Baron, R.A. and Neuman, J.H. (1996), 'Workplace violence and workplace aggression: Evidence on their relative frequency and potential causes', *Aggressive Behaviour*, 22(3), 161–73.

Bauman, Z. (1991), *Modernity and Ambivalence*, Cambridge: Polity.

Bauman, Z. (1993), *Postmodern Ethics*, Cambridge: Blackwell.

Beale, D. and Hoel, H. (2010), 'Workplace bullying, industrial relations and the challenge for management in Britain and Sweden', *European Journal of Industrial Relations*, 16(2), 101–18.

Beale, D. and Hoel, H. (2011), 'Workplace bullying and the employment relationship: Exploring questions of prevention, control and context', *Work, Employment and Society*, 25(1), 5–18.

Bender, K. and Sloane, P.J. (1998), 'Job satisfaction, trade unions, and exit-voice revisited', *Industrial and Labor Relations Review*, 51, 222–40.

Bjorkqvist, K., Osterman, K. and Hjelt-Back, M. (1994), 'Aggression among university employees', *Aggressive Behaviour*, 20, 173–84.

Blase, J., Blase, J. and Du, F. (2008), 'The mistreated teacher: A national study', *Journal of Educational Administration*, 46, 263–301.

Bolton, S.C. (2007), 'Dignity in and at work: Why it matters', in S.C. Bolton (ed.), *Dimensions of Dignity at Work*, Oxford: Butterworth-Heinemann, 3–16.

Bowie, V. (2010), 'An emerging awareness of the role organizational culture and management style can play in triggering workplace violence', in M.R. Privitera (ed.), *Workplace Violence in Mental and General Healthcare Settings*, Sudbury, MA; Toronto: Jones and Bartlett.

Bowling, B. (1999), *Violent Racism*, Oxford: Clarendon Press.

Brandth, B. and Kvande, E. (2001), 'Flexible work and flexible fathers', *Work, Employment and Society*, 15(2), 251–67.

Budd, T. (1999), *Violence at Work: Findings from the British Crime Survey*, London: Home Office.

Burnes, B. and Pope, R. (2007), 'Negative behaviours in the workplace: A study of two Primary Care Trusts in the NHS', *International Journal of Public Sector Management*, 20(4), 285–303.

Catley, B. and Jones, C. (2002), 'Deciding on violence', *Reason in Practice*, 2(1), 23–32.

Chappell, D. and Di Martino, V. (2006), *Violence at Work*, Geneva, Switzerland: International Labour Office.

Cortina, L. and Magley, V.J. (2009), 'Patterns and profiles of response to incivility in the workplace', *Journal of Occupational Health Psychology*, 14(3), 272–88.

Coyne, I., Seigne, E. and Randall, P. (2000), 'Predicting workplace victim status from personality', *European Journal of Work and Organizational Psychology*, 9, 335–49.

Creegan, C. and Robinson, C. (2008), 'Prejudice in the workplace', in A. Park, J. Curtice, K. Thomson, M. Phillips, M. Johnson and E. Clery (eds), *British Social Attitudes – The 24th Report*, London: Sage.

Croteau, J.M. (1996), 'Research on the work experiences of lesbian, gay, and bisexual people: An integrative review of methodology and findings', *Journal of Vocational Behavior*, 48, 195–209.

Cunningham, I., James, P. and Dibben, P. (2004), 'Bridging the gap between rhetoric and reality: Line managers and the protection of job security for ill workers in the modern workplace', *British Journal of Management*, 15, 273–90.

D'Cruz, P. and Noronha, E. (2009), 'Experiencing depersonalised bullying: A study of Indian call-centre agents', *Work Organisation, Labour and Globalisation*, 3(1), 26–46.

De Cuyper, N., Baillien, E. and De Witte, H. (2009), 'Job insecurity, perceived employability and targets' and perpetrators' experiences of workplace bullying', *Work & Stress*, 23(3), 206–24.

Denney, D. (2010), 'Violence and social care staff: Positive and negative approaches to risk', *British Journal of Social Work*, 40(4), 1297–313.

Denney, D. and O'Beirne, M. (2003), 'Violence to probation staff: Patterns and managerial responses', *Social Policy and Administration*, 37(1), 49–64.

Devine, F. (1992), *Affluent Workers Revisited*, Edinburgh: Edinburgh University Press.

Dibben, P., James, P. and Cunningham, I. (2001), 'Senior management commitment to disability: The influence of legal compulsion and best practice', *Personnel Review*, 30(4), 454–67.

Eakin, J. (2005), 'The discourse of abuse in return-to-work: A hidden epidemic of suffering', in C. Petersen and C. Mayhew (eds), *Occupational Health and Safety: International Influences and the New Epidemics*, New York: Baywood.

Einarsen, S. (1999), 'The nature and causes of bullying', *International Journal of Manpower*, 20, 16–27.

Einarsen, S. (2000), 'Harassment and bullying at work: A review of the Scandinavian approach', *Aggression and Violent Behavior*, 5(4), 379–401.

Einarsen, S. and Raknes, B.I. (1997), 'Harassment in the workplace and the victimisation of men', *Violence and Victims*, 12(3), 247–63.

Einarsen, S. and Skogstad, A. (1996), 'Bullying at work: Epidemiological findings in public and private organizations', *European Journal of Work and Organizational Psychology*, 5, 185–201.

Einarsen, S., Raknes, B.I. and Matthiesen, S.B. (1994), 'Bullying and harassment at work and their relationships to work environment quality: An exploratory study', *European Work and Organizational Psychologist*, 4, 381–401.

Einarsen, S., Aasland, M.S. and Skogstad, A. (2007), 'Destructive leadership behaviour: A definition and conceptual model', *The Leadership Quarterly*, 18, 207–16.

Einarsen, S., Hoel, H. and Notelaers, G. (2009), 'Measuring exposure to bullying and harassment at work: Validity, factor structure and psychometric properties of the Negative Acts Questionnaire–Revised', *Work & Stress*, 23(1), 24–44.

Einarsen, S., Hoel, H., Zapf, D. and Cooper, C.L. (2011), 'The concept of bullying and harassment at work: The European tradition', in S. Einarsen, H. Hoel, D. Zapf and C.L. Cooper (eds), *Bullying and Harassment in the Workplace: Developments in Theory Research and Practice*, London: CRC Press.

Elston, M., Gabe, J., Denney, D., Lee, R. and O'Beirne, M. (2003), 'Violence against doctors: A medical(ised) problem? The case of National Health Service general practitioners', in S. Timmermans and J. Gabe (eds), *Partners in Health, Partners in Crime: Exploring the Boundaries of Criminology and Sociology of Health and Illness*, Oxford: Blackwell.

Escartín, J., Rodríguez-Carballeira, A., Zapf, D., Porrúa, C. and Martín-Peña, J. (2009), 'Perceived severity of various bullying behaviours at work and the relevance of exposure to bullying', *Work & Stress*, 23(3), 191–205.

Estrada, F., Nilsson, A., Kristina, J. and Wikman, S. (2010), 'Violence at work: The emergence of a social problem', *Journal of Scandinavian Studies in Criminology and Crime Prevention*, 11(1), 46–65.

Expert Advisory Group on Workplace Bullying (2005), *Report of the Expert Advisory Group on Workplace Bullying*, Dublin: The Stationery Office.

Fevre, R. (2001), *The Demoralization of Western Culture*, London: Continuum.

Fevre, R. (2003), *The New Sociology of Economic Behaviour*, London: Sage.

Fevre, R., Robinson, A., Jones, T. and Lewis, D. (2008), *Work Fit for All – Disability, Health and the Experience of Negative Treatment in the British Workplace*, Insight Report No. 1, London: Equality and Human Rights Commission.

Fevre, R., Nichols, T., Prior, G. and Rutherford, I. (2009), *Fair Treatment at Work Report: Findings from the 2008 Survey*, Employment Relations Research Series No. 103, London: Department for Business, Innovation and Skills.

Fevre, R., Grainger, H. and Brewer, R. (2010), 'Discrimination and Unfair Treatment in the Workplace', *British Journal of Industrial Relations*, 49(S2), S207–35.

Fevre, R., Robinson, A., Jones, T. and Lewis, D. (2010), 'Researching workplace bullying: The benefits of taking an integrated approach', *International Journal of Social Research Methodology*, 13(1), 71–85.

Fevre, R., Robinson, A., Lewis, D. and Jones, T. (forthcoming), 'The ill-treatment of disabled employees in British workplaces', *Work, Employment and Society*.

Flannery, R. (1996), 'Violence in the workplace 1970–1995: A review of the literature', *Aggression and Violent Behaviour*, 1, 57–68.

Ford, R. (2008), 'Is racial prejudice declining in Britain?', *British Journal of Sociology*, 59(4), 609–36.

Foster, D. (2007), 'Legal obligation or personal lottery? Employee experiences of disability and the negotiation of adjustments in the public sector workplace', *Work, Employment and Society*, 21(1), 67–84.

Foster, D. and Fosh, P. (2010), 'Negotiating "difference": Representing disabled employees in the British workplace', *British Journal of Industrial Relations*, 48(3), 560–82.

Fox, S. and Stallworth, L.E. (2005), 'Racial/ethnic bullying: Exploring links between bullying and racism in the US workplace', *Journal of Vocational Behaviour*, 66, 438–56.

Glasø, L., Matthiesen, S.B., Nielsen, M.B. and Einarsen, S. (2007), 'Do targets of workplace bullying portray a general victim personality profile?', *Scandinavian Journal of Psychology*, 48, 313–19.

Goffman, E. (1956), 'The nature of deference and demeanour', *American Anthropologist*, 58(3), 473–502.

Goffman, E. (1968), *Stigma – Notes on the Management of Spoiled Identity*, Harmondsworth: Penguin.

Goffman, E. (1972), *The Presentation of Self in Everyday Life*, Harmondsworth: Penguin.

Goldthorpe, J., Lockwood, D. Bechhofer, F. and Platt, J. (1969), *The Affluent Worker in the Class Structure*, London: Cambridge University Press.

Grainger, H. and Fitzner, G. (2007), *The First Fair Treatment at Work Survey: Executive Summary – Updated*, Employment Relations Research Series No. 63, London: Department of Trade and Industry.

Greenberg, J. (1997), *Occupational Crime*, Chicago: Nelson-Hall.

Hanmer, J. and Itzin, C. (with Quaid, S. and Wrigglesworth, D.) (eds) (2000), *Home Truths about Domestic Violence: Feminist Influences on Policy and Practice: A Reader*, London: Routledge.

Harris, B. and Leather, P. (2011), 'Levels and consequences of exposure to service user violence: Evidence from a sample of UK social care staff', *British Journal of Social Work*, first published online on 8 September 2011, doi:10.1093/bjsw/bcr128.

Harris, K.J., Harvey, P. and Booth, S.L. (2010), 'Who abuses their coworkers? An examination of personality and situational variables', *The Journal of Social Psychology*, 150(6), 608–27.

Harvey, M., Treadway, D. and Heames, J.T. (2006), 'Bullying in global organizations: A reference point perspective', *Journal of World Business*, 41(2), 190–202.

Harvey, M., Treadway, D., Heames, J.T. and Duke, A. (2009), 'Bullying in the 21st century global organization: An ethical perspective', *Journal of Business Ethics*, 85, 27–40.

Hauge, L.J., Skogstad, A. and Einarsen, S. (2007), 'Relationships between stressful work environments and bullying: Results of a large representative study', *Work & Stress*, 21(3), 220–42.

Hauge, L.J., Skogstad, A. and Einarsen, S. (2010), 'The relative impact of workplace bullying as a social stressor at work', *Scandinavian Journal of Psychology*, 51, 426–33.

Health and Safety Executive (2007), *Managing the Causes of Work-Related Stress – A Step-by-Step Approach Using the Management Standards*, Sudbury, MA: HSE Books.

Heames, J.T., Harvey, M.G. and Treadway, D. (2006), 'Status inconsistency: An antecedent to bullying behaviour in groups', *International Journal of Human Resource Management*, 17(2), 348–61.

Hearn, J. and Parkin, W. (2001), *Gender, Sexuality and Violence in Organizations: The Unspoken Forces of Organization Violations*, London: Sage.

Hershcovis, S.M. (2010), 'Incivility, social undermining, bullying … oh my!: A call to reconcile constructs within workplace aggression research', *Journal of Organizational Behavior*, 32, 499–519.

Hochschild, A. (1983), *The Managed Heart: Commercialization of Human Feeling*, Berkeley: University of California Press.

Hodson, R. (2001), *Dignity at Work*, Cambridge: Cambridge University Press.

Hodson, R., Roscigno, V.J. and Lopez, S.H. (2006), 'Chaos and the abuse of power: Workplace bullying in organizational and interactional context', *Work and Occupations*, 33(4), 382–416.

Hoel, H. and Beale, D. (2006), 'Workplace bullying, psychological perspectives and industrial relations: Towards a contextualized and interdisciplinary approach', *British Journal of Industrial Relations*, 44(2), 239–62.

Hoel, H. and Cooper, C. (2000), *Destructive Conflict and Bullying at Work*, Unpublished report, Manchester: Manchester School of Management, University of Manchester Institute of Science and Technology.

Hoel, H. and Salin, D. (2003), 'Organisational antecedents of workplace bullying', in S. Einarsen, H. Hoel, D. Zapf and C. Cooper (eds), *Bullying and Emotional Abuse in the Workplace: International Perspectives in Research and Practice*, London: Taylor and Francis.

Hoel, H., Rayner, C. and Cooper, C.L. (1999), *Workplace Bullying: What We Know, Who Is to Blame, and What Can We Do?*, London: Taylor and Francis.

Hoel, H., Cooper, C. and Faragher, B. (2001), 'The experience of bullying in Great Britain: The impact of organizational status', *European Journal of Work and Organizational Psychology*, 10(4), 443–65.

Hoel, H., Faragher, B. and Cooper, C. (2004), 'Bullying is detrimental to health, but all bullying behaviours are not necessarily equally damaging', *British Journal of Guidance and Counselling*, 32(3), 367–87.

Hoel, H., Glasø, L., Hetland, J., Cooper, C.L. and Einarsen, S. (2010), 'Leadership styles as predictors of self-reported and observed workplace bullying', *British Journal of Management*, 21, 453–68.

Hubert, A.B. and Van Veldhoven, M. (2001), 'Risk sectors for undesirable behaviour and mobbing', *European Journal of Work and Organizational Psychology*, 10(4), 415–24.

Hunt, R. and Dick, S. (2008), *Serves You Right: Lesbian and Gay People's Experiences of Discrimination*, London: Stonewall.

Hutchinson, J. and Eveline, J. (2010), 'Workplace bullying policy in the Australian public sector: Why has gender been ignored?', *The Australian Journal of Public Administration*, 69(1), 47–60.

Ironside, M. and Seifert, R. (2003), 'Tackling bullying in the workplace: The collective dimension', in S. Einarsen, A.H. Hoel, D. Zapf and C.L. Cooper (eds), *Bullying and Emotional Abuse in the Workplace: International Perspectives in Research and Practice*, London/New York: Taylor and Francis.

James, P., Cunningham, I. and Dibben, P. (2002), 'Absence management and the issues of job retention and return to work', *Human Resource Management Journal*, 12(2), 82–94.

James, P., Cunningham, I. and Dibben, P. (2006), 'Job retention and return to work of ill and injured workers: Towards an understanding of the organisational dynamics', *Employee Relations*, 28(3), 290–303.

Jiménez, B.M., Muñoz, A.R. Gamarra, M.M. and Herrer, M.G. (2007), 'Assessing workplace bullying: Spanish validation of a reduced version of the negative acts questionnaire, *The Spanish Journal of Psychology*, 10(2), 449–57.

Jones, T., Robinson, A., Fevre, R. and Lewis, D. (2011), 'Workplace assaults in Britain: Understanding the influence of individual and workplace characteristics', *British Journal of Criminology*, 51, 159–78.

Keashly, L., Hunter, S. and Harvey, S. (1997), 'Abusive interaction and role state stressors: Relative impact on student residence assistant stress and work attitudes', *Work & Stress*, 11, 175–85.

Lee, D. (2002), 'Gendered workplace bullying in the restructured UK civil service', *Personnel Review*, 31(2), 205–27.

Lewis, D. (2003), 'Voices in the social construction of bullying at work: Exploring multiple realities in further and higher education', *International Journal of Management and Decision Making*, 4(1), 65–81.

Lewis, D. (2004), 'Bullying at work: The impact of shame among university and college lecturers', *British Journal of Guidance and Counselling*, 32(3), 281–300.

Lewis, D. and Gunn, R.W. (2007), 'Workplace bullying in the public sector: Understanding the racial dimension', *Public Administration: An International Quarterly*, 83(3), 641–65.

Leymann, H. (1990), 'Mobbing and psychological terror at workplaces', *Violence and Victims*, 5, 119–25.

Leymann, H. (1996), 'The content and development of mobbing at work', *European Journal of Work and Organizational Psychology*, 5(2), 165–84.

Leymann, H. and Gustafsson, A. (1996), 'Mobbing at work and the development of post-traumatic stress disorders', *European Journal of Work and Organizational Psychology*, 5(2), 251–76.

Liefooghe, A.P.D. and Mackenzie-Davey, K. (2001), 'Accounts of workplace bullying: The role of the organization', *European Journal of Work and Organizational Psychology*, 10(4), 375–92.

Lim, S., Cortina, L.M. and Magley, V.J. (2008), 'Personal and workgroup incivility: Impact on work and health outcomes', *Journal of Applied Psychology*, 93, 95–107.

Lopez, S.H., Hodson, R. and Roscigno, V.J. (2009), 'Power, status, and abuse at work: General and sexual harassment compared', *Sociological Quarterly*, 50, 3–27.

Lutgen-Sandvik, P., Tracy, S.J. and Alberts, J.K. (2007), 'Burned by bullying in the American workplace: Prevalence, perception, degree and impact', *Journal of Management Studies*, 44(6), 837–62.

Malinauskienė, V., Obelenis, V. and Đopagienė, D. (2005), 'Psychological terror at work and cardiovascular diseases among teachers', *Acta Medica Lituanica*, 12(2), 20–5.

Matthiesen, S.B. and Einarsen, S. (2004), 'Psychiatric distress and symptoms of PTSD among victims of bullying at work', *British Journal of Guidance and Counselling*, 32(3), 335–56.

Mayo, E. (1933), *The Human Problems of Industrial Civilization*, New York: Macmillan.

Mayo, E. (1949), *The Social Problems of Industrial Civilization*, London: Routledge and Kegan Paul.

McCarthy, P. (1996), 'When the mask slips: Inappropriate coercion in organisations undergoing restructuring', in P. McCarthy, M. Sheehan and W. Wilkie (eds), *Bullying: From Backyard to Boardroom*, Alexandria, Australia: Millennium Books.

McCarthy, P. (2003), 'Bullying at work: A postmodern experience', in S. Einarsen, A.H. Hoel, D. Zapf and C.L. Cooper (eds), *Bullying and Emotional Abuse in the Workplace: International Perspectives in Research and Practice*, London/New York: Taylor and Francis.

McCarthy, P. and Mayhew, C. (2004), *Safeguarding the Organisation against Violence and Bullying: An International Perspective*, Basingstoke: Palgrave MacMillan.

McCormack, D., Djurkovic, N., Casimir, G. and Yang, L. (2009), 'Workplace bullying and intention to leave among schoolteachers in China: The mediating effect of affective commitment', *Journal of Applied Social Psychology*, 39(9), 2106–27.

McKenna, B., Smith, N.A., Poole, S.J. and Coverdale, J.H. (2003), 'Horizontal violence: Experiences of registered nurses in their first year of practice', *Journal of Advanced Nursing*, 42(1), 90–6.

Meek, C.B. (2004), 'The dark side of Japanese management in the 1990s: Karoshi and ijime in the Japanese workplace', *Journal of Managerial Psychology*, 19(3), 312–31.

Mikkelsen, E.G. and Einarsen, S. (2002), 'Basic assumptions and symptoms of post-traumatic stress among victims of bullying at work', *European Journal of Work and Organisational Psychology*, 11(1), 87–111.

Milczarek, M. and European Agency for Safety and Health at Work (2010), *Workplace Violence and Harassment: A European Picture*, A European Risk Observatory Report, Luxembourg: Publications Office of the European Union.

Neuman, J.H. and Baron, R.A. (2003), 'Social antecedents of bullying: A social interactionist perspective', in S. Einarsen, H. Hoel, D. Zapf and C. Cooper (eds), *Bullying and Emotional Abuse in the Workplace: International Perspectives in Research and Practice*, London: Taylor and Francis.

Nielsen, M.B., Skogstad, A., Matthiesen, S.B., Glasø, L., Aaslan, M.S., Notelaers, G. and Einarsen, S. (2009), 'Prevalence of workplace bullying in Norway: Comparisons across time and estimation methods', *European Journal of Work and Organizational Psychology*, 18(1), 81–101.

Nielsen, M.B., Einarsen, S. and Matthiesen, S.B. (2010), 'The impact of methodological moderators on prevalence rates of workplace bullying. A meta-analysis', *Journal of Occupational and Organizational Psychology*, 83, 955–79.

Nielsen, M.B., Notelaers, G. and Einarsen, S. (2011), 'Measuring exposure to workplace bullying', in S. Einarsen, H. Hoel, D. Zapf and C.L. Cooper (eds), *Bullying and Harassment in the Workplace: Developments in Theory, Research and Practice*, London: CRC Press.

Notelaers, G. and De Witte, H. (2003), 'De relatie tussen werkstress en pesten op het werk en welbevinden op het werk' [The relationship between work stressors, workplace bullying and well-being], in W. Herremans (ed.), *Arbeidsmarktonderzoekersdag, 2003 Vrij Universiteit Brussel* (pp. 139–63), Reeks: De Arbeidsmarkt in Vlaanderen. Leuven, Steunpunt Werkgelegenheid, Arbeid en Vorming 26 mei 2003, VUB.

Notelaers, G., Einarsen, S., De Witte, H. and Vermunt, J.K. (2006), 'Measuring exposure to bullying at work: The validity and advantages of the latent class cluster approach', *Work & Stress*, 20(4), 288–301.

O'Beirne, M., Gabe, J., Denney, D., Elston, M. and Lee, R. (2003), 'Veiling violence: The impacts of personal and professional identities on the discourse of work-related violence', in R. Lee and E. Stanko (eds), *Researching Violence: Essays on Methodology and Measurement*, London: Routledge.

O'Beirne, M., Denney, D. and Gabe, J. (2004), 'Fear of violence as an indicator of risk in probation work – Its impact on staff who work with known violent offenders', *British Journal of Criminology*, 44(1), 113–26.

O'Connell, P.J. and Williams, J. (2001), *National Survey of the Experiences of Employees. Report of the Task Force on the Prevention of Workplace Bullying*, Dublin: Department of Enterprise, Trade & Employment.

O'Connell, P.J., Calvert, E. and Watson, D. (2007), *Bullying in the Workplace: Survey Reports 2007*, Dublin: Economic and Social Research Institute.

Parker, R. and Aggleton, P. (2003), 'HIV and AIDS-related stigma and discrimination: A conceptual framework and implications for action', *Social Science and Medicine*, 57, 13–24.

Parkins, I.S., Fishbein, H.D. and Ritchey, P.N. (2006), 'The influence of personality on workplace bullying and discrimination', *Journal of Applied Social Psychology*, 36(10), 2554–77.

Pearson, C.M., Andersson, L.M. and Wegner, J.W. (2001), 'When workers flout convention: A study of workplace incivility', *Human Relations*, 54(11), 1387–419.

Peyton, P.R. (2003), *Dignity at Work: Eliminate Bullying and Create a Positive Working Environment*, Hove, England: Brunner-Routledge.

Phillips, C. and Bowling, B. (2007), 'Ethnicities, racism, crime and criminal justice', in M. Maguire, R. Morgan and R. Reiner (eds), *The Oxford Handbook of Criminology*, Oxford: Oxford University Press (4th edition).

Piirainen, H., Rasanen, K. and Kivimaki, M. (2003), 'Organizational climate, perceived work-related symptoms and sickness absence: A population-based survey', *Occupational and Environmental Medicine*, 45(2), 175–84.

Quine, L. (1999), 'Workplace bullying in NHS community trust: Staff questionnaire survey', *British Medical Journal*, 318, 228–32.

Quine, L. (2002), 'Workplace bullying in junior doctors: Questionnaire survey', *British Medical Journal*, 324, 878–9.

Rafferty, C. (2001), 'Bullying at work', in P. McCarthy, J. Rylance, R. Bennett and H. Zimmerman (eds), *Bullying from Backyard to Boardroom*, Sydney, Australia: Federation Press.

Raver, J.L. (2008), 'The dark side of employees' behaviour: Evaluating our questions, answers, and future directions', Professional Development Workshop conducted at the Academy of Management Conference, Anaheim, CA, August.

Rayman, P. (2001), *Beyond the Bottom Line*, New York: Palgrave.

Rayner, C. (1997), 'Incidence of workplace bullying', *Journal of Community and Applied Social Psychology*, 7(3), 181–91.

Rayner, C. and Lewis, D. (2011), 'Managing workplace bullying: The role of policies', in S. Einarsen, H. Hoel, D. Zapf and C.L. Cooper (eds), *Bullying and Harassment in the Workplace: Developments in Theory Research and Practice*, London: CRC Press.

Richman, J.A., Shinsako, S.A., Rospenda, K.M., Flaherty, J.A. and Freels, S. (2002), 'Workplace harassment/abuse and alcohol-related outcomes: The mediating role of psychological distress', *Journal of Studies on Alcohol*, 63, 412–19.

Robinson, A. (2010), 'Domestic violence', in F. Brookman, M. Maguire, H. Pierpoint and T. Bennett (eds), *Handbook on Crime*, Cullompton, England: Willan.

Rodríguez-Muñoz, A., Moreno-Jiménez, B., Vergel, A.I.S. and Hernández, E.G. (2010), 'Post-traumatic symptoms among victims of workplace bullying: Exploring gender differences and shattered assumptions', *Journal of Applied Social Psychology*, 40(10), 2616–35.

Roethlisberger, F.J. and Dickson, W.J. (2003 [1939]), *Management and the Worker*, London: Routledge.

Roscigno, V.J., Hodson, R. and Lopez, S. (2009), 'Workplace incivilities: The role of interest conflicts, social closure and organizational chaos', *Work, Employment and Society*, 23(4), 727–73.

Roscigno, V.J., Lopez, S. and Hodson, R. (2009), 'Supervisory bullying, status inequalities and organizational context', *Social Forces*, 87(3), 1561–89.

Salin, D. (2001), 'Prevalence and forms of bullying amongst business professionals: A comparison of two different strategies for measuring bullying', *European Journal of Work and Organisational Psychology*, 10(4), 425–41.

Salin, D. (2003), 'Bullying and organisational politics in competitive and rapidly changing work environments', *International Journal of Management and Decision Making*, 4(1), 35–46.

Salin, D. (2008), 'The prevention of workplace bullying as a question of human resource management: Measures adopted and underlying organizational factors', *Scandinavian Journal of Management*, 24, 221–31.

Salin, D. and Hoel, H. (2011), 'Organisational causes of workplace bullying', in S. Einarsen, H. Hoel, D. Zapf and C.L. Cooper (eds), *Bullying and Harassment in the Workplace: Developments in Theory, Research and Practice*, London: CRC Press.

Sayer, A. (2007), 'Dignity at work: Broadening the agenda', *Organization*, 14(4), 565–81.

Schat, A.C.H. and Kelloway, E.K. (2003), 'Reducing the adverse consequences of workplace aggression and violence: The buffering effects of organizational support', *Journal of Occupational Health Psychology*, 8(2), 110–22.

Schur, L., Kruse, D., Blasi, J. and Blanck, P. (2009), 'Is disability disabling in all workplaces?', *Industrial Relations*, 48(3): 381–410.

Sennett, R. (1999), *The Corrosion of Character*, New York: W.W. Norton.

Serantes, N.P. and Suárez, M.A. (2006), 'Myths about workplace violence, harassment and bullying', *International Journal of the Sociology of Law*, 34(1), 229–38.

Sheard, L. (2011), '"Anything could have happened": Women, the night-time economy, alcohol and drink spiking', *Sociology*, 45 (4), 619–33.

Skogstad, A., Matthiesen, S.B. and Einarsen, S. (2007), 'Organizational changes: A precursor of bullying at work?', *International Journal of Organizational Theory and Behaviour*, 10(1), 58–94.

Spector, P.E., Coulter, M.L., Stockwell, H.G. and Matz, M.W. (2007), 'Relationships of workplace physical violence and verbal aggression with perceived safety, perceived violence climate, and strains in a healthcare setting', *Work & Stress*, 21, 117–30.

Strandmark, M. and Hallberg, L.R.-M. (2007), 'The origin of workplace bullying: Experiences from the perspective of bully victims in the public service sector', *Journal of Nursing Management*, 15, 332–41.

Tehrani, N. (2011), 'Workplace bullying: The role for counselling', in S. Einarsen, H. Hoel, D. Zapf and C.L. Cooper (eds), *Bullying and Harassment in the Workplace: Developments in Theory, Research and Practice*, London: CRC Press.

Tepper, B.I. (2000), 'Consequences of abusive supervision', *Academy of Management Journal*, 43(2), 178–90.

Tombs, S. (2007), 'Violence: Safety crimes and criminology', *British Journal of Criminology*, 47(4), 531–50.

Tsuno, K., Kawakami, N., Inoue, A. and Abe, K. (2010), 'Measuring workplace bullying: Reliability and validity of the Japanese version of the negative acts questionnaire', *Journal of Occupational Health*, 52, 227–40.

Tuckey, M.R., Dollard, M.F., Saebel, J. and Berry, N.M. (2010), 'Negative workplace behaviour: Temporal associations with cardiovascular outcomes and psychological health problems in Australian police', *Stress and Health*, 26(5), 372–81.

Upson, A. (2004), *Violence at Work: Findings from the 2002/3 British Crime Survey*, London: Home Office.

Vaill, P. (1989), *Managing as a Performing Art*, San Francisco, CA: Jossey-Bass.

Vartia, M. (1996), 'The sources of bullying – Psychological work environment and organizational climate', *European Journal of Work and Organizational Psychology*, 5(2), 203–14.

Vartia, M. and Hyyti, J. (2002), 'Gender differences in workplace bullying among prison officers', *European Journal of Work and Organizational Psychology*, 11(1), 113–26.

Waddington, P.A.J., Badger, D. and Bull, R. (2005), *The Violent Workplace*, Cullompton, England: Willan.

Walby, S. (2005), *Improving the Statistics on Violence against Women*, Geneva, Switzerland: UN Division for the Advancement of Women.

Walker, C. and Fincham, B. (2011), *Work and the Mental Health Crisis in Britain*, Chichester: Wiley-Blackwell.

Woodhams, C. and Corby, S. (2003), 'Defining disability in theory and practice: A critique of the British Disability Discrimination Act 1995', *Journal of Social Policy*, 32(2), 1–20.

Wright Mills, C. (1959), *The Sociological Imagination*, Oxford: Oxford University Press.

Zapf, D. (1999), 'Organizational, work group related and personal causes of mobbing/bullying at work', *International Journal of Manpower*, 20(1/2), 70–85.

Zapf, D. and Einarsen, S. (2003), 'Individual antecedents of bullying: Victims and perpetrators', in S. Einarsen, H. Hoel, D. Zapf and C.L. Cooper (eds), *Bullying and Emotional Abuse in the Workplace: International Perspectives in Research and Practice*, London: Taylor and Francis.

Zapf, D. and Einarsen, S. (2011), 'Individual antecedents of bullying: Victims and perpetrators', in S. Einarsen, H. Hoel, D. Zapf and C.L. Cooper (eds), *Bullying and Harassment in the Workplace: Developments in Theory Research and Practice*, London: CRC Press.

Zapf, D. and Gross, C. (2001), 'Conflict escalation and coping with workplace bullying: A replication and extension', *European Journal of Work and Organizational Psychology*, 10(4), 497–522.

Zapf, D., Knorz, C. and Kulla, M. (1996), 'On the relationship between mobbing factors, and job content, social work environment, and health outcomes', *European Journal of Work and Organizational Psychology*, 5(2), 215–37.

Zapf, D., Einarsen, S., Hoel, H. and Vartia, M. (2003), 'Empirical findings on bullying in the workplace', in S. Einarsen, H. Hoel, D. Zapf and C.L. Cooper (eds), *Bullying and Emotional Abuse in the Workplace: International Perspectives in Research and Practice*, London: Taylor and Francis.

Zapf, D., Escartín, J., Einarsen, S., Hoel, H. and Vartia, M. (2011), 'Empirical findings on prevalence and risk groups of bullying in the workplace', in S. Einarsen, H. Hoel, D. Zapf and C.L. Cooper (eds), *Bullying and Harassment in the Workplace: Developments in Theory Research and Practice*, London: CRC Press.

Index